The Novel and the Nazi Past

American University Studies

Series I
Germanic Languages and Literature

Vol. 28

PETER LANG
New York · Berne · Frankfurt am Main

Donna K. Reed

The Novel
and the Nazi Past

PETER LANG
New York · Berne · Frankfurt am Main

Library of Congress Cataloging in Publication Data

Reed, Donna K., 1944–
   The novel and the Nazi past.

   (American University Studies.   Series I, Germanic
Languages and Literature; vol. 28)
   Revision of thesis (Ph.D.)
   Bibliography: p.
   Includes index.
   1. German fiction – 20th century – History and
criticism.   2. National socialism in literature.
3. Mann, Thomas, 1875–1955. Doktor Faustus.   4. Böll,
Heinrich, 1917–   . Billard um Halbzehn.   5. Grass,
Günter, 1917–   . Blechtrommel.   I. Title.
II. Series.
PT772.R38   1984   833'.914'09358   83-49004
ISBN 0-8204-0064-5
ISSN 0721-1392

CIP-Kurztitelaufnahme der Deutschen Bibliothek

Reed, Donna K.:
The novel and the Nazi past / Donna K. Reed. –
New York; Berne; Frankfurt am Main: Lang,
1984.
   (American University Studies: Ser. 1,
   Germanic Languages and Literature; Vol. 28)
   ISBN 0-8204-0064-5

NE: American University Studies / 01

© Peter Lang Publishing, Inc., New York 1985

Printed by Lang Druck, Inc., Liebefeld/Berne (Switzerland)

To Eugene and Benjamin

Acknowledgments

I should like to thank the many people who helped to bring this book into existence.

The book began as a Ph.D. dissertation. A Fulbright Fellowship enabled me to start my research in Munich, Germany. Numerous stimulating discussions there with advanced students at the University and one especially useful meeting with the novelist and critic Reinhard Baumgart helped me to develop and sharpen my ideas. My dissertation advisor at Harvard, Henry Hatfield, provided all the necessary guidance throughout. A dissertation group in Berkeley, California, conducted by Shirley Hecht, gave me and other women the rare opportunity to share and solve common problems that arose in the process of writing. One of its members, Susan Sterling, who is now a writer of fiction, continued to critique my writing and to discuss my work with me, often with an almost uncanny ability to elicit insights I was just beginning to pursue.

Several others have helped particularly with the revision of the manuscript for publication. The editors of *New German Critique*, especially David Bathrick, read and carefully criticized an earlier version of the *Mittelstand* chapter before it was published in their journal. Russell Berman of Stanford University and my colleagues at the University of California in Davis, Roland Hoermann and Karl Menges, also read chapters and responded with a variety of thought-provoking comments. The University of California awarded me a Faculty Research Grant to edit the manuscript for publication; Mary Doty has mastered the computer for me. Lastly, Kate Gross has given excellent editorial assistance.

But it is to my husband, Eugene Lunn, who is a professor of European Intellectual History at Davis, that I owe the greatest debt. From the beginning his knowledge of German history and culture have been invaluable in helping me to formulate, analyze, and further develop my ideas. He was exceptionally adept at grasping the social and historical implications of my literary interpretations and then directing me to texts that would most aptly expand and enrich my analyses. He has labored with me to improve many passages in my book. And his ardent interest in the subject often sustained me in my efforts.

Contents

Introduction

In 1943 a famous German expatriot in southern California embarked upon what he called his wildest book. Struggling to come to grips with the Nazi atrocities, the seventy-year-old exile Thomas Mann looked inward and backward to his own and his country's cultural past. From such painful reflection originated the novel about which the author cared the most: "I am attached to this book as I am to no other. Whoever does not like it, I do not like anymore. Whoever shows himself sensitive to the extreme emotional tension under which it was created, to him belongs all my gratitude." [1]

Thirteen years later, Günter Grass, then a relatively unknown poet, left his home in Berlin for Paris to write the novel of the Nazi era which was to make him known. The thirty-year-old Grass became highly conscious of his native tongue in French-speaking surroundings. The book, which was to be praised for its lively, graphic language, took on distinct contours after the author's visit to postwar Danzig.

Also in the late fifties, Heinrich Böll, a recognized postwar writer, began to assemble the various scraps of paper which were to become his most formally conscious work to date, intensifying the combination of concrete, surface realism and symbolism only suggested in his earlier writing. Embracing the last fifty years of German history, Böll's novel seems almost a retort to those critics who had praised his *Irish Journal* for finally leaving the Nazi past behind.

All three of these novelists attempted to come to terms with Nazism. In the immediate wave as well as the subsiding wake of organized madness emerged three of the best known postwar

---

1. Thomas Mann, "Das mir nächste meiner Bücher," *Gesammelte Werke*, XI (Oldenburg: Fischer, 1960), p. 686.

German novels: *Doctor Faustus, The Tin Drum,* and *Billiards at Half-Past Nine.*

Mann viewed *Doctor Faustus* as the novel to end all novels, but critics acclaimed *The Tin Drum* and *Billiards at Half-Past Nine* as the revival of this "dead" genre. The lively, concrete realism of Grass's and Böll's prose contributed of course to the alleged revitalization of the novel. And if there was a crisis of the novel, it was in part a crisis of the German language in the immediate postwar period. Numerous statements made by individual writers, literary critics, and linguists attest to the difficulty of writing in the language which had been so misused for twelve years. The Group 47, a writers' association that became increasingly influential during the 1950s in forming West German literature, was dedicated to the creation of a new literature; but even some of its members still wrote with a style and language that they themselves had decried. The process of decontamination in literary as well as daily usage was not completed overnight. Like other members of this group, Grass and Böll were keenly aware of Nazi language distortion; they attempted to use unrhetorical, uncontaminated, often colloquial German. In addition, not only formal problems but also psychological and socio-historical perceptions had to be worked through in the fifties to make possible the production of two works of literature comparable to the work of that towering figure of twentieth-century German prose, Mann.

In the first decade after the defeat of Nazi Germany, literature reflected primarily the omnipresent state of physical and spiritual ruin.[2] Although some older writers attempted implicitly to justify their "inner emigration" at first, the younger postwar writers consciously fixed their eyes upon the undisguised devastation surrounding them to analyze the heretofore disguised senselessness of their

---

2.   The following introductory description of the postwar confrontation with the Nazi past provides background for the three main novels of this study and thus confines itself to the Federal Republic. Postwar literary and historical developments in the German Democratic Republic will be traced in the Epilogue as context for the discussion there of Christa Wolf's *Patterns of Childhood.*

war experiences. As Manfred Durzak has written, to varying degrees nearly all the works which appeared in these first ten to thirteen years could be called "confessional literature" or "literature of ruins" ("Bekenntnis-" or "Trümmerliteratur"). [3] This literature is characterized by a consciously simple and unpoetic prose, but the style, as Group 47 spokesman Hans Werner Richter explains, is not a product of the writers' naiveté or technical incompetence but of their awareness "that only the method and intention of the pioneer are appropriate to the new beginning of prose in our country. The method of taking stock. The intention of truth. Both at the price of poetry. Where the beginning of existence is, is also the beginning of literature." [4] However much these writers fell back on earlier literary traditions, aesthetic requirements of form were secondary to the existential statement of truth. This moral impetus dominated West German prose of the first postwar decade.

What is often classified as the literature of *Vergangenheitsbewältigung* ("coming to terms with or confronting the past") appears in these years as such confessions or "literature of ruins." In Böll's *Where Were You, Adam?* (1951) and Richter's *The Defeated* (1949), the reader follows along through the war at the side of one simple, unheroic, unindoctrinated soldier. In *The Cherries of Freedom* (1953), Andersch prunes away at the fictive aura, which still remains in Böll's and Richter's narratives, and calls his book "A Report." Even when such writers move beyond the war experience to focus on the present, the overriding moral impetus behind their works still subordinates narrative artistry. In *Death In Rome* (1954), Koeppen attacks his opportunist Nazi figure so viciously that this "Judejahn" becomes a caricature, a stereotypic incarnation of evil. Gaiser's *The Dying Chase* (1953) underscores the artistic-moral dichotomy from the opposite perspective. Reading this author's romantic description of the tragedy of an ongoing

---

3.   Manfred Durzak, *Der deutsche Roman der Gegenwart* (Stuttgart: Kohlhammer, 1971), p. 11.

4.   Hans Werner Richter, *Almanach der Gruppe 47* (Reinbek: Rowohlt, 1962), p. 10.

lost war, one inevitably recalls the Nazi aesthetics of death and violence. The other writers thus appear justified in their fear of an aesthetic as opposed to moral account of the war experience.

Toward the end of the fifties, the sense of "pioneering" a new literature for a new society began to exhaust itself. For one thing, that new West German society was growing more affluent and less desolate. As Durzak stresses, the year 1959 marked a turning point away from the unpoetic diction and narrative structures of the first years.[5] In this year appear Böll's *Billiards at Half-Past Nine*, Grass's *The Tin Drum*, and Johnson's *Speculations about Jacob*. Never abandoning their moral perspective, Böll and others of his generation turn from their directly confessional phase to more artistic and experimental development of narrative techniques. With Grass and Johnson a younger generation emerges with its initial, original literary attempts. The end of the fifties marks a sharp caesura in narrative themes and artistic quality of postwar West German prose. The Nazi past does not disappear from these novels, but it appears in its larger societal and historical context where society before and after the Nazis is portrayed.

The Tin Drum and *Billiards at Half-Past Nine* thus seem to be comparable to Mann's *Doctor Faustus* as artistically sophisticated novels of the epoch.[6] Precisely their high literary quality, however, would make these works suspect to the critic and social philosopher Theodor Adorno. Implying partial agreement with the attitudes of the early fifties, he pronounced his now famous dictum that it is barbaric, after Auschwitz, still to write poetry. Works of lesser artistic quality would more easily avoid the grotesque paradox of an

---

5.   Durzak, pp. 11-12.

6.   Although Böll's novel has not continued to draw as much critical attention as the other two, it nonetheless culminates the development of his literary technique in the fifties, one which had been highly representative of other writers of that decade. See, for example, James H. Reid, *Heinrich Böll: Withdrawal and Reemergence* (London: Wolff, 1973), p. 49, and Frank Trommler, "Realismus in der Prosa," *Tendenzen der deutschen Literatur seit 1945*, ed. Thomas Koebner (Stuttgart: Kröner, 1971), pp. 223-224.

aesthetic portrayal of barbarism. If poetry *after* Auschwitz is barbaric, then literature *about* fascism certainly runs the same risk. Conceding that the "profuseness of suffering must not be forgotten," Adorno nevertheless maintained that art offers a kind of solace which immediately transforms and betrays the real feelings of grief. Out of the victims of Nazism "something is prepared, works of art, which are thrown as feed to the world that murdered them." Further, artistic portrayal always possesses the potential to create aesthetic enjoyment; stylistic structuring gives meaning to the unthinkable.[7]

From Adorno's perspective, would these three novels thus appear barbaric? In all his discussions in Californian exile with Mann about *Doctor Faustus*, such an opinion of the writer's work does not emerge. And yet particularly Mann's as well as Böll's art would offer solace to the mournful, and structure meaning out of the incredible. Even Grass's looser form and satire imposes a grotesque though not often aesthetically pleasing meaning upon the unthinkable. And "cultural possessions" they have all become. Yet does not each of these novels at different points fall silent before the unthinkable, expressing a helpless sense of incredulity? Leverkühn's final cantata, for example, ends with "silence and night," though Zeitblom cannot resist imagining some "hope beyond the hopelessness" of that darkness. Throughout Böll's novel recurs the phrase "what for what for what for." In the "Faith, Hope, Love" chapter, Oskar's description of the Crystal Night culminates in a repeated "But I, I don't know." To differing degrees, each writer lets remain incredible that one part of Nazism which cannot be left otherwise: the mass murder in the camps. To leave clouded whatever of fascism can be clarified would be dangerous. Although art does distort fascist inhumanity in that it stylizes and organizes its subject, the alternative, as Reinhard Baumgart concludes, would be "to

---

7. Theodor Adorno, *Noten zur Literatur*, III (Frankfurt am Main: Suhrkamp, 1965), p. 126.

look away and to be quiet -- perhaps in the opinion that the bar-barous happens because of barbarians, not because of us and those like us. And such burying of one's head in the sand would only betray that from which it feels itself untouched: inhumanity." [8]

Mann rewrites the Faust myth to depict the doom of the land of Goethe. Böll focuses less on the Nazi annulment of cultural humanist traditions; he portrays the impact of Nazism through the eyes of the unassuming, humble folk who manage to retain their simple humanity amidst fascist inhumanity. The banality of Nazi evil Grass sifts through the mind of a misshapen gnome, who nei-ther condemns nor embraces but simply magnifies the grotesque contours of that evil. Unquestionably, the Nazis perpetrated crimes of a magnitude rarely witnessed in the history of humankind. An impossible but imperative task confronts these three writers: to describe that inhumanity.

The following pages will examine the three major writers' con-frontations with inhumanity. Their shared endeavor to comprehend and portray how it all could happen provides a prism through which to view and compare the novels, however much they may differ. For the novelists' attempts to understand the reign of Nazi society and its ideology affect the literary composition of the works: the choice of main characters and milieu, the development of the writers' own aesthetics, and the overall formal structuring of the novels. The following chapters will illuminate the resulting common features of Mann's, Grass's, and Böll's portraits of Nazi society and culture. In the first chapter, the focus of all three upon an historically pivotal social group, the middle classes of German society, is analyzed. Seeking security from their economically and socially threatened position in the 1920s, this *Mittelstand* provided a crucial base of mass support for the NSDAP. Chapter Two examines the interplay of art and politics in the authors' responses to fascism, particularly as they develop an aesthetics to combat Nazi culture: Mann's reckoning with the land of Beethoven amassed under Hitler, the

---

8.   Reinhard Baumgart, *Literatur für Zeitgenossen* (Frankfurt am Main: Suhrkamp, 1970), pp. 35-36.

sensitivity of Grass and Böll to Nazi "aestheticization" of politics. The third chapter correlates the novelists' approaches to Nazi ideology with the whole shape of their novels, which range from self-contained to open. Finally, the Epilogue studies the continuing confrontation with Nazism in novels since these three classics.

Despite their status as classics on Nazism, *Doctor Faustus, The Tin Drum*, and *Billiards at Half-Past Nine* have never been compared extensively and have only recently been individually viewed from an interdisciplinary perspective. Until the mid-seventies, most criticism of fictional works on the Third Reich acknowledged the concern with the Nazi past, but focused primarily on formal and textual content analysis. Critics thus often relegated Nazism to the category of a literary theme instead of discussing the literary treatment of a complex historical, social, and political phenomenon. [9] Recent scholarship on Grass especially has begun to incorporate historical and sociological analyses of Nazism. [10] This book contributes

---

9.   Notable early exceptions are primarily broad overviews of postwar literature, which include appropriately historical but necessarily limited examinations of *Vergangenheitsbewältigung*: Reinhard Baumgart, *Literatur für Zeitgenossen* (Frankfurt am Main: Suhrkamp, 1966); Peter Demetz, *Postwar German Literature* (New York: Pegasus, 1970); Durzak, *Der deutsche Roman der Gegenwart*; *Tendenzen der deutschen Literatur seit 1945*, ed. Koebner; Hans Mayer, *Deutsche Literatur seit Thomas Mann* (Reinbek: Rowohlt, 1967).

10. A valuable collection of essays, *Gegenwartsliteratur und Drittes Reich. Deutsche Autoren in der Auseinandersetzung mit der Vergangenheit*, ed. Hans Wagener (Stuttgart: Reclam, 1977), reflects new developments in an interdisciplinary approach to literature on Nazism. Several recent contextual studies of the individual writers, especially Grass, will be treated in the coming chapters. (The only other published book in English on *Vergangenheitsbewältigung* in German literature will not be drawn upon. Hamida Bosmajian's *Metaphors of Evil* [Iowa City: University of Iowa Press, 1979], is a morally sensitive and humane study of the problem posed by Adorno, how to give form to the inexpressible, but it is not interdisciplinary and only discusses one of the novels examined in this book, Uwe Johnson's *Anniversaries*. I have just learned that another book, *The Uncompleted Past*, by Judith Ryan, [Wayne State University Press] will appear after my own manuscript goes to press and thus too late to be considered in this study. Perhaps the two books will complement each other well since current announcements suggest that Ryan's study focuses primarily on ethical questions of individual responsibility, an issue discussed, but not central to my own book.) There will be no attempt made here to pursue another recent

to that effort, but I would caution against implicitly expecting literature to be history or sociology. Furthermore, these disciplines should be used not only to critique but also to illuminate fictive characters and events in a way sympathetic to the author's apparent intentions. Such an interdisciplinary approach, which integrates pertinent extra-literary scholarship with formal analysis, is necessary to understand literary treatment of a subject like Nazism. These three novels will be explicated, compared, and measured against historical, socio-psychological and philosophical interpretations of Nazism. The evolution of each novel's style and entire structure will be traced to the writer's historical approach. This comparative and interdisciplinary method should enable us to appreciate and assess more critically the achievements of each work.

---

approach which focuses on the reception of the literature among the German reading public; an excellent example of this method is Rainer Nägele, *Heinrich Böll. Einführung in das Werk und in die Forschung* (Frankfurt am Main: Athenäum Fischer, 1976).

CHAPTER ONE

The *Mittelstand* Protagonist

Socio-Historical Context

"This one time I knew what I wanted and the task I set myself: nothing less than the novel of my epoch." (EDF, 704)[1] This was Thomas Mann's intent in writing *Doctor Faustus*. Written without such stated intentions, Heinrich Böll's *Billiards at Half-Past Nine* and Günter Grass's *The Tin Drum* could also be called novels of the epoch. With a design less grand, less imposing, Böll and Grass also attempt to come to terms with the last fifty years of German history.

Nazism is viewed in broad historical perspective from the distanced vantage point of 1959, when *Billiards at Half-Past Nine* and *The Tin Drum* appeared, and from the geographical distance of the exile Thomas Mann in America. Portrayal of this larger social context in the twentieth century poses problems for the novelist, however, as anyone acquainted with the "crisis" or "death" of the novel knows. One basic source of this crisis is the difficulty in depicting the great complexity of modern society. But if twentieth-century society is opaque, then Nazi Germany, whose deeds defied the limits of what was thought humanly possible, appears to be more so. What parts of this vast society will each writer include? Will he try to confine his focus to those most responsible, or provide a cross-section of Nazi supporters from various social strata? Who is responsible? Whose story shall he tell?

---

1.   Such notes in parentheses refer to the page numbers of the following editions of the novels: *Doktor Faustus* (Frankfurt am Main, 1960), abbreviated DF; the *Entstehung*: EDF; *Die Blechtrommel* (Frankfurt am Main, 1960), abbreviated Bt; *Billard um halb zehn* (Munich, 1959), abbreviated Bil. All translations are my own.

As early as the late twenties, Ernst Bloch foresaw: "Now more than ever, the moist humus for ideology is in the petite bourgeoisie."[2] Certainly the late development of constitutional government in Germany contributed to a general political immaturity not limited to the lower middle and middle classes. The importance of their support, however, in the Nazi rise to power has been further emphasized by postwar historians.[3] Karl Dietrich Bracher has

---

2.   Quoted in Reinhard Baumgart, "Kleinbürgertum und Realismus," *Neue Rundschau* 75, 4 (1964), 656.

3.   Recruitment and voting statistics provide a concrete measure of the importance of the *Mittelstand* as a social basis of Nazism. In 1930, over 70% of party members came from these urban and rural lower-middle-class and middle-class groups: white-collar workers, 25.6%; self-employed, 20.7%; officials, 8.3%; civil service employees, 6.6%; teachers, 1.7%; and farmers, 14.0% (George Mosse, *Nazi Culture* [New York, 1968], p. 346.) Furthermore, a new standard work on the composition and leadership of the Nazi party, Michael H. Kater, *The Nazi Party: A Social Profile of Members and Leaders, 1919-1945* (Cambridge: Harvard University Press, 1983), shows strong over-representation of the lower middle classes in proportion to their percentage of the population. This meticulously researched statistical study confirms the lower middle class thesis for both the rank and file and the leadership (p. 236). Such party statistics correlate, on the whole, with the data on Nazi electoral support. If we take 1928 as a beginning, and the highpoint of Nazi electoral success, July, 1932, as a conclusion, the following revealing pattern emerges:

Votes (in millions) at general elections

Parties	1928	*July, 1932*
Working-class (SPD and KPD)	12.3	13.1
Middle-class (excluding Centre)	12.9	4.0
Catholic Centre	3.7	4.5
National Socialists	0.8	13.7

While the Left and the Catholic Centre gained slightly, it was the middle-class parties from whose loss of nine million votes the Nazis gained the major share of their massive new voting strength. An additional factor in the Nazi increase of thirteen million was their appeal to many younger, new voters (Geoffrey Barraclough, "The Rise of National Socialism," *Fascism: Three Major Regimes*, ed. Heinz Lubasz [New York, 1973], p. 74). Whereas this thesis on the significance of *Mittelstand*-support originated in the late twenties and was widely accepted in the sixties and seventies, recently attempts have been made to question and qualify it, notably Richard Hamilton, *Who voted for Hitler?* (Princeton: Princeton University Press, 1982). Hamilton argues against a theory of *the* lower middle classes, indicating geographical and religious differences in voting patterns: the middle strata along with all other groups apart from workers voted

written: "It was the rural and urban 'middle class,' in the broad sense of the term, which started and carried out the breakthrough of the NSDAP. The 'panic of the middle class,' which set in with the outbreak of the economic crisis, was sharpened by the fact that the middle class felt threatened not only economically but, more important, socially as well."[4] The face of the petit bourgeois was so visible in the Nazi party that Joachim Fest's book *The Face of the Third Reich* profiles essentially the rise of the *Kleinbürger* to power. Far behind such a Himmler or a Hitler, the bewildered, fearful faces of Alfred Matzerath, Zeitblom, and even the Fähmel family could all fill in the background of this picture of the Third Reich. Coming to terms with the Nazi past in these three novels has meant understanding the role and responsibility of an historically pivotal social group.

The central role of the *Mittelstand* does need, however, to be viewed in a larger historical context. To any party which wished to retain governmental power in this historical situation, mass support was indispensable. No modern society, especially one which had

---

heavily for the Nazis after 1930 in Protestant and Catholic small towns and especially rural areas; the Nazi vote was lower in the big cities, and the mixed districts there, combining lower middle and working classes, voted only 30% for the Nazis (much less than the rich districts). The last point -- the focus of Hamilton's study -- is inconclusive, however: Hamilton himself emphasizes the virtual impossibility of determining voting tendencies of the lower middle classes in the large cities, since they had no distinctive base there, but lived in mixed districts with working class people. Although Hamilton shows that middle strata support for the NSDAP was not monolithic, and that the Protestant rich also voted heavily for the Nazis, more studies will be necessary to truly question the *Mittelstand* thesis. Finally, even if the thesis in the future will have to be highly qualified, it has been a very influential one ever since the 1930s; it is therefore understandable that Mann, Böll, and Grass developed fictional versions of an interpretation that many contemporary historians, political scientists, sociologists, and social psychologists endorsed.

4. Karl Dietrich Bracher, *The German Dictatorship*, trans. Jean Steinberg (New York: Praeger, 1970), p. 157. Another now standard history, Gordon Craig, *Germany 1866-1945* (Oxford: Oxford University Press, 1980), argues the same thesis, as does Heinrich August Winkler's monographic work on the subject, *Mittelstand, Demokratie und Nationalsozialismus* (Cologne: Kiepenheuer & Witsch, 1972).

already tasted democracy, would tolerate any longer the traditional elites governing without a believable claim to represent more than their own interests. On the other hand, although he had won the support of the middle classes, Hitler came into office in 1933 not on an irresistible wave of popular acclaim but, rather, as part of a process of back-room political dealings with the old elites. As Alan Bullock has emphasized, the Nazis would never have come to power "legally," through a "revolution from above," without the willingness of the German Right already in control between 1930 and 1933 to accept them as a partner in government. [5] These representatives of the old ruling classes of Imperial Germany mistakenly expected to be able to control Hitler for their own ends and ensure their own power through his mass support. What the Army leaders, the industrialists and businessmen, and the upper classes of the German Right wanted was to regain their "old position as the ruling class; to destroy the hated republic and restore the monarchy; to put the working classes 'in their places'; to rebuild the military power of Germany; to reverse the decision of 1918 and to restore Germany -- their Germany -- to a dominant position in Europe." [6]

Their massive blunder was nearly equaled by the disastrous policy pursued by Moscow until 1933. Following the Moscow line, the Communist party (KPD) gave priority to elimination of the Social Democrats (SPD) as the rival working-class party. Totally underestimating the Nazi threat, the Communists believed that their path to power would be aided by the elimination of the SPD and by a Nazi take-over which would soon collapse. Though more aware of the possibility of a powerful Nazi dictatorship, the Social Democrats had become a sclerotic trade-union party without leaders capable of organizing a successful opposition to Hitler. [7] The ineffectiveness and failure of the German Left to unite undoubtedly facilitated the rise of the National Socialists to power. Unwilling, of course, to join with its opposite on the political spectrum, the

5.   Alan Bullock, *Hitler: A Study in Tyranny* (New York: Bantam, 1953), p. 213.

6.   Ibid., p. 215.

7.   Ibid., p. 214.

traditional German Right turned to the nationalist middle class masses radicalized and mobilized by the Nazis. The Nazi program seemed close enough to the desires of the old elites, once it was shorn of its extreme elements, which the respectable Right allowed itself to believe would disappear after the Nazis shared governmental responsibility. But it was precisely because Hitler's program was backed by thirty-seven percent of the population that the old elites contracted to rule with him. Within this conjuncture of historical forces, the massive middle class backing of the Nazis became critical.

Tracing the actual intrigues behind closed doors, scrutinizing the political tactics of the traditional Right or the disunited Left -- such pursuits are the task of the historian. However significant in the scramble for political power these details are, they indicate little about the human experience in the existential social milieu in which Nazi party members and voters lived. The question inevitably emerges: what gave rise to this crucial support? Focus on the *Mittelstand* and their milieu uncovers the most important social sources of the support. It is their story that unfolds in these three novels.

Although it may seem impossible to discuss such different figures as the Matzerath family, the Fähmels, and Zeitblom as belonging to one social stratum, the term *Mittelstand* characterizes all of them and captures perhaps best what Bracher refers to as "'middle class,' in the broad sense of the word." The use of such a broad term, literally middle estate, to describe social groups with such divergent economic interests, styles of living and life expectations, and so lacking in the kind of relative political unity displayed by great landowners, big businessmen, and workers, does have some justification. In his analysis of these middle strata, Hermann Lebovics states: "Even if the concept of a middle estate with its implications of a pre-industrial society organized in *Stände*, or corporate bodies, could represent no economic or social reality after the middle of the nineteenth century, it could, and did, represent a unity of aspiration and of fear for the future."[8] As Germany experienced with increasing intensity and tempo the consequences of capitalist industrialization in the second half of the nineteenth century, common fears worked to form the beginnings of unity in the middle strata of society. Unlike the unity of industrialists or the labor movement, it was a negative unity. Fears of economic irrelevance and, above all, loss of status stalked the middle classes.[9] Hitler's middle- and lower-middle-class faithfuls wanted to strike out against the classes both above them and below, against the capitalists with their trusts and department stores, and against the industrial workers with their unions.[10]

The term *Stand*, which has pre-industrial roots, implies precisely this concern with status, as opposed to class, which refers more to economic level. Users of the word *Stand* often want to de-emphasize their economic condition -- for example, *Mittelstand* professional people who wish to compensate for their poor economic situation with thoughts of status. Such usage indicates too a view about society in general, which is not seen here as structured according to economic forces. As Lebovics says, to many members of the middle classes in this period the view that society was nothing more than aggregates of economic power in conflict was abhorrent: "They preferred to view society as an organism in equilibrium. And, of course, they liked to conceive of themselves as the heart, or, better, the soul of the social body."[11]

Lebovics designates three main groups of this variegated *Stand*.[12] The most numerous group was the old *Mittelstand*: peasant proprietors, artisans, and small businessmen in (broadly speaking) "pre-industrial" occupations. This group could not compete with

---

8. Hermann Lebovics, *Social Conservatism and the German Middle Classes 1914-1933* (Princeton: Princeton University Press, 1968), p. 5.

9. Ibid., p. 5.

10. Heinz Lubasz, "Hitler's Welfare State," *New York Review of Books*, December, 1968, p. 33.

11. Lebovics, p. 9.

12. Ibid., pp. 6-7.

larger firms which could buy and sell in bulk; they suffered more than their larger competitors from market economy fluctuations because they were rarely able to get favorable legislation or create monopolies. Their restless, status-seeking mentality is reflected in Grass's small shopkeeper Matzerath. The second group, the new middle class who held jobs created mostly by industrialization, does not appear in the three novels. The third division included those who had taken up pursuits that had been held in great esteem in the days before industry transformed German national life: state officials, university students, lawyers, doctors, school teachers, architects. These individuals were involved in activities only indirectly related to the capitalist economy of Germany. Although economic downswings had no direct effect upon such positions, intellectually aware members of such occupational groups could not fail to realize to what degree their own status and economic position depended upon the continuation of the social structure in which, before 1914, they had found a comfortable place. [13] Consequently they identified themselves with the status quo of a society which in retrospect appeared stable, harmonious, and legitimately stratified. Clearly recognizable in this description is Mann's Zeitblom. Although social status and economic position are less salient concerns for the "spiritually" oriented Fähmels in Böll's novel, their whole provincial style of living, rooted in the nineteenth century, is threatened by modern society. Even though the novels' figures in this third level of the *Mittelstand* are professionals, they, like many of their historical counterparts, have no power connections within or without the small towns in which they reside. Such teachers and architects have had as little influence on socio-political developments as the *Kleinbürger*-grocer. Circumscribed by their small milieu, the perspective, mentality and values of this group of the middle estate often resemble those of the *Kleinbürger*.

The *Mittelstand* thus appears to include persons of varying incomes, status, and values. The term *Mittelstand* actually encompasses a complex and differentiated group of people who nonetheless shared particular problems. They all feared economic or social

---

13.   Ibid., pp. 7-8.

irrelevance. Naturally those persons on the lower rungs of the hierarchy within their own occupations felt the threat most keenly. As a Gymnasium schoolmaster, not a university professor or respected scholar, Zeitblom parallels within his profession the small businessman Matzerath who is outranked by larger firms. In a comparable position within the educational hierarchy to Matzerath in the business world, Zeitblom is likely to feel more insecure and old-fashioned than his superiors in the ranks of intellectuals, when his humanist philosophies appear superseded in the growing "mass" society about him. Thus the teacher or architect who held a philosophy more appropriate to the previous century could bear some resemblance to the small tradesman whose self-esteem and status also rested in that older social structure.

Such brief sociological descriptions only begin to hint at the social, political, and historical significance of the novels' protagonists. The foregoing analysis of the *Mittelstand* should initially ground the novels' major characters in their extra-literary social context. Any critical evaluation of literary attempts to come to terms with the Nazi past must measure these attempts against sociological and historical analyses of the period. With differing degrees of social understanding and different interpretations of Nazism, these three writers have all given members of the *Mittelstand* central roles in their novels of the epoch. Their views of the role of the *Mittelstand* are in each case a key to their understanding of Nazism.

The Mittelstand Misapprehends History

For the novel of his era, Mann reviews in the light of historical circumstances the artist-bourgeois conflict that appears in so many of his stories. The author's previous mistrust of either polar figure appears to find vindication in their fascist variations. A revised Wagner, the bourgeois counterpart to the Faustian artist, unwittingly simulates here the petit bourgeois protagonist. Serenus Zeitblom, as narrator of *Doctor Faustus*, tries to comment on the petit bourgeois milieu while still subject to its historically generated psychology. Most critics, focusing as they do on the humanist or undaemonic character of Zeitblom, fail to analyze him also as a member of the *Mittelstand*. [14] Certainly Zeitblom would not have marked time with Alfred Matzerath; Zeitblom is not a Nazi. And yet he is an ambivalent opponent of National Socialism, impotent at best in his dissent. Zeitblom's weakness and ambivalence in the face of Nazism derive in no small part from a middle class perspective.

In his conception of Zeitblom, Mann transforms a bourgeois humanist into the slightly comic character of an old-fashioned pedant. To mitigate the torment of the novel's subject, the author shields himself with humor; he narrates through a caricature of the humanist burgher in himself. Mann's reckoning with his epoch is a reckoning with himself seen historically. In *Story of a Novel* he refers to directly confessional aspects of the work and emphasizes that Zeitblom and Leverkühn "have far too much to conceal, namely the secret of their identities" (EDF 740). For Mann, then, the novel becomes a settlement with the artist and the burgher in himself, with both identities seen as representative of his epoch, an epoch coming to an end in Nazism. Mann's parody of his *Bildungsbürger* Zeitblom often transforms him into a *Bildungsphilister*. In making

---

14. Two notable exceptions, which do analyze Zeitblom's position in the social structure, are: Inge Diersen, *Untersuchungen zu Thomas Mann*, 5th ed. (Berlin: Rütten & Loening, 1965); Eugen Barbu and Adrei Ion Deleanu, "Serenus Zeitblom," *Sinn und Form Sonderheft zu Thomas Mann* (Berlin: Rütten & Loening, 1965), pp. 134-143.

this philistine the mediator of the social reality leading up to Nazism, Mann creates a schoolmaster within that reality whose understanding of Nazism reflects his social circumstances. Zeitblom mirrors the mentality of the threatened *Mittelstand* in the pre-Nazi period.

Zeitblom's introduction of himself explicitly emphasizes his roots within the *Mittelstand*: "It was in the modest rank of a semi-professional middle class ['*Mittelstand*' in the original] that I came into the world. My father, Wohlgemut Zeitblom, was an apothecary, though the most important in town." (DF, 14) Already Zeitblom appears to be among those who prefer the implications of social and cultural status in the word *Stand* to the economic reference of the world *Klasse*: the *Mittelstand* of his father was half professional, his apothecary the most important in the town square. The "scholar" Zeitblom, the "man of the fine arts," tends to be above materialistic considerations. Zeitblom's pride rests rather in his own intellectual contemplations, which inform his perspective and writing style throughout the novel. The limitations of his intellectual understanding of the epoch derive, in part, from his *Stand*: Zeitblom, the intellectual, remains a *Kleinbürger*.

Characteristic of Zeitblom's narrative are pedantic diversions such as the following passage: "I will not look back, and I will take care not to count how many pages I have amassed between the last Roman numeral and the one just written. The disaster, a surely totally unanticipated one, has come to pass, and it would be useless to expend myself in its behalf in self-accusation and excuses." (DF, 96) And so forth. To "brighten up the gloomy material" (EDF, 700), Mann lets the laughable, painstaking pedant step forward. Interesting here is the discrepancy between the unimportance of the subject matter and the importance lent to it through Zeitblom's thorough, detailed analysis, and the inappropriately pathetic word "disaster." Totally overestimating the significance of such details as the number of pages per chapter is in itself harmless enough. Such absorption with petty details, however, or, on the other hand, assimilation of large, complex problems into a narrow trivializing perspective characterizes Zeitblom's thinking on many less harmless social and political issues.

Zeitblom's political views can be explained in part by the context in which he writes. Constantly fearing that one of his own sons could report him for his work on a biography of a banned "decadent" composer, this inner emigrant is necessarily cautious in criticizing the National Socialists. In remembering a positive youthful experience with the learned town rabbi, for example, Zeitblom writes, as late as 1943: "It may be the result of this youthful experience, but also because of the keen-scented receptivity of Jewish circles for Leverkühn's work, but I have never, precisely in the Jewish problem and its management, been able to agree fully with our Führer and his paladins; and this fact was not without influence on my resignation from the teaching staff here." (DF, 14-15) Such fear and caution understandably obscure Zeitblom's vision to pass over direct confrontation with Nazi language and its manipulative aims. He approaches the "Jewish problem," the bureaucratic term for the proposed liquidation of an entire "race," as a question with pros and cons to be weighed intellectually. His use of Hitler's euphemisms facilitates here his already strong tendency toward somewhat philistine philosophizing. Indeed, without realizing the implications of his statements, Zeitblom appears to argue that people who embody such valuable qualities as some Jews he has known should be permitted to live. Even in Germany today, according to Hannah Arendt, there are more than a few people, especially among the cultural elite, who still deplore the fate of "prominent" Jews only, "who still publicly regret the fact that Germany sent Einstein packing, without realizing that it was a much greater crime to kill little Hans Cohn from around the corner, even though he was no genius." [15]

Zeitblom's recognition of the Nazi threat to the scholarly and artistic pursuits he values did motivate him to resign from his teaching position. This act undoubtedly represents more opposition to the Nazis than many teachers of his day were able to muster. The reasons for his resignation, however, omit the reality that millions of human beings were being slaughtered who had a right to live whether or not they were learned or cultured. Precisely

---

15. Hannah Arendt, *Eichmann in Jerusalem* (New York: Viking Press, 1965), p. 134.

through his verbal distancing techniques, the well-intentioned Zeitblom could be grouped close to the unassuming figure of Alfred Matzerath warming his fingers on the synagogue fire. Just as the Crystal Night means for Matzerath that something is "going on" in the city, so also Zeitblom at the outset of the novel unintentionally absorbs the problem of genocide into the framework of his everyday life and normal intellectual routine. Only in 1945 when full information about the camps was made public does he specify genocide as a source of his general sense of horror expressed throughout the war. The initial susceptibility of the well-meaning schoolmaster to Nazi manipulation of thought evolves in part out of his penchant for abstract thinking, but it also attests to the "success" of their techniques. Even Zeitblom, who retires when the Nazis come to power, has not entirely escaped their infiltration of the mind.

Similar instances of such philistine intellectualization abound in *Doctor Faustus*. In each case, the same pattern of thought appears as above: social and political issues of massive import are distilled down to the reclusive proportions of the pedant. Since Zeitblom's priorities revolve primarily around writing his biography of Leverkühn, he perceives the war or Nazism as background disturbances: "I may say that the times are not precisely favorable to the steady pursuance of such a work as this. And, moreover, just during the Munich disorders and executions, I got an influenza with fever and chills, which for ten days confined me to my bed." (DF, 230) The war atrocities almost appear to be in the same category with Zeitblom's flu: both have impeded his progress on the biography. History-making events have been assimilated to the small world of Zeitblom's book. Precisely this kind of parody, which provides comic relief for Mann, reveals the narrowness of Zeitblom's perspective. As in the Matzerath family, radio or newspaper reports about the course of the war are the sole means of contact for Zeitblom with the world outside his hermitage in Freising.

Not only his biography, but also Adrian's music takes precedence for Zeitblom over all political, social and moral considerations. As quoted above, memories of a learned town rabbi and the Jews' receptivity to Adrian's compositions dissuade Zeitblom from supporting genocide. Just as disturbing is that the "learned" biographer often admits that his desire for the immortalization of Adrian's work actually motivates his opposition to Nazism. His hope for preservation of Leverkühn's music is part of a broader concern for German culture. His conception of culture and the resulting questionable opposition to Nazism evolve out of his position in the *Mittelstand.*

This Wilhelmian scholar's notion of culture is exclusive; "real" art is not easily accessible to the masses. Rebelling against Adrian's impassioned hopes for an art intimate to all humanity, Zeitblom maintains: "Art is of the mind and spirit [Geist], which do not at all need to feel obligated to the society, the community. . . . An art that goes in unto the folk, which makes the needs of the crowd, the little man, and small minds its own, sinks into poverty." (DF, 429) Zeitblom saw fascism as just that: small-mindedness and the impoverishment of *Geist.*

Often in the novel, what he rightly identifies in fascism is also a threat to traditional culture: fascism is primitive, barbaric, crude, common. The same threat, however, this "moderate man and son of culture" perceives in communist and democratic popular movements. Only reluctantly, in the last years of the war, does he begin to alter his view of "mob rule": "The dictatorship of the proletariat appears to me, the German burgher, as an ideal situation, compared now with the dictatorship of the scum of the earth. To my knowledge, Bolshevism has never destroyed any works of art." (DF, 451) The cultured aesthetic distaste implied in the term scum or dregs of society (*Abschaum*) is not so much inaccurate as utterly inadequate in itself as an understanding of Nazism and its rise to power. Zeitblom's respect here for Bolshevism does not imply the social insight that Lukács suggests. [16] Behind both his weak preference for communism or democracy and his disgust with Nazism is his desire to preserve culture as he conceives of it. He is helpless to fight or even understand much of fascism beyond the threat it poses to traditional culture.

---

16. Georg Lukács, *Essays on Thomas Mann,* trans. Stanley Mitchell (New York: Grosset & Dunlap, 1964), p. 86.

In his aversion to the Nazis as common, Zeitblom represents many teachers and professors of his time whose sense of status was offended by "the democratic leveling mania." The motives behind their rejection of Nazism as described by W. F. Haug resemble Zeitblom's: "Of the reasons given for opposition to fascism, not political, but those motives resting on high estimation of one's own status dominate." [17]

The destruction of high culture menaces all that Zeitblom has ever stood for and believed in. As the cultured burgher, Zeitblom faces irrelevance. He is indeed a part of the *Mittelstand* group (as described by Lebovics) whose status depended upon the continuation of a social structure which before 1914 had afforded them a comfortable place. In Zeitblom's own nineteenth-century epoch of bourgeois humanism, the respect paid to the educated, cultured individual supported the schoolmaster's own sense of dignity and worth. Thus, Zeitblom later agrees when the Kridwiss-Kreis decries the loss of value that the (once privileged) individual suffers after World War I; typically ignoring any rational social analysis, these men speak of "the ruthlessness with which *life* today strides over the individual." (DF, 484-Emphasis added)

Zeitblom's more fanatic counterparts appear in such contemporary "intellectual" circles. Mann draws upon his own analysis of Lagarde and the George-circle when he portrays in the Kridwiss-Kreis the intellectual milieu of a politicized *Mittelstand*. In the political discussions of these philistines, as Lukács has pointed out, the "'small world' is confronted by no 'great' one; it reduces the themes and dimensions of the 'great world' to its own eccentric, esoteric, reactionary and increasingly barbaric philistinism." [18] Such caricatures of the *Bildungsbürger* are even more convinced than Zeitblom that their bourgeois traditions are at an end. Affirming the decay of their culture, these Sorel-enthusiasts join in the attack on the positivistic scholarship of their day, and gleefully proclaim

---

17. Wolfgang Fritz Haug, *Der hilflose Antifaschismus* (Frankfurt am Main: Suhrkamp, 1970), p. 77.

18. Lukács, *Essays*, p. 62.

the irrational sources of social cohesion. Their love of organic community and disdain for "merely critical" reason imply a hatred of
modern socio-economic rationalization. In his analysis of similar
university "mandarins" in this period, Fritz Ringer identifies the
source of these passions as the hatred of "class" society which had
replaced the status patterns of an earlier age: "This is the area in
which mandarin antimodernity began to resemble some of its
lowbrow variants. Large segments of the middle and lower middle
classes were also victimized by the sudden disequilibrium between
class and status elements in German social stratification. On a
pretheoretical level, common resentments created ideological
affinities." [19]

Leverkühn's apocalyptic music echoes in Zeitblom's ears while
he listens horrified to these descendents of bourgeois traditions
incanting their own end. The venerated cultural tradition has
become separated from the majority of the people and thus increasingly introverted, esoteric, inhumane, and barbaric. The "inwardness" of its burgher and artists has no "outward" potential. Just as
his author intended (EDF, 700-701), Zeitblom becomes less and less
successful at denying the relationship between the bombs outside
which frighten him and the biographical material inside. What
Mann has Zeitblom recognize is this: the irrational or daemonic elements which had seemed upsetting but fascinating in art are mur-
derous in their social and political manifestations. [20]

This narrator concludes that art and its admirers must be politically and socially responsible. And Zeitblom begins about halfway through the novel to expand his narrative to include much
more of the world outside. Only through recognizing the daemonic
in both the political and cultural realms does he gradually cease to
relegate Nazism to a marginal position in his thoughts and,

19. Fritz Ringer, *The Decline of the German Mandarins: The German Academic Community, 1890-1933* (Cambridge, Massachusetts: Harvard University Press,
1969), p. 447.

20. See Mann's speech, "Deutschland und die Deutschen," for further exposition of
the writer's links between Faust, "inwardness," and fascism.

therefore, in the novel. More pages devoted, however, to Zeitblom's understanding of fascism as barbaric or daemonic do not compensate for the inadequacy of this limited interpretation. The "son of culture" represents the reprehensible defenselessness of the German idealist tradition.

Does such cultivated disdain for fascism extend beyond the humanist schoolmaster? Does the author share his views or is he critical of them? As the novel progresses, the parody evident in so much of Zeitblom's narrative seems to be increasingly absent from his discussions about fascism. Passages like the one previously quoted condemning Nazism as "mob rule" resemble Zeitblom's competent discussions of Adrian's music in their sober, thoughtful tones. For these interpretations of music and politics, he has been given a language which asks to be taken seriously. The narrowness of Zeitblom's political understanding is not offset by parody or other passages in the novel: communism and democracy are presented as the saviors of traditional high culture, fascism as the harbinger of irrational barbarism. These particular political attitudes suggest finally those of the novel and its author. As a bourgeois pedant in "inner emigration," who still speaks of the Allies as "our enemy," Zeitblom appears to lack the insights of the exiled patrician bourgeois. With the increasingly unparodied language in the second half of the novel, however, Zeitblom does repeat, often in overstated or flattened form, his author's attitudes. In accordance with his own narrow concerns, for example, the biographer confesses that his desire for recognition of Leverkühn's music motivates his opposition to Hitler's regime. Here Zeitblom's "anti-fascism" is a limited version of Mann's defense of high vs. mass culture--a defense which Zeitblom also duplicates directly in his unparodied condemnation of Nazism as impoverishment of the cultured *Geist*. Zeitblom's language, free of irony, often expresses attitudes the author articulated in letters and speeches.

Mann's early social views, of course, derived from his patrician background and literary position within the cultivated circles of the prewar Wilhelmian era. In this milieu he, like Zeitblom, was committed to the defense of traditional high culture against the democratic "rabble." Such views found expression during the war in the

Observations of an Unpolitical Man which excoriated western "materialistic" democracy. By 1922, however, Mann had adjusted to Germany's new parliamentary regime and had implicitly resigned himself to the passing of the patrician society of his youth. Like his narrator, he began to argue for a more politically responsible commitment on the part of those supporting high cultural ideals and in addition found some solace in the cultural views of Social Democrats. [21] It is clear in all this, however, that by evading the issue of socialist economics and its attempt to democratize society radically, and by finding in socialism the repository of traditional culture, Mann never entirely left his earlier attitudes behind. The patrician motive behind his "Confession to Socialism" is not difficult to find. Whereas many critics praise Mann's anti-fascism without closer examination of its motives, Isaac Deutscher acknowledges the writer's courageous sincerity but also notes that one of the impulses which moved him into opposition and exile was "the antagonism of the cultivated patrician bourgeois to the savage plebeians, the *Kleinbürger* and *Lumpenproletarier* who were running amok in the shadow of the swastika." [22]

Exile in California might have encouraged Mann's tendency to overgeneralize from his own cultural background when analyzing Germany. Viewed in America as the spokesman for his country and the authority on Nazism, Mann used his own experience and soul-searching as a microcosm of "the German trauma." Mann's concentration on his own past, nonetheless, did evolve into the depiction of a *Mittelstand* response to fascism. The *Bildungsbürger* of Mann's background, steeped in traditions of inwardness, was as politically inexperienced and impotent as the less educated *Kleinbürger* that Grass knew so well.

Both Mann and Grass describe the social milieu they know best. The son of the more educated Lübeck senator and grain company proprietor would understandably emphasize different origins

---

21. Thomas Mann, "Rede vor Arbeitern in Wien," *Gesammelte Werke*, XI (Oldenburg: Fischer, 1960), pp. 890-910.

22. Isaac Deutscher, *Marxism in our Time* (Berkeley: Ramparts Press, 1971), p. 285.

of Nazism than would the son of a suburban grocer. Whereas Mann pursues what he sees as the philosophical sources of Nazi ideology at great length, Grass shows less interest in the search for its alleged intellectual precursors. Lagarde and Sorel are granted little acclaim in the homes of bakers and grocers. In Grass's novel the aura of fascism is represented by the fetid air of a petit bourgeois living room instead of the chilling salon atmosphere where educated conversation heralds the apocalypse. Grass's focus on his milieu reveals the banality of the middle class Hitler-faithfuls and thus de-demonizes the same movement which the Kridwiss-Kreis hails as the delicious dissolution of the world.

Just at the intellectuals in *Doctor Faustus*, including Zeitblom, are fascinated by the daemonic, other provincial characters in the novel personify it. According to Zeitblom, the strange hermits in Kaisersaschern and something of the hysteria of the later Middle Ages left hanging in the air make mystical, symbolic acts like book-burnings not unthinkable. Where Grass sees the good-natured, average shopkeeper warming his hands on the fire caused by the burning of the synagogue, Mann might see a vixen hag. Mann, along with Zeitblom, focuses on the daemonic, irrational sides of provincialism; its backward-looking elements he sees manifested in the communal hysteria of Nazism. [23]

---

23. Thomas Mann, "Deutschland und die Deutschen," *Schriften zur Politik* (Frankfurt am Main: Suhrkamp, 1970), pp. 165-167.

The Petit Bourgeois Makes History

Mann pokes fun at his antiquated bourgeois narrator; Grass lets his narrator mock the petit bourgeois environment. Not so myopically grounded in middle class attitudes and tradition, Oskar jeers at what Zeitblom embodies. And yet this imp of a narrator can speak for his milieu as well as, if not better than, Zeitblom does for all the petty philistines. As the voice of the *Kleinbürger*, Oskar slides back and forth between more and less obvious satire of him, intermittently suggesting a sympathetic insider's view. More mobile than the realistic schoolmaster, the fantastic dwarf at times appears to speak for the petit bourgeois, while quietly satirizing him; at other moments, Oskar's mocking attack is more direct. For example, Oskar can faithfully recall in detail all courses of a family dinner from the potato schnapps to the fruit pudding with sour cream. Here he hints at an ironic distance, reproducing the obsessive absorptions of the *Spiessbürger* in a suffocatingly small world where the food at family festivities is at least as important as the brewing world war. In contrast, a similar obsessive devotion to carpet-beating is criticized more vigorously by the same narrator. To defend his ears from the thunder overwhelming the back yards, Oskar drums in competition with the rug-beating housewives and their "hymn to cleanliness."

In their angry protests against the twelve years of Nazism, many postwar writers (Böll included) tended to reduce the Nazis to "the others," while conscientiously exploring problems of anti-fascism. Mann avoids such a reductive, uncomprehending view of the fascists through the personal self-scrutiny behind the characterization of Leverkühn and Zeitblom; he also, nonetheless, permits readers to exclude themselves from the indictment of both the composer and his admirer by linking their fascist propensities to exotic pacts with the devil or a fascination with daemonic irrationalism. Whereas Grass also maintains that a writer must be able to identify with the figures he creates, including the SS-men, he says the writer must love all these characters in a literary, cool and distanced way--quite dispassionate in comparison with Mann. Precisely that sympathetic but detached attitude, Grass continues, determined his literary creations, "including the figure Oskar

Matzerath, who, in the midst of the petite bourgeoisie, as part of them, and as their mouthpiece, tells his story." [24] To encourage the reader's critical understanding of these Nazi supporters, in *The Tin Drum* Grass has given the *Kleinbürgertum* a narrator who knows them so intimately that he can both imitate and slyly satirize them.

Even the physical appearance of the grotesque gnome suggests he is a satirical facsimile of the petit bourgeois. As a dwarf, he is the "little man" in extreme. All the little Matzeraths, Greffs, and Meyns line up feeling proud and "bigger" behind the mission of the swastika. Oskar's size suggests not only the little men outsized by socio-historical developments, but also a resultant childishness in their behavior which the Nazis encouraged. In contrast to those about him, Oskar consciously chooses his roles: when he appears childish, he is playing out deliberately the naiveté and self-absorption that others unconsciously embody. When he mimics their faith in a Santa Claus-Hitler and their indifference to the suffering of others, he represents the infantilism of an epoch. [25] The misshapen dwarf provides an exaggerated mirror image of these grotesquely evasive little folk.

Like all these arrogant "little men," Oskar declares himself a hero. One can still write a novel nowadays, he maintains, because individuality is not a thing of the past. He and his keeper Bruno "are still far from being a nameless, heroless mass." (Bt, 11) Such self-perception satirizes a view most common among the sheltered, anti-modern middle classes. The *Mittelstand* that Lebovics describes did not acknowledge modern mass society when they viewed themselves as the heart and soul of the social body, instead of part of a "nameless, heroless mass." As shall be discussed later, a novel portraying Nazi manipulation of the nineteenth-century attitudes of

---

24. Heinz Ludwig Arnold, "Gespräch mit Günter Grass," *Text und Kritik* 1/1a (Günter Grass issue), October, 1971, p. 5.

25. Michael Hollington, *Günter Grass: The Writer in a Pluralist Society* (London: Boyars, 1980), pp. 43-45. "Childish" is not to be confused here with "child-like," another aspect of Oskar which brings out positive though often repressed sides of adults around him. This is discussed in Chapters 2 and 3.

the middle classes will understandably satirize characteristics of the nineteenth-century novel.

As an ordinary, full-sized human being, Oskar would not have the mobility necessary to play satirically in the various poses of the petit bourgeois. Perhaps even more important, a manifestly grotesque "little man" can expose best the seemingly apolitical, naive, and petty little men who nonetheless made catastrophic history. To put it simply, Grass meets the grotesque with the grotesque. That is, an outrageous narrator and extraordinary situations are necessary in the novel to unmask the extremity of everyday Nazi reality. Thus the irreal gnome helps to create fantastic, grotesque situations which reveal as strange, in a manner reminiscent of Brecht, what the estranged, that is, adapted, ordinary reader had perhaps accepted as normal. Fantastic episodes provide a fresh, critical look at what passed for ordinary reality in the Third Reich.

The rostrum scene illustrates how the fantastic reveals hidden realities. Unlikely as such a delightful disruption of a Nazi rally is, one of its effects is to make the *Kleinbürger*-Nazis look ridiculous in what Böll would call their "bourgeois earnestness." The passersby gathered in front of the rostrum prefer the playful dancing rhythm of Oskar's drum to the strict march beat of the Nazis. The drummer boys are also drawn into Oskar's waltz, to the frustration of their corps leaders, Löbsack, and other party dignitaries. Later, while the drummers suffer punitive drills, the indignant Löbsack paces up and down the meadow: "About-facing on the heels of his boots, he had succeeded in eradicating all the grass and daisies at each end of his resolute marching path." (Bt, 99) Significantly, Oskar's dancers had left the daisies untouched. Having repressed natural instincts, a compulsive official like Löbsack fears the natural vitality around him. In Wilhelm Reich's analysis of lower-middle-class behavior of this period, the military exhibitionism of rhythmically perfect parades becomes a substitute gratification for suppressed sexual needs. [26] Not fantasy for fantasy's sake, the

---

26. Wilhelm Reich, *The Mass Psychology of Fascism*, trans. from the manuscript of the revised and enlarged third edition (Albion, Michigan: Albion Press, 1970), p. 26.

unreal, the unlikely points to the psycho-social sources of automaton militarism. [27]

Thus, the dwarfish drummer provides the perspective to view the real eccentrics and the dangerously real grotesque in his environment. Of the three novelists, Grass is the most avowedly conscious of the historical significance of his petit bourgeois characters. According to Geno Hartlaub in an interview with the writer, Grass became aware while working on his novels that "extensive areas that one usually considers unpolitical depend in reality very much on politics -- the suffocating domain of the petits bourgeois, for example, with their false idylls of family festivities, their ineradicable need for security, their delusions of grandeur, and their equation of social ascent with general progress." In *The Tin Drum* specifically, Grass says that he tried to show "how latently political the unpolitical petits bourgeois have been as pillars of a *Weltanschauung* like that of the Nazi regime." [28]

Oskar's view of his family from underneath the card table and the marriage bed takes in scene after scene of this confined musty milieu. Screened from the upheavals of modernization, people appear to exist just as they have for centuries. World-shaking events take place outside this little apartment on the city outskirts and find their way into it only through the radio reports of

27. Cf. Franz Schonauer, "Günter Grass. Ein literarischer Bürgerschreck von gestern?" *Zeitkritische Romane des 20. Jahrhunderts*, ed. Hans Wagener (Stuttgart: Reclam, 1975), pp. 342-361. In claiming that Grass uses history only to stimulate his wild fantasies, Schonauer overlooks the psycho-social and historical revelations of these fantastic scenes.

28. Geno Hartlaub, "Wir, die wir übriggeblieben sind. . . ," in *Von Buch zu Buch - Günter Grass in der Kritik*, ed. Gert Loschütz (Neuwied and Berlin: Luchterhand, 1968), p. 212. But Norbert Mecklenburg, "Faschismus und Alltag in deutscher Gegenwartsprosa. Kempowski und andere," *Gegenwartsliteratur und Drittes Reich*, ed. Hans Wagener (Stuttgart: Reclam, 1977), p. 27; and Helmut Koopmann, "Günter Grass. Der Faschismus als Kleinbürgertum und was daraus wurde," *Gegenwartsliteratur und Drittes Reich*, ed. Hans Wagener (Stuttgart: Reclam, 1977), pp. 171-174, judge the novel to be ahistorical, Grass's stated intentions notwithstanding. They miss in Grass the socio-historical sources of *Kleinbürger* support for Hitler analyzed in the following pages.

submarine victories, emergency announcements, etc. Hitler's rise to power is registered in little household details: vacuum cleaning replaces rug beating in the back yard; Hitler's picture now stares opposite Beethoven's in the living room. Oskar's narrative reveals the seeming discrepancy between the barely comprehended events of world history and the daily predominant concerns of the *Kleinbürger*. Such political naiveté and privatism, however, prove themselves not at all incongruous with national politics. These attitudes make the petits bourgeois receptive to ideologies promising to better their lot; they turn out in full-dress support of Hitler. The "negative unity" of the middle classes is being politicized. The one-time "unpolitical" *Kleinbürger* is making history. [29]

Generally frustrated as the unrepresented "little man" and particularly restless on a Sunday at home, Alfred Matzerath eagerly escapes from the confines of his stuffy living room to the Nazis' outdoor rally meetings. Deftly characterized in a few scenes strewn throughout the book, Matzerath personifies the insecure, loyal conformist, "who always shouts, laughs, or claps when others shout, laugh, or clap." (Bt, 123) He joins the Nazi party out of this internal pressure to conform ("when that was still quite unnecessary") and out of a need for social status rather than for material, opportunistic aims ("gained nothing" - Bt, 123). Certainly his unrewarding work in the grocery has not won him social esteem: he comments at his son's birth, "Now we finally know what we've been working ourselves to death for." (Bt, 35) His harbored resentments and aggressions are assuaged by the status feeling he attains when he dons a uniform. Oskar, poring over old photos, notes the proud though tragic gaze of Father Matzerath in World War I uniform. Alfred looks "demoralized" in the interwar years. His neighbor Meyn (another representative figure: all the storm troopers--SA--in Markus's store resemble him) is similarly disoriented after World War I; he seeks order and social recognition as an SA member. [30]

29. Gertrude Cepl-Kaufmann, *Günter Grass: eine Analyse des Gesamtwerkes unter dem Aspekt von Literatur und Politik* (Kronberg/Ts.: Scriptor, 1975) and Frank Richter, *Günter Grass: Die Vergangenheitsbewältigung in der Danzig-Trilogie* (Bonn: Bouvier, 1979) both miss the epochal resonance of this privatism.

30. Heinz Hillmann, "Günter Grass's 'Blechtrommel.' Beispiel und Überlegungen

Although Matzerath is not a fanatic mass murderer, he nonetheless shares with a Höss or a Himmler the public-private split. Reserving any vestiges of humanity he has for the private world, he proudly follows orders in the outside one. After all, as Matzerath announces upon leaving for the rally, "Duty is duty, and schnapps is schnapps."

The invasion of the Red Army brings this dutiful party member's life to a fitting end. Having anxiously swallowed his party pin to conceal it from the Russians, the red-faced Matzerath involuntarily provokes a suspicious Russian to shoot at him. His ensuing death has no greater consequence than that the termites in the cellar have to make a detour around the corpse. Pretentious bravery, stupidity, and hubris have all been shot down simultaneously. As Grass says, petty aggressions, a false sense of self-importance: such characteristics can be almost lovable within the private realm, but become dangerous and grotesque when the *Kleinbürger* takes over the political leadership.[31] The braggart Matzerath, choking to death on the Nazi party (-pin needle), finds in this sense a justly grotesque end. Such scenes as well as the gnome who describes them mirror the disproportions of a regime of "giant-dwarfs."[32]

---

zum Verfahren der Konfrontation von Literatur- und Sozialwissenschaften," *Der deutsche Roman im 20. Jahrhundert*, vol. 2, ed. Manfred Brauneck (Bamberg: C. C. Buchners, 1976), pp. 7, 8, 12, 13, 15. When Hillmann argues, however, that Grass makes the causes of petit bourgeois support of Hitler seem ahistorical by omitting their economic misery, he underestimates the importance of Meyn's and Matzerath's needs for social status, typical of *Mittelstand* thinking at this time, which tended to assimilate economic questions to those of status. Hillmann also seems implicitly to expect the novel to contain all the factual details of a work of sociology or history. Similar criticisms to Hillmann's are made by Silke Jendrowiak, *Günter Grass und die "Hybris" des Kleinbürgers* (Heidelberg: Winter, 1979), p. 294.

31. Hartlaub, "Wir, die wir übriggeblieben sind. . . ," p. 212.

32. The expression is borrowed from the title of the novel *Die Riesenzwerge* (1964) by Gisela Elsner.

Like their midget mouthpiece Oskar, all the little folk in this environment are "dwarfed" by the larger corporate system around them. These small shopkeepers see the world from below, unlike the department store owner or factory owner. Each one seeks his or her outlet for the energies pent up in this small domain. Whenever Oskar feels hostile with the omnipresent suffocation, he attacks with his sing-scream. When the city theater appears to him like something out of his own kitchen, like a "monstrously blown-up neo-classical coffee mill," he cannot resist destroying the glass of the building that annoys him. Oskar's family and friends are less aware than the fantastic imp of the exact sources of their frustration; they seek outlets similar to Alfred Matzerath's uniformed flight to the Nazi rally.

From the oppressive boredom of this life, Oskar's mother flees to romantic rendezvous with Bronski. Agnes and Jan seek their fulfillment in less rigid, more playful, sensual activities than those of Alfred and his goose-stepping comrades. As her suicide attests, however, Agnes cannot successfully escape the petty hostilities and everyday despair. The other little bakers and grocers vent their energies in the fanatic, industrious pursuit of various labors and hobbies. Gretchen Scheffler's endless embroidery is one example. Matzerath's tireless culinary endeavors culminate in achievements like a pork roast prepared with concentrated dedication: Oskar notes how Alfred "cut slice after slice, his features so full of unabashed tenderness over the tender, succulent meat that I had to avert my eyes." (Bt, 250)

Another exemplary family in the neighborhood is the Greffs. While Lina Greff slovenly and acridly decays from the monotony of their life together, her husband busily devotes himself to his grocery, boy scouts, folk song fests, sports, and home-spun inventions. Reminiscent of *Wandervogel* and "Vater Jahn" types, Greff shares their romantic idealism and nationalism. His excessive idealism spills over into flowery descriptions of the foods he sells. Unable to talk about vegetables as vegetables, this vegetarian would wax eloquent to a customer about a potato, describing the "swelling, bursting vegetable flesh, always devising new forms and yet so chaste." (Bt, 239) Casting his simple vegetable-seller's role in idealized hues, he would wisely smile as he explained that his shop apron was "God's green gardener's apron." (Bt, 240) Thus the famous idealist inwardness of the *Bildungsbürger* manifests its infamous potential in the *Kleinbürger*.

Greff attacks all his "leisure" activities with the same missionary zeal that he inflicts upon his boy scouts. "Nature," Oskar quips, meant "asceticism" to the vegetarian. In fanatic pursuit of a routinized hobby, Greff engages in wintry morning baths in a hole in the frozen Baltic, all the while singing nationalist military songs. Such missionary dedication to athletics relieves Greff's latent homosexual desires. Often several naked youths were seen with the singing, shouting greengrocer in the icy Baltic. But the group's rigorous swimming and hiking is to end when the boys all go off to war. Greff is then confronted with the harsh, banal realities of his existence; he grows listless. When he receives a summons to appear in court on a morals charge, presumably an indicator of Nazi suppression of homosexuality, even more brutal realities confront his evasive idealism. Greff too commits suicide.

Such are the strange but all too common anachronistic misfits holed up in the outskirts of Grass's Danzig. All the romantic heroism, political naiveté, privatism, hubris, and conformism which help to mobilize a movement behind Hitler appear in Oskar's neighborhood. It is this kind of "stunted" environment which provided the moist humus for Nazi ideology.

In the last chapter of Book One, "Faith, Hope, Love," emerge the most searing images of uncomprehending complicity which summarize Grass's view of the petits bourgeois in the Third Reich. Here smug little creatures are absorbed in their own daily affairs; not one "who sets up his soup kettle on the bluish flames suspects that disaster is bringing his supper to a boil." (Bt, 160) They remain unaware that their new savior Hitler is in reality the gasman. Their undiscerning faith, hope, and love for the gasman-savior the author counters here with reason and information: "Love knows no time of day, hope is without end, and faith knows no limits, only knowledge and ignorance are subject to times and limits." (Bt, 166)

Ingenious as a description of the *Kleinbürgertum* in this period, *The Tin Drum* is nonetheless not an analysis of the causes of petit bourgeois privatism, political naiveté, etc., nor need it be. Pleas for reasonableness, knowledge "subject to times and limits," however, would probably have converted few to moderation in the twenties. If the Weimar Republic could have successfully answered the needs of the petits bourgeois instead of permitting them to be victimized, they would have been less likely to misperceive their salvation in National Socialism. Exhortations to Matzerath and Greff to be reasonable and informed would have fallen on deaf ears just as the Kridwiss-Kreis dismissed Zeitblom's injunctions to be rational.

Although Böll is more sympathetic to radical social change than the moderate Grass, he nonethless seems nearly convinced that what is necessary will never come. Thus the little folk in *Billiards at Half-Past Nine* retire to a marginal idyll which Böll paints much less critically than Grass does his misshapen milieu. Grass's unthinkable and yet real world emerges brilliantly through the fantastic facsimile of the *Kleinbürgertum*, Oskar. It is as if no uncorrupted human agent could be found fit to mirror and expose the social reality of the Nazi epoch.

The Petit Bourgeois Watches Others Make History

As survivors of the Nazi epoch, Böll's narrators grapple with memories of a past which often seems one with the present. They, like Zeitblom, have had to withdraw from the political public world corrupted by Nazi "beasts." These gentle lambs, as the author calls them, do not perceive the same kind of apocalypse, however, that the bourgeois humanist does. Such dramatic terminal points do not define history or everyday experience in the perspective of Böll's narrators. On the contrary, life before and after 1933, as well as before and after 1945, seems, in its essentials, painfully unchanged. The romantically tragic predictions of Mann's novel bear little resemblance to the simple assertions and observations offered by Böll's figures. Mann wrote *Doctor Faustus* in view of the rubble of 1943-1946, of course, not the "reconstructed" Germany of the fifties.

Like Grass, Böll de-demonizes Mann's Germany which stares, possessed of the devil, into the abyss. Unlike the more iconoclastic Grass, Böll de-mystifies Nazism as a means to another end, not as an end in itself. Having revealed the banality behind the ideology, Böll moves on to other explanations for the course of Germany's recent history. He sees a deeper pattern which is sustained while ideologies come and go. The decent, kind, and gentle folk are victims, Böll seems to argue, destined in our time to be persecuted by the vain, ambitious careerists. A pessimistic version of the Catholic moral tradition, with an emphasis on the seemingly eternal sacrifice of the lambs to the wolves (or to primarily buffalos in the novel), appears to be behind Böll's ahistorical presentation.

Then too the magnitude of the sacrifice under Hitler has gripped the minds of survivors in *Billiards at Half-Past Nine*, so that for them the past lives on in the present. As Lawrence Langer observes, in their narration "the act of recollection, instead of forging links with the past, only widens the exasperatingly impassable gulf between the dead and the living, creating a void which makes new beginnings for the future equally impossible, until some way of reconciling the fate of those dead with the present can silence the influence they continue to exert on the living." [33]

Not only through their riveted memories does the past continue in the present. As an old waiter whispers, the current political situation makes them wonder if perhaps the Nazis did win after all. The fifties in West Germany did witness a massive reinstatement of former Third Reich officials. In 1952 Adenauer admitted publicly that two-thirds of the senior government officials were former Nazi party members. Hans Globke, once the co-author of the official commentary on the Nazi Nuremberg Race Laws and now Adenauer's chief personal advisor, was a notorious example of this "restoration" of Nazis. [34] In order to emphasize the similarities before and after 1945, Böll omits the differences. Less impressed

---

33. Lawrence Langer, *The Holocaust and the Literary Imagination* (New Haven: Yale University Press, 1975), p. 270.

34. David Childs, *Germany since 1918* (New York: Harper & Row, 1971), p. 146.

than Grass with the change from a terrorist totalitarian to an allegedly democratic state, he stresses mainly that the ambitious careerists reign again; the humble, simple people are relegated to the sidelines.

Once again a novel of this era is narrated from a petit bourgeois perspective. One of the most striking aspects of this work, which was written to confront Germany with its fascist past, is that very few historical names or events appear. Unlike Grass who enjoys mentioning world events to expose the private, narrow perspective of his *Kleinbürger*-family, Böll shows much sympathy for the sheltered, day-to-day life of the Fähmels. He seems to support the reclusive and alienated perspective by which his characters view historic events as an intrusion. What happens in this provincial milieu, moreover, is according to Böll the appropriate material for the novelist.

Given four years after the publication of *Billiards at Half-Past Nine*, Böll's Frankfurt lectures explicitly provide the social context of the novel's aesthetic intentions. Nazi distortion of language and thought motivate Böll's "Aesthetics of the Humane," his search for a viable language and a livable society. Throughout the lectures, Böll repeatedly returns to his major concern: the inhumanity in everyday German life, what he calls the lack of neighborliness and "Nicht-wohnen-Können" (inability to live or dwell) of the Germans. Humanity he finds in the little folk whom others ridicule as provincial. In his opinion, "It appears quite so, that provincialism may for a good while be our only possibility of creating intimate terrain, building neighborliness, being able to live." [35] A sense of homelessness and lack of community which is traceable to the Hitler years has been perpetuated by the wealthy consumer society of today. Literature following the war reflects this homelessness; it is no surprise that "so little eating takes place in German literature, just as little home living, rarely is money spoken of . . ." [36]

---

35.   Heinrich Böll, *Frankfurter Vorlesungen* (Munich: Deutscher Taschenbuch Verlag, 1968), p. 53.

36.   Ibid., p. 97.

Implementing in the novel his own suggestions, Böll shows us, for example, the compulsive gourmet in the careerist Nettlinger as seen through the eyes of the victimized Schrella. Further, the subject of money is raised directly: Nettlinger's crude attempts to bribe Jochen reveal his insensitivity to the hotel porter's more humane priorities. The narrative perspective also conforms to Böll's purposes: no people are better able to expose the inhumanity of others than those who exemplify the "neighborliness." Even the hotel milieu, potentially representative of various social groups, is seen from the small man's (Jochen's) viewpoint and value system.

Böll pleads for provincialism in these lectures and in the novel. Like Mann and Grass, the son of the Cologne carpenter portrays the social milieu he knows best. For Böll, the little world of the Fähmels would be the ideal world in which the individual could still live according to humane, moral principles. For all the sympathy one feels, however, for the Fähmels' gentle neighborliness, the gap between them and the rest of society remains immense and would most likely be closed by the powerful groups on the outside and not by the isolated little folk themselves.

The situation in the novel is structured in such a way that people like the Wackes and the Nettlingers are set against the Schrellas and the Fähmels in a small German town over three generations. What at first seem to be inconsequential though brutal quarrels between high school boys gradually take on larger historical implications. The cruel bullies -- the "buffalos" in the narrative -- grow up to be Nazis, and in the postwar period they again assume positions of power and leadership. The "lambs," who are gentle and kind as children, grow up to be terrorized and exploited by the Nazis.

As the beastly "others," the Nazi careerists are viewed unsympathetically from the outside. The reader learns only of their oppressive impact on the lambs, of their stupid brutality. Opportunist capitalists and petty officials all appear in the novel like the zealous automatons of the petite bourgeoisie. It is primarily in opposition to the assiduous, hard-working oppressors that the victims define their values. Johanna's aversion to the pervasive petit bourgeois virtues is central, for example, to her appraisal of Heinrich Fähmel as a prospective husband. To assure herself that while he was singing his chest did not expand and contract like the others' in an arrogant, earnest manner, she sneaked into choir practice. But Johanna feared that he would not pass the most difficult test of wearing a uniform for the Kaiser's birthday celebration: "How would he look, marching past down there, decked out with history, heavy with destiny?" (Bil, 108) Heinrich did not conform here or elsewhere. Keenly aware of the self-impressed seriousness of the little ruling men, Johanna and Heinrich prize each other as exceptions and attempt to shield one another from the smug "respectability" of their surroundings.

As a young girl Johanna recognizes that the need for honor and order evolved out of the deep despair and insecurity gripping this *Stand* in the middle: "They were neither rich nor poor enough to discover the only permanent thing: transience -- which I longed for, although I was brought up for permanent ideals: marriage, faithfulness, honor, the bedroom where only duty lay, not pleasure." (Bil, 127) Just as Grass has Oskar expose the compulsive rigidity of the Nazis when he disrupts their orderly marching music, Johanna perceives the "character armor" protecting the typical middle-class Nazis.

The Fähmels react against this fanatical earnestness with various kinds of playfulness. Free from such dutiful responses, they treasure natural grace and pleasure in their living: Heinrich is described as a ballet master; he and Johanna remember that all is a playful game and thus remain above the others' over-inflated sense of self-importance; Heinrich cultivates his secret smile, his sense of irony. Moving from the sheltered, apolitical, preindustrial milieu of his boyhood into the more modern town, Heinrich does initially exemplify a more relaxed, sovereign, less pompously serious attitude toward his career. At first his country boy's naiveté facilitates his confident play for success at the architect's competition. His sheltered background does blind him, however, to the ominous social and political developments as well as his own role as essentially the most dedicated manipulator of all in his meteoric rise to the top. He has played his careerist enemies' game, even if by his own rules.

Thus Heinrich is another naive petit bourgeois caught and deeply immersed in the contradictions of the changing world. Only at the close of the narrative does he come to recognize his implicit collusion with the beastly activities when he openly declares his opposition instead of "secretly smiling." Like other *Mittelstand*-professionals in small towns, he has had as little influence on the national (or local) socio-political developments as the suburban grocer. Defined by his small milieu, his perspective and values are often *kleinbürgerlich*.

Although the Fähmels are not ambivalent toward Nazism like Mann's Zeitblom, they nonetheless galvanize no effective resistance. The lambs are at least an anti-Nazi group, which does not exist in Böll's earlier works and marks his own emergence in the late fifties from previous social-political withdrawal. In future novels he will gradually expand the size if not the power of this small alternative society. [37] But Robert's group, in which a few individuals help each other to fight against others' brutality, still falls far short of organized resistance. Furthermore, they themselves do not see such action as political. "The others make history," as Johanna says. Reaffirming the heritage of an apolitical idealism which contrasts "spirit" and "power" in absolute terms, the Fähmels withdraw into their inwardness. Without the cultural background of the *Bildungsbürger*, the Fähmels nonetheless share with Zeitblom his political naiveté. Like others of the *Mittelstand* Lebovics describes, the Fähmels perceive social and political power from a spiritual, ethical perspective. Banned into exile as a political fugitive, Robert Fähmel speculates about himself: "Had he ever been active politically?" (Bil, 114) Robert feels rather that humane, moral impulses motivated him and his group to protect Schrella. Such group action was all too rare, took great courage, and indicated acute moral if not political sensitivity to Nazi behavior. Sadly, such political inexperience in the atomized middle classes facilitated their exploitation and manipulation by the Nazis.

---

37.   James H. Reid, *Withdrawal and Reemergence* (London: Oswald Wolff, 1973), pp. 51, 84.

In each of Böll's narrators' reflections about his or her past, problems of political impotence and action are raised. While such questions await answers, the tempo and structure of the novel begin to change. Reflections about the past are embodied in long monologues which seem almost indifferent to the present. After memories ranging over the past fifty years have thus been invoked, the narrating figures step out of their isolation and their memories and move into the present. More dialogues appear; time is often noted; action quickens.[38] The tension thus created explodes with the shot from Mother Fähmel's revolver. After such a climax has been reached, the drama begs resolution.

Full resolution does not materialize.[39] On the surface not much seems very different at the end of the novel from the beginning. Mother Fähmel will return to the sanatorium, Schrella to Holland. Large questions still await answers. Does the return to the present include the political present? Does the move out of

---

38. Disregarding the social and political content of the novel, the following contains, nonetheless, a thorough, detailed stylistic analysis of Böll's novel: Klaus Jeziorkowski, *Rhythmus und Figur. Zur Technik des epischen Konstruktion in Heinrich Bölls "Der Wegwerfer" und "Billard um halb zehn"* (Bad Homberg: Gehlen, 1968).

39. In his sensitive study *The Holocaust and the Literary Imagination*, Lawrence Langer argues that the very magnitude of the mass murder in the camps paralyzes both the will of Böll's characters and the aesthetic form which conveys their dilemma (pp. 281-284). The subject, however, of this novel of an epoch embraces more than the holocaust, which tends to emerge only intermittently within memories spanning events of half a century. The holocaust appears assimilated into the history of suffering visited upon the lambs of this society, even if Böll does recognize its unprecedented quality. The sufferers' ruminations about powerlessness remain unresolved and find form in the anticlimactic closing of the novel. While the magnitude of the holocaust itself paralyzes, as Langer contends, the Fähmels' thoughts dwell on several phenomena of Nazism which, while related to the concentration camps, are far more comprehensible. Political inexperience in a large part of the populace, economic and social insecurity stalking the middle strata: these and other circumstances, which become visible through the Fähmels' memories, may indeed be comprehended. Unfortunately, the Fähmels never grasp how their own powerlessness, a problem that haunts them throughout, stems from comprehensible social and political circumstances.

isolation embrace more than the immediate family? Will Robert's adoption of Hugo make any difference to anyone but Hugo and the family? The long, reflective monologues which grapple with the past result in partial answers, personal more than social solutions.

Heinrich Fähmel, for example, has learned that "irony would never suffice" to shield him from fascism in the past or its remains in the present. At Johanna's suggestion, he cancels the Café Kroner birthday celebration, along with his daily breakfast there; he is about to destroy his own legend to prevent a monument to himself. That is, he will no longer let it appear that he is reconciled to the society which could murder Edith; he will not pretend to be its great architect. The building plans of his past can best serve now stacked as seats in the atelier for his birthday guests. For the first time, a man like the butcher Gretz who could deliver his own mother to the Nazis is turned away. Although Heinrich's gestures are only symbolic, they are public. Such unflinching demonstration of his refusal to be reconciled is an active change from his previous quiet collusion.

These symbolic public gestures (Heinrich's new stance of protest, Johanna's assassination attempt, Robert's adoption of the persecuted Hugo) express the Fähmels' irreconciliation. Such genuine moral outrage at the atrocities of the past, unatoned for and insidiously integrated into the present, was all too rare among the Fähmels' contemporaries. Symbolic acts will probably effect little desired change, however, in their society. This "solution" would appear then to re-confirm the problem: the simple, gentle people will continue to look on, and suffer, and protest while the others "make history."

The political implications of a novel cannot be resolved by an author who sympathizes with the apolitical attitudes of his characters. Peter Demetz has commented that Böll suggests in actuality a commitment that is far less political than he would have us believe: "The trouble is that Böll's good people are good German petits bourgeois who do not want to get involved with the daily business of politics; traditionally unable to think except in the most extreme terms, they continue to dream of an absolute idyll and are

unwilling to soil their hands with something disturbingly relative." [40] Böll creates no satisfying alternatives for his *Kleinbürger*
because he, like them, probably sees none. Durzak has pointed also
to the seeming contradictions in Böll's public image: "on the one
hand, the combative social critic, who fearlessly takes a stand, and
on the other, the literary apologist for the moral, virtuous
Kleinbürger." [41] Böll's social criticism, however, is often that of an
"irreconcilable" addressed to a society which is viewed as totally
lacking in the humanity he finds in his little folk. As he criticizes,
he seems to foresee continuation of an irreconcilable dichotomy of
humanity vs. inhumanity; he would thus seal for his *Kleinbürger*
the very fate that he laments.

Elements of Nineteenth-Century Realism

Although Böll is concerned about the inescapable lot of the decent
little people, he still would not prophecy their end. Having survived
the total apocalypse that Mann foresaw when writing his novel
between 1943 and 1946, Böll and Grass neither project Germany's
end in the depths of hell, nor do they predict the death of a culture
and the novel form it produced. Yet, of course, not only those with
Mann's view of fascism have proclaimed the death of the novel. To
be more precise: it is the inherited form of the nineteenth-century
novel, which grew and took on shape with its bourgeois reading
public, that has been called into question today. That nineteenth-
century middle-class consciousness lingered on in the socio-political
attitudes which Hitler manipulated. Cannot elements of that bourgeois novel be transplanted into twentieth-century prose to give life
to the inherited milieu and characters that facilitated fascism?

Many interrelated aspects of that narrative form now initially
appear inadequate. This novel's very core, the *Fabel*, consists of a
conflict between the characters and their environment. Such depiction of reality, however, perpetuates what Adorno referred to as the

---

40. Peter Demetz, *Postwar German Literature* (New York: Pegasus, 1970), p. 198.

41. Manfred Durzak, *Der deutsche Roman der Gegenwart* (Stuttgart: Kohlhammer,
1971), p. 26.

anachronistic bourgeois illusion that the individual is essentially
alone and society acts upon him or her from the outside. [42] Other
theoreticians now find the novel's realism suspect. The realistic
novel scene which mirrors in the particular the general society of
the nineteenth century cannot represent the twentieth. As Erich
Kahler asserts in his article "Untergang und Übergang der
epischen Kunstform," the complexity of today's social reality defies
the limits of sensory awareness. [43] The enormous growth in population and industrialization by the end of the nineteenth century, and
the increasing complexity of the social network, of institutions,
classes, mass media, etc., made that century's realistic mode of
representation impossible for the society which followed. In the
1920s Brecht saw that the simple and direct mimesis of reality
reflected nothing about real social conditions: "The actual reality
has slid into the functional effect of what appeared to be reality." [44]
Not only the growth of modern society but also the world wars
changed the face of a comprehensible nineteenth-century world. In
the *Entstehung und Krise des modernen Romans*, Wolfgang Kayser
notes that World War I first disclosed the limitations of the novel
form, which could only oversimplify or distort that event. [45] Since
Mann, Böll, and Grass were confronted with an even more modern
and complex war and society, they appear to attempt the impossible.
And yet fascism, with its sources of support in a social group decidedly anti-modern, permits portrayal of the nineteenth within the
twentieth century, and thus permits a kind of realistic style reminiscent of the day when the bourgeois novel thrived.

In developing a workable definition of "realism" in his book
Mimesis, Erich Auerbach describes the nascent European form of
realism in the nineteenth century as "a serious representation of

---

42. Quoted in Baumgart, "Kleinbürgertum und Realismus," p. 654.

43. Erich Kahler, "Untergang und Übergang der epischen Kunstform," *Neue Rundschau* 64, 1 (1953), pp. 1-3.

44. Quoted in Baumgart, "Kleinbürgertum und Realismus," p. 654.

45. Wolfgang Kayser, *Entstehung und Krise des modernen Romans* (Stuttgart: Metzler, 1954), p. 26.

contemporary everyday social reality against the background of a constant historical movement." [46] In German nineteenth-century novels, however, the historical background of events appears to be completely immobile. In Germany itself, at least until the late 1860s, there was still a provincial and old-fashioned quality to life, a seeming resistance to historical change, the image of which persisted in the novel until the 1880s. Life continued to be more firmly rooted in the individual, the idiosyncratic, the traditional for much longer than was the case in France. Thus it "yielded no subject matter for a realism so generally national, so materially modern, so intent upon an analysis of the emerging destiny of European society, as the realism of France." [47] The previous discussion of the *Mittelstand* has seen frequent reference to the nineteenth century in Germany and its bourgeois traditions. These *Mittelstand* figures respond to fascism with a socio-political understanding rooted in that tradition. It is thus appropriate that all three of these novels contain elements of the provincial German realism that Auerbach describes. In the novels of Mann and Grass, such passages are parodied to indicate the limitations of such provincialism. [48]

To the degree that the historical background portrayed is not immobile or entirely omitted, the three novels also slightly resemble French nineteenth-century realism. Much less disconcerted by the crisis of the novel than the predominantly French advocates of the *nouveau roman*, these German writers incorporate elements of both countries' nineteenth-century traditions in their novels of the epoch. [49] No other method of description or choice of milieu could be

---

46. Erich Auerbach, *Mimesis*, trans. Willard Trask (Garden City, New York: Doubleday & Co., 1957), p. 457.

47. Ibid., p. 455.

48. While recent scholarship suggests that heretofore ignored shades of irony and humor in nineteenth-century realistic works render them less poetic or saccharine than previously supposed, they nonetheless would eschew the grotesqueries in the parodic portions of these novels about Nazism.

49. The following analysis makes no attempt to equate totally the styles of Grass, Mann, and Böll with that of the nineteenth-century realists. Clearly many aspects of the three novels would not be included in such an equation. These authors are aware of the older mode's shortcomings as a narrative form

more appropriate to their depiction of society before and during the Third Reich.

The aspects of twentieth-century reality omitted from these novels are striking. Rarely does a factory or hotel, automobile or airplane play a part in the action. (The hotel scenes in *Billiards at Half-Past Nine* do show modern cosmopolitan society, always from the perspective, however, of the *Kleinbürger* Jochen.) Reinhard Baumgart notes the significance of the scenery chosen in the novels of Grass and Böll: the intimate living room, untouched nature, the local beach or pub, the back courts. The real life models here are more often the suburb or small town rather than the city or the world made "smaller" and international by airlines.[50] While Amsterdam, Stalingrad, and other parts of the world are referred to, they are distant, marginal, and never themselves pictured as integral scenes of the life represented in the novels. The people here are anchored in Germany and know little of the other countries that, for instance, Frisch's Homo Faber visits regularly. They manage at home to evade the impersonal technology of World War II. Furthermore, the bustling modern city, even the center of Nazi power, Berlin, has no place in the worlds portrayed here. The back courts and the grocery store of the suburbs, not Danzig proper, are the environs of the Matzeraths. Zeitblom and Adrian move through towns described like medieval museums (Halle, Leipzig); they remain, even in Munich, in the musty, old-fashioned ambience of

---

appropriate for the twentieth century. The artifice Oskar, for example, avoids for his author all the difficulties that the nineteenth-century narrator encounters, who can portray the actions of his characters only the way the general public is able to see. The seemingly imposed and complex symbolic constructs in both *Doctor Faustus* and *Billiards at Half-Past Nine* attempt to point beyond the small milieu to larger, more complicated interpretations of Hitler's rise to power. Indeed, more than one critic has praised Böll's novel for its similarities with the French *nouveau roman*, for example: Karl August Horst, "Überwindung der Zeit," in *Der Schriftsteller Heinrich Böll*, ed. Werner Leugning (Munich: Deutscher Taschenbuch Verlag, 1969), pp. 67-71. More examples of the many departures from the nineteenth-century novel could be listed. But the purpose here is to identify those elements which do in all three novels resemble the realism of the previous century.

50. Baumgart, p. 652.

nineteenth-century salons. Without a name, the town in *Billiards at Half-Past Nine* takes on shades of the poetically irreal villages of "O" in nineteenth-century novels. With so much of the mobile, cosmopolitan modern world left out, the milieux described in these novels remain relatively small and clearly circumscribed.

Whereas, as Kahler says, the complexity of modern social reality is not simply observable, the enclosed environs set apart by these writers can be concretely reproduced. The sensory awareness of a Grass leaps with gusto upon all that is so reproducible in, for instance, the little baker's domicile: "those ornamental coverlets, cushions embroidered with coats of arms, Käthe Kruse dolls lurking in corners, stuffed animals, . . . knitting, crocheting, embroidery, plaiting, knotting, and lacework. This sweetly cute, delightfully cozy, stiflingly tiny abode, overheated in winter and poisoned with flowers in summer . . ." (Bt, 71) Grass considers the regional element important in his novels. Precisely because such provincialism remains so concrete, his works, he maintains, find responsive readers in far corners of the world where one has no idea whatever of Danzig.[51] Indeed, the common judgment of critics that the postwar West German episodes in the novel are unconvincing may result from their lack of so many magnified realistic details. The provincial scene and the mode of living of its petit bourgeois inhabitants do not provide much access to the social reality of post-Nazi Germany.[52]

Mann's *Wandervogel*-like students seek surroundings far away from the rapidly changing cities; although parodied by Mann, these hills and valleys appear as reproducible as they were when Raabe's hermits wandered there. In Böll's novel, concentrated focus on every detail of the school ball game, for example, effects concrete representation of an episode which will have larger socio-political implications. History itself, viewed securely from Johanna's balcony, is marching by below. Similarly, in Stifter's *Turmalin* a

---

51.   Hartlaub, "Wir, die wir übriggeblieben sind . . .," p. 214.

52.   Baumgart, p. 661.

century before, the window of the warm living room provides the view of the large, frightening world outside. The small milieu, isolated from the larger society and thus historical events, dominates in the provincial realism that Auerbach characterizes. Reappearing with similar realistic description in these novels, however, such milieux in the period between 1914 and 1945 reflect an isolation of the middle strata which is of great political significance in the new era of mass democracy or its manipulation. Focus on this strata in the pre-fascist and fascist periods, which because of its pivotal role is not in fact marginal to the course of historical development, relieves the novelist from portrayal of broader, less reproducible social reality and thus retains descriptive elements of nineteenth-century realism.

What Auerbach calls realism, "a serious representation of contemporary everyday social reality," prevails in these novels, but in a limited sense. In contrast to the nineteenth century, social reality contemporary to the three writers contains much more than the overheated, close living room or the medieval-like village. Concentration on such small scenes reveals, however, the background of the little folk who more or less support the overall social-political reality of 1933-1945: Nazism. Historically speaking, such tacit or active support is vital for Nazi success in its drive for mass mobilization, a situation very different from the simply elitist politics of the nineteenth century. In literary terms, the little folk themselves come to life in these pages to a degree impossible in novels which encompass a much broader, more changeable modern world. Where Homo Faber remains an abstract model, for example, these figures take on real contours.

Shielded from the confusing upheavals of modernization, the *Kleinbürger* seem to carry on their business and pleasure much as their ancestors did in pre-industrial times. Unlike the *Grossbürger*, or workers, whose lives draw them out into larger and more anonymous social realms, the *Kleinbürger* remain close to home, always among the same friends, neighbors, and relatives. In intimate, interpersonal scenes their personal characteristics emerge.

Individuals interact here, not political parties or large corporate groups. People are understandable and accountable to one another; they can appear in the novels as individualized beings, not parts of an amorphous mass.

None of these writers copies this reality thoughtlessly. Grass exposes most mercilessly the anachronistic petit bourgeois consciousness. As Baumgart has said, Grass transforms the understandably provincial personalities of Keller's Seldwyla into twentieth-century parodies of themselves by lining up snapshots such as that of Father Matzerath drunkenly addressing the portraits of Hitler and Beethoven in the living room. Revealing the decay of bourgeois tradition into a parody of itself, such novel figures mimic their burgher roles like frenzied marionettes.[53]

Though not intended by Baumgart, the above description could well fit the schoolmaster Zeitblom also. Himself a parody of his own tradition, Zeitblom seems to imitate the humanist burgher with a kind of pedantic exactness. Reproducible as a figure out of the previous century, Zeitblom is alive from the first as an individualized, almost eccentric being. Lukács has compared Zeitblom to the inward Raabe eccentrics who criticized and yet could not resist Bismarck: "It is Zeitblom then who gives this modern and universal tragedy a provincial, old-fashioned, typically German stamp."[54]

Böll applauds the outdated consciousness of his little folk. Portrayed without parody, the gracious old architect Fähmel is as clearly recognizable as part of a real *Kleinbürger*-milieu as are his daydreams about his future family: "birthday celebrations, funerals, weddings and silver weddings, christenings . . ." (Bil, 61) His perspective bound to his immediate surroundings, the young Fähmel really believes that he has his own happiness entirely in his own hands. At first his environment confirms his feeling: relatively calculable relationships, for example, with single, idiosyncratic indi-

---

53. Baumgart, p. 656.

54. Lukács, *Essays*, p. 85.

viduals, not an anonymous bureaucratic structure, are crucial to the
acceptance of his plans for St. Anton. When the Fähmels later feel
misused and hurt by the outside world, they withdraw. The
resigned folk in Storm, Grillparzer, or Stifter (Böll mentions Stifter
frequently in his Frankfurt lectures) are their historical relatives. [55]

Appearing in all three of these novels, then, are the little people who would also be "at home" in the pages of Stifter, Storm,
Keller, Raabe. Focus on their limited living sphere offers the novelist certain advantages. The smaller the milieu, the more observable
and reproducible it is. The more isolated this realm is from historical upheavals and constant modernization, the more frozen and pic-
torial it is. In short, representation of the *Mittelstand* facilitates
certain nineteenth-century modes of realistic description. These
novelists are to a degree spared the dilemma of the modern writer:
how to portray anonymous modern society. Pivotal because
anachronistic, the historical protagonist of the Third Reich becomes
a literary one.

---

55. Baumgart, p. 655; Reid, *Withdrawal and Reemergence*, p. 83, also notes a similar
     espousal of eccentric individualism in Böll and Raabe: their regrets at missed
     opportunities after a war generate their irredeemable protest against the ma-
     terialist, superficial, and standardized societies of their days.

CHAPTER TWO

The Aesthetic Aversion to Nazism

Politics Made Aesthetic

Artists can perceive what people with less aesthetic sensitivity may overlook. They may be primarily repulsed by the plebeian crudity of the Nazis, as was Thomas Mann. Or they may have an eye for the Nazis' own artistry: while communism politicized art, Walter Benjamin commented in 1936, fascism "aestheticized" politics.[1] Both Grass and Böll detect the manipulation intended in the imposing architecture of pseudo-classical antiquity and in the unified geometric formations of crowds at a mass meeting. Understanding such aesthetic manipulation can help clarify the mass hysteria associated with fascism. The well-known images of euphoric faces crying "Heil Hitler!" result in large part from the Nazis' careful cultivation of mass propaganda techniques.

In politics as in art: where content is lacking or cannot be revealed, the attempt is often made to substitute formal artistic structures for it. As Brecht observed in the late 1930s, the Nazis became in effect aesthetic formalists, substituting rhetoric for real social change. Aware of the power of language to shape perceptions, Brecht cited the Nazis' manipulative use of the word *Volk*, for example, to conjure up a mystical unity which distracted attention from immediate social, economic, and political needs.[2] The more

---

1. Walter Benjamin, "The Work of Art in the Age of Mechanical Reproduction," in *Illuminations*, trans. Harry Zohn (New York: Harcourt, Brace and World, 1968), p. 244.

2. Bertolt Brecht, "Bemerkungen zum Formalismus," *Gesammelte Werke*, 19 (Frankfurt am Main: Suhrkamp, 1967), p. 318.

distance that exists between ideology and social reality, the more ideological enthusiasm must be aroused, lest the regime collapse.[3] Whereas the Nazis did at first make good on a few of their promises to better the lot of, for example, small businessmen and peasants, the deteriorating situation for these groups in the long run could have been evident to the impartial observer. As the historian David Schoenbaum has concluded, the Third Reich skillfully and consistently perpetuated a vision of social reality unlike any objective appraisal of that reality. Contrary to their promises, by 1939 the concentration of capital in relatively few hands was greater, while the rural population had declined, not increased. Similarly, industry's share of the GNP was up, agriculture's down. Industrial labor was better off, and small businesses worse. When officially interpreted, however, Nazi society showed an unparalleled unity, with opportunities for all classes, a "new deal" and the good old days all in one.[4] Imparting such interpretation was the job of Nazi propaganda.

The Nazis themselves viewed their propaganda as art. In the Nuremberg Party Convention of 1934, Goebbels proclaimed: "May the shining flame of our enthusiasm never be extinguished. This flame alone gives light and warmth to the creative art of modern political propaganda. Rising from the depths of the people, this art must always descend back to it and find its power there. Power based on guns may be a good thing; it is, however, better and more gratifying to win the heart of a people and to keep it."[5] Since the only so-called creative art which the Nazis allowed in their theaters and museums was that which created an "enchanted world of the Ideal," in Goebbels' words,[6] it is no surprise that their creative

---

3.   Siegfried Kracauer, *From Caligari to Hitler* (Princeton: Princeton University Press, 1947), p. 300.

4.   David Schoenbaum, *Hitler's Social Revolution* (Garden City, New York: Doubleday & Co., 1967), pp. 285-286.

5.   Quoted in Kracauer, p. 299.

6.   Quoted in George Mosse, *Nazi Culture*, trans. Salvator Attanasio and others (New York: Grosset & Dunlap, 1968), p. 157.

propaganda did much the same. Though illusory, however, this art was not identifiable merely as theater or museum pieces, but pretended to be reality: the myths had to rise "from the depths of the people," had to incorporate the people's deepest needs and enlist their full allegiance. In contrast to old-fashioned pre-fascist despots who were content with "power based on guns," the Nazis attempted to blot empirically perceptible reality out of the minds of their subjects and to construct a new, illusory world which appeared to answer to all their wants. The more people have lost the ability or courage to perceive the mystifications, the more they will comply with the directors of the staged reality. While proclaiming the revival of a genuinely Germanic way of life, unpolluted by western modernization, the men around Goebbels mobilized all the most modern means of communication at their disposal (radios, public loudspeakers, films, newsreels) to spark and fan the flame of enthusiasm for this new "beautiful illusion" (*Schein*).

With such means of technical reproduction, the Ministry of Propaganda had at its command the channels by which to invade the daily life of the population. The Ministry pressured manufacturers to build cheap radio sets, so that every German could afford one. The radios were made in such a way that no foreign broadcasts could be received.[7] Newsreels for the cinema were cleverly spliced to conform with the myth being perpetuated. As Benjamin has pointed out, the propagandistic importance of mechanical reproduction of parades, sports events, and war maneuvers cannot be overestimated. When such events are captured and presented by the camera and sound recording, the "masses" are brought face to face with themselves. Fascism saw its salvation in giving these masses not their rights, but instead a chance to express themselves, to become the stars of the art which is propaganda.[8] Leni Riefenstahl's film *Triumph of the Will* is an excellent example of the Nazis' creation of a mythical reality and their ability to then "document" it in their art. Symbols chosen for their stimulative power

7.   Ibid., p. 139.

8.   Benjamin, p. 243 and p. 253.

abound: waving swastika banners, the dancing flames of bonfires and torches, Hitler descending out of the clouds in a roaring machine -- these and numerous other devices combine to create a state of ecstasy in all the participants (on both sides of the screen). As Siegfried Kracauer noted, the innumerable rows of various party formations composed living ornaments across the huge festival grounds, and -- most important for the viewers -- symbolically presented these masses as instrumental superunits. The Nuremberg rally of 1934 (which was to draw attention away from the Nazi purges of the early summer) helped to create the impression of a monolithic new order. Then this bastard reality, instead of being an end in itself, served as the set for a film that was to assume the character of an authentic documentary. [9]

Exposed to the unending bombardment of propaganda, day after day, Böll and Grass became aware of the "artistry" of the Nazis. The rhythm of life changed. There was always a reason for celebration, marches, and demonstrations -- all of which were accompanied by constant fuss and fanfare. From distant California, Mann focused more on the result of their techniques: mass hysteria. Aware of the same artistry, this faraway observer chose rather to examine the past cultural roots of irrationalism in Germany, which proclaimed the superiority of the subconscious, the primitive in man, to the intellect. Mann incorporated adherents of the movement into an artist figure who in effect prophesies such mass irrationalism on a higher plane. In contrast, the fictive artists of Böll and Grass do not prefigure such hysteria; they discern, rather, its aesthetic manipulation. (Because Böll and Grass concentrate more on the aestheticization of politics outlined here, they will be discussed first.) There is an important aesthetic component in the aversion of all three writers to Nazism. But aesthetic repulsion takes different forms: Böll and Grass respond to the sensory bombardment of Nazi culture, Mann to what offends his idea of beauty and culture.

---

9.   Kracauer, pp. 301-302.

To fend off the "enchanted world of the Ideal," the artists in *The Tin Drum* and *Billiards at Half-Past Nine* develop a counter-aesthetics. They combat illusionary art with an art which exposes and destroys the mystifications for them. The pseudo-monumentality of Nazi art could only be countered by an art which is unassuming and simple. The titles of the novels indicate their choices. Oskar and the disillusioned architect Robert Fähmel respond to the rigid fuss and fanfare with games of drumming and billiards. While not developing a specific counter-aesthetics, Leverkühn in his last cantata creates a magic square game which highlights Mann's high cultural approach. In each case these games crystallize their authors' aesthetic responses to Nazism.

Moral Aesthetics

Thinking back on his adolescence, Böll relates why he resisted a friend's encouragement to join the Hitler Youth: "I didn't do it, not only for moral reasons (because I believed I knew in what direction developments would lead), not only for political reasons, but also for aesthetic ones: I didn't like this uniform, and I've never had a love of marching." [10] No lack of energy diverted the young man from following the example of his friends. What dismayed him, rather, were the marching columns of enforced uniformity. During the war, he says, his superiors always ordered him to string along at the back of his regiment because "I could never keep in step . . . . I will freely admit that I felt relatively good back there, where I didn't need to engage in singing and warbling, where I was also spared shoulder-slapping as well as scolding -- there was also more time in the rear to think, indeed to dream. . ." [11] It was the sensory bombardment of militaristic display which particularly disturbed the young man. Barked military orders and incessant "warbling"

---

10. Heinrich Böll, "Zu Reich-Ranickis 'Deutsche Literatur in West und Ost,'" *Aufsätze - Kritiken - Reden II* (Munich: Deutscher Taschenbuch Verlag, 1969), p. 49.

11. Ibid., p. 49.

and singing rang in his ears; the feel of shoulder-slapping and rigid goose-stepping marshalled his body; the sight of marching uniforms regimented his perception. Nazi indoctrination repelled Böll in its attempt to regulate all of his senses.

Böll's sensitivity to the Nazis' art of propaganda informs many passages in *Billiards at Half-Past Nine*. His narrators discern especially the rhythmic devices of Nazi propaganda which instrument the new tempo of daily life. As the Fähmels recognize, the baton which directed this change in tempo orchestrated an arrangement of reality that was an illusion.

The Nazis' move toward a total culture, a *Gleichschaltung* in all realms of public and private life, required that no individual fall out of step with the movement they were creating. They aimed to anesthetize individual thought, to exhaust the potential for reflective or skeptical thinking. Although the Fähmels' isolation and individualism renders them politically impotent, it also contains a positive subversive potential. Always on the sidelines, Johanna is in a position to observe the process of indoctrination with clear insight: "I was afraid; like a watchful bird with sharp eyes I stood there above on the balcony; . . . and I observed as the epoch marched by below." (Bil, 121).

Feeling distinct from her contemporaries, Johanna recognizes a ritualistic rhythm in the parades which acclaimed Hindenburg as their leader. She takes the magic out of the *Machtergreifung* by focusing on the militarist ceremonies in the pre-Nazi period when old imperialist military leaders aided the Nazi entry into the government. Johanna watches horrified as those below "prayed the litany: respectable, respectable, honor-loyalty, defeated and yet undefeated; order . . ." (Bil, 121) With this frequently repeated string of words, Böll recreates the proud, dogged rhythm of marching feet. The hebetude produced by many feet tramping together vitiated individual thought. Tired and thoughtless, marchers together felt an illusion of solidarity and power otherwise absent from their lives. The rhythmic feeling spurred them onward and engendered a mystic unity of national passion. Attempting to erase the loss of World War I, they came to believe they were "defeated and yet undefeated." The litany replaced reality.

At party conventions and mass meetings, the Nazis employed various geometric forms to impress observers as well as participants. Marching formations, for example, appeared to advance in a heavy, machine-like movement. The participants themselves appeared like automatons, robots; each person was geared to the rhythm of the larger complicated machine. Attached to such a large, imposing formation, the individual goose-stepper enjoyed previously unknown feelings of power. In the formation of these robots, the human element was aesthetically stylized into an impersonal mechanical design. Thus in Böll's novel the Nazi convert, Otto, "was now only Otto's husk that quickly received a different content." (Bil, 109) The human content of his mind has been replaced by inhuman formulas of power: "Even in this brain, power had already become a formula, denuded of utility, freed from instincts, it was almost without hatred, was effected automatically: blow by blow." (Bil, 116) Otto has become the machine-man, wielding his newly acquired power automatically.

The sense of power and the compelling excitement felt through rhythmic body movements: these feelings born of marching find their analogue in sports. Recognizing the sense of pride and power which athletics affords, the Nazis encouraged sports and cultivated the heroic image of the mighty, muscular Aryan, which image compensated for individual feelings of inadequacy. Here too Johanna detects a rhythmic ritual in the physical exercises of sportsmen: "That was like a fugue -- precise, stimulating, and still there were stretches of great boredom in them." (Bil, 102) This fugue-like repetition in athletic training took on a compulsive, compensatory character: "His exercises smelled like fanaticism; this strong, slender boy's body smelled like the earnest sweat of those who haven't experienced love yet; her brothers Bruno and Friedrich had smelled like that when they got off their bikes . . . and tried in the garden to relax fanatical leg muscles with fanatical compensatory exercises." (Bil, 102) Fanaticism, repugnant to Johanna, became in the Hitlerian scheme a phenomenon to be encouraged, inculcated.

While evoking the march rhythm discussed above, the words "respectable," "defeated and yet undefeated" seem to drum key ideas into the minds of the marchers that Johanna observes. As the NSDAP became increasingly skillful in modern techniques of mass propaganda, it learned "to clothe its vague theories in terse and easily remembered phrases and slogans, to implant facts by suggestive repetition, to stir up irrational, subconscious emotions by means of simple symbolism, and to direct the dynamic of the movement toward pithy notions of the enemy." [12] The emphasis on mass meetings and parades suggests the absolutely secondary role the press played in molding the opinion of the masses. The suggestive power of the spoken word -- the written form was much less forceful -- was in the forefront. [13] Aware early of such tactics of indoctrination, Mother Fähmel attempts to erase from her son's memory the line "Must have a weapon" that Heinrich was to learn for school. The military march rhythm in which such slogans as "honor/loyalty," "defeated and yet undefeated" are repeated in the novel reflects how these easily remembered phrases were implanted. The drilling-in of these symbolic mottos systematically weakened individuals' power of resistance and thus instilled in the "masses" the forcible rule of the Hitlerian "stronger will."

The rhythmical patterns conveying these slogans suggest not only parades and military drilling of propaganda but also the religious aesthetics which the Nazis adopted. As *Triumph of the Will* graphically shows, festivities in the Third Reich were set up in the form of recitations, responses, and choruses: the Christian liturgical framework was adapted to the content of the Nazi world-view. [14] The public celebrations on which Böll focused were important as "confessions of faith." A writer as genuinely religious as he, trained in the traditions of the Catholic Church, would be especially aware of the Nazis' appropriation of its rituals. Thus Johanna describes in religious terms the phrase-mongering of those parading by below:

---

12.   Bracher, p. 150.

13.   Ibid., p. 152.

14.   Mosse, p. 96.

the marchers "prayed the litany." In fact, the militarists and the Nazis partake in the sacramental ceremonies of the buffalos and not the sacrament of the community of true believers, the lambs. The ceremonial forms of Catholicism have been arrogated to a false and beastly "religion."

Clearly, Böll's narrators have keen eyes and ears for Nazi methods of mass indoctrination. The strategy behind marching, rigorous sports training, and slogan-chanting does not escape them. They see and hear the Nazis' manipulation of the senses. Their awareness, however, does not come simply from an aesthetic sensitivity. It is their moral integrity as provincial, isolated individualists that makes them resist Nazi ceremonial appeals. Stemming from this, the Fähmels' neighborly friendliness and mutual trust cause them to be repelled by the Nazi attempt to sow mutual distrust (for the purposes of effective spying) among the population. These characters thus become a model of the aesthetic beauty of provincial values which Böll contrasts with Nazi aesthetics. Such values make up in part what Böll means in his Frankfurt lectures by the "Aesthetik des Humanen."

In literature, according to Böll, "morals and aesthetics prove themselves congruent, inseparable also, . . . from whatever viewpoint an author may set about describing the humane." [15] Böll's "Aesthetics of the Humane" addresses itself to what is aesthetically valid not only as a subject of literature but also as a way of life. Thought and language, however, he tells his student listeners, have been poisoned by the Nazis. If this general atmosphere is to be decontaminated, "if humanitarianism is to arise again, then laborious, detailed work must be carried out, boring, burdensome, requiring much patience -- beginning in the school readers, in kindergarten. It is that which is in store for you -- to build an aesthetics of the humane, to develop forms and styles appropriate to the morals of the situation." [16]

---

15. Böll, *Frankfurter Vorlesungen*, p. 84.

16. Ibid., p. 37.

Adhering to their moral values, the Fähmels exemplify ways of life which are aesthetically humane. As morally motivated artists, they develop an aesthetics directly opposed to the Nazi art of propaganda. Böll chooses his words carefully: both Nazi buffalos and victimized lambs engage in activities described as litanies, formulas. Thus, rituals themselves are not evil, however much the Nazis may have contaminated the practice; indeed, the Fähmels counter the Nazis' aesthetics with their own.

Robert Fähmel had wanted to become an architect, like his father. As a youth, he dreamed of the houses and churches he would build. Instead, in his maturity he destroys buildings, even one that his father had designed. Robert becomes a demolition expert, an artist of destruction, and as such bears some resemblance to the artists Oskar Matzerath and Adrian Leverkühn. Robert's father Heinrich, who grew up in the Wilhelmian era, perceived himself as part of a relatively stable society, one in which he could establish himself enough in order to develop his craft: building. Robert, who was born in 1916 (one year before Böll), experiences no political regime to which he would wish to contribute monuments: neither the Weimar Republic, nor the Third Reich, nor the Bonn Republic. The Third Reich is for him (as for Böll) the culmination of a society destructive of all he values as well as of his own youth and the potentially creative period of his life.

Robert immerses himself intermittently in formulaic worlds to escape from the "aesthetics of the inhumane" in the Nazi and postwar society. Mathematical formulas, a useful obsession in his occupation, appeal to him in their precision; they become particularly beautiful combined with dynamite as tools to destroy inhumane values. Such formulaic thinking is not limited to his demolition work, however; his correct personal conduct, described by his secretary as "polite arithmetic," maintains an impersonal distance. Instead of raw, personal feelings, Robert mainly remembers the geometric movements of people in his past: "His memory had never relied on words and images, only on movements. Father, that was his gait, the coquette curve that the right pant leg described with every step." (Bil, 31) Such movements capture for this mathematician the essence of a passing moment, the behavior of another person. His formulas also protect him from feelings, many of which are painful reminders of life under Nazi rule. For example, returning to his father's abbey in 1958, he is worried that memories of destroying it during the war will be revived. Relieved, he notes: "his anxiety had been groundless; memory did not become feeling, but remained formula; it didn't dissolve in bliss or grief and didn't terrify his heart; his heart was not involved." (Bil, 191) Robert suffered at the hands of proto-Nazi bullies. He lost friends like Ferdi, who had attempted to assassinate the bullies' leader, and lost his wife, who died in a bombing raid. To numb all this pain, he has translated his emotions into formulas.

Casting immediate situations into concrete geometric forms also enables Robert to compare past and present history in the abstract. Events subsumed into the same formal system appear analogous enough to illuminate each other. One who thinks like Robert has a much deeper understanding of the Nazi past than one who quickly adjusts to each situation as new, unrelated to the past it evolved from. The opportunist Nettlinger has no need or ability to perceive such meaningful abstractions. His own transformation, for example, from Schrella's former persecutor to his present benefactor suggests to Nettlinger an image worthy of note. (Since Schrella's name was still on a list of political enemies left over from the Third Reich, he had been "mistakenly" imprisoned upon his return to Germany. Nettlinger is seeing to his release.) Schrella disagrees with Nettlinger: the story is not an image because "images mean an abstraction, and . . . the role that you played then . . . you play now; the roles are -- pardon -- the same. For then making me harmless meant locking me up; today making me harmless means letting me go free. I'm afraid that Robert, who thinks much more abstractly than I do, for this reason has no desire to see you." (Bil, 150) Robert would not be deceived by the apparent differences in Nettlinger's official behavior. Nettlinger, proud of his current commitment to democracy, does not admit that both of his roles simply further his career with the particular government in power. Unlike the formulas of the lambs, those of the buffalos discourage reflection and awareness, and encourage the zealous automaton. Robert's absorption in formulas, in his personal system of signs and symbols, stands in direct contrast to Nazi aesthetic forms which were designed to obliterate any personal, individual viewpoint.

Unlike the former Nazis and other Germans who "forget" or repress the past, Robert constantly incorporates past into present; his mind remains in possession of many different points in time. Like his father and mother, he appears occasionally to confuse the remembered past with the present, or to let memory supersede. Johanna in the sanatorium provides the most extreme example of this confusion: she pretends that her husband has dyed his hair gray, for instance, and that clocks and calendars do not exist. Such preoccupation with memories provides only a temporary escape from the unbearable present. [17] The tendency to mix past and present represents a protest against the realities of both.

Robert's counter-aesthetics culminate in destruction. In opposition to Nazi society and its formulas for automatons, Robert employs his formulas to demolish its inherited cultural monuments. To the inhumanity of this society he sets a monument of rubble. Such a memorial is to stand for those destroyed, the victims: Robert "sowed formulas that contained exactly what he wanted: dust and ruins, revenge for Ferdi Progulske, for the waiter called Groll, the boy who had thrown his notes into the mailbox." (Bil, 114) Not intended to have any political impact, his act expresses symbolic moral protest. By demolishing the abbey, he proposes his symbol for this society.

During an interrogation by an American soldier Robert reveals the meaning of his actions. The American asks him why he unnecessarily demolished the abbey, which had obstructed no German military field of defense fire. Robert remembers a midsummer

---

17. Klaus Jeziorkowski, *Rhythmus und Figur* (Bad Homberg: Gehlen, 1968), has contributed a thorough formal analysis of the time structures in this novel. He also argues, in contrast to Therese Poser, "Heinrich Böll -- 'Billard um halb zehn,'" in *Möglichkeiten des modernen deutschen Romans*, ed. Rolf Geissler (Berlin: Moritz Diesterweg, 1965), that the ritualistic withdrawals are not escape from, but rather necessary preparation for, the present.

festival during the war. While Robert and his family watched, his Nazi brother Otto lit the ceremonial fire, and then a half dozen monks led the crowd in singing a Nazi song. All around the fire, he could see that "the heated faces of the young men and women shown wildly in the solstice fire that Otto had been allowed to light, and all of them sang what the honorable monk . . . intoned: 'Our frail bones are trembling.' Wailing with torches in their hands, they went back down the hill . . ." (Bil, 136) Anger at the monks who lent authenticity to ceremonies and public confessions of Nazi faith motivated his protest, as did his more general anger at this fabricated, imposed, and total world which tolerated no individual dissent and infiltrated every household, including his own. The monks, and this entire culture, do not deserve its monuments. Robert presents it with a counter-memorial of ruins, aesthetically perfect from his perspective: "You must admit that it was a perfect demolition." (Bil, 137) His art of destruction opposes in retrospect the Nazi art of propaganda.

In the remaining forties and fifties, Robert continues to remember and destroy. Böll's own nostalgia for 1945-48, when a new and more just society appeared possible, may account for an apparent preference for ruins in his fiction.[18] While others endeavor to reconstruct West Germany, to rebuild her material wealth, Robert destroys according to contract, living and working in isolation from the society he cannot accept. Once grimly opposed to the official murderers and militarists of the Third Reich, he continues to act in opposition to his former oppressors, now dressed up as democrats, and to all the other opportunists who find it so easy to forget. Robert stands in sharp contrast to the busy, colorful hotel crowd through which he moves each morning on his way to the reserved billiards room. This billiards game represents the quintessence of Robert's adverse behavior.

---

18. James H. Reid, *Heinrich Böll: Withdrawal and Reemergence* (London: Wolff, 1973), p. 15 and Christian Linder, *Böll* (Reinbek bei Hamburg: Rowohlt, 1978), pp. 89-90.

Throughout the novel, many of the lambs view particular activities in their lives as a game. In defining themselves against the self-impressed earnestness they see about them, they adopt a playful stance, toward their jobs, for instance, like Father Fähmel in his youth, or toward traditional obligations to a marriage partner, like Mother Fähmel. Robert's billiard game is the most concrete realization of this generally playful attitude.

The essence of Robert's counter-aesthetics, his game is pursued at specified hours, like a ritual: "For the porter this had already become a ceremony, almost a liturgy, part of his flesh and blood; every morning at exactly half-past nine to take the key from the board, . . . and a half-minute later Hugo came, the older of the two boys, and asked: 'As always? . . .'" (Bil, 17) Hugo functions as a sympathetic listener in this liturgy, not a partner. Robert plays billiards alone and unconcerned with the official rules. Competition and winning points do not interest him; he plays because of his personal fascination with the geometric figures outlined by the billiard balls. Indeed, the same laws of statics and balance which he applies in calculating the demolition point of a building engage him here: "The swirling lines were all tied to angles, bound to geometric laws and physics; the energy of the hit that he gave the ball with the cue and a little frictional energy, everything a question of dimensions." (Bil, 30) In striking contrast to the loud, pompous ceremonies and parades which provoked him to take up demolition, Robert's personal ritual in this game is "light, quiet music without a melody, painting without a picture, scarcely color, only formula." (Bil, 30) The quiet, ebbing rhythm and the soft rolling sounds of this prose diverge strongly from the rigid marching beat of the Nazi litany: "respectable, respectable, honor-loyalty, order. . ." Thus Robert's and Otto's formulas directly oppose each other.

Robert pursues a personal and individual rhythm, both in the game proper and in the ritual around it. In this hour and a half, he immerses himself in the constantly fleeting figures of the billiard balls. Simultaneously, he relates to Hugo his memories of people and events that are also arranged geometrically, anchored as figures in his mind. The game as Robert plays it symbolizes an alternative thought process, one which withdraws from the flow of contemporary time into its own rhythm and into the past. As Hugo experiences it, Robert's daily hour-and-a-half stay, as well as the game itself, lends a sense of eternity and timelessness:

> Had it not always been like this? Had he not already stood here centuries ago at the white lacquered door panel, hands folded behind his back, watching the quiet game, listening to the words which sent him back sixty years, forward twenty, back again ten and then suddenly flung him out into the reality of the calendar outside? White over green, red-white over green, always within the border that bound only two square meters of green felt -- that was clean, dry and exact, between half-past nine and eleven . . . (Bil, 43)

The almost hypnotic rhythm of "white over green, red-white over green . . ." combines with Robert's words to carry Hugo backward and forward in time while he remains in this room. The movements of the balls, like the calculations for demolition, are clean, dry and exact. The formulaic channels enable Robert to remember by protecting him from the feelings which might otherwise force him to repress his memories. Such stories of the past also implicate the present when they fling Hugo "out into the reality of the calendar outside."

Toward the end of the novel, as dialogues replace monologues, a sense of urgency replaces the slow, dreamy flow of memory. For the first time in the novel, Robert plays billiards with a partner, his returned friend Schrella. Hugo observes that the isolated, timeless world has vanished: "This was the perpetual present." (Bil, 225) The game, once "a kind of prayer wheel, a litany struck over the green felt with cues and balls" (Bil, 226), has lost its hypnotic appeal: "The spell had vanished. The precision was diminished, the rhythm disrupted, while the clock so exactly answered the question *when*?: 6:51 on September 6, 1958." (Bil, 226) Robert's ritual has fulfilled its function: unlike those who tried to take up life as though the Third Reich had not occurred, Robert has indelibly printed it in his memory. He has paid tribute to his pain and is ready to receive other people and the present. He can now give up his counter-ritual, the billiards game at half-past nine.

The games of Robert's father and mother serve similar functions for them. Like their son, they carry on a kind of sovereign game with time. Johanna's withdrawal into a sanatorium especially resembles Robert's magic rituals. To protect herself as a dissenter against the Nazis, Johanna enters the Denklingen Asylum during the war and remains there until she makes one brief excursion back into society on the sixth of September, 1958. Johanna calls the sanatorium an enchanted castle, giving her residence there a fairy-tale atmosphere, an unreal air. Indeed, she insists that her visitors play a game with her: they enact various scenes out of the family's past as if they were taking place in the present. It is as if the atmosphere were bewitched; time has stood still here, as in a fairy tale. Through this game in the "enchanted castle," Johanna gains sovereignty over time and prepares to enter, if only briefly, into the present.

Here too the game loses its magic; it can no longer protect one from the present because it has finally integrated the past. Johanna says to her husband: "Come, old man, let's not play blind man's bluff anymore. I'm not going to cover your eyes any longer: you are eighty today, I am seventy-one, and at ten to twelve meters one has pretty good accuracy." (Bil, 204-205) The game with time, the counter-world of magic, enables her in the end to act, to procure a weapon. Gathering all her memories and pain, she will act upon them: "Come back to me, you years, you weeks and days, you hours and minutes" (Bil, 205), all of which culminates in readiness for the present: "The time is ripe!" (Bil, 208)

Out of the counter-rituals to Nazism evolve Johanna's and Robert's counter-symbols. Robert's monument of ruins finds its analogue in Johanna's assassination attempt. Incensed at the bogus world of parades and ceremonies, Robert offers that society and its postwar aftermath their real symbol: the ruins of any semblance of previous civilization. Johanna remembers the pre-Nazi period of indoctrination. She wants "revenge for the word that was the last to leave the innocent lips of my son: 'Hindenburg'" (Bil, 118). As Böll's "aesthetics of the humane" would suggest, her symbolic protest, like Robert's, is morally motivated: "I must have a weapon, must have a weapon. The Lord says 'mine is the vengeance,' but why shouldn't I be the Lord's instrument?" (Bil, 117) Deliberately repeating the refrain of the nationalist-military verse which her son had learned, Johanna feels morally justified in using a weapon in her counter-action. After dismissing the older Nettlinger as a possible target ("I'm not going to shoot into a museum." [Bil, 215]), Johanna's eyes light upon the "buffalo face" of an important minister across the way at a public celebration. Identifying an enemy purely by looks, she chooses this minister as the target of her revenge. He appears to her as a new version of the older "respectable, respectable" ideals. Seeing in the perpetrators of such "virtues" the murderers of her children, she decides to prevent the murder of her grandchildren. Thus her assassination of him would be "not murder of a tyrant but of respectability." (Bil, 215)

Clearly, the elimination of one minister, however objectionable he is, will transform little of the society which Mother Fähmel opposes. Further, her reasons for the assassination would most likely remain unknown to the public or be discredited as the thinking of a mad woman. Individual acts of violence can generate a still more repressive "law and order" response. All of these political considerations, as well as the problem of moral reprehensibility, are absent from the novel, however. Like Robert's demolition of Saint Anthony's, Johanna's assassination attempt remains a symbolic expression of her feelings. That her symbolism may well remain private and therefore be easily neutralized is indicated by the hotel officials' hopes that such a "happening" will make good copy: "Such a scandal can immediately send a hotel zooming. The headlines will be buzzing." (Bil, 233) The Fähmels' deeds express moral implacability without practical expectations, and thus remain isolated symbols of their private counter-aesthetics.

The counter-rituals of all the Fähmels culminate in symbolic acts through which they enter the present. Johanna turns the militarist's weapon back upon him. Heinrich destroys his own legend about himself when he cancels his Café Kroner breakfasts. Robert adopts Hugo; the small, alternative community of this humane family is increased by one member. Giving up their counter-rituals, they break out of their isolation through figurative gestures.

Artificially Amoral Aesthetics

Both Böll and Grass transplant their sensitivity to Nazi aestheticized politics into the artist figures of their novels. While these authors discern the same craft behind the propaganda, their fictive artists and their game-like counter-aesthetics serve diverging functions in the novels. Both writers scrutinize the effects of public celebrations, of arrogated religious aesthetics. The billiard or drumming games their narrators play recall the Nazi past. Having withstood personal pain and the loss of loved ones, however, Böll's artist family requires their counter-liturgies to protect them from the Nazis and their "aesthetics of the inhumane." Consequently, the billiards game is intended to present a rhythm and ritual which is humane. The beat of Oskar's drum jars and exposes the harmony of Nazi litanies, however, and only occasionally implies Grass's model of the humane. One does not identify with, or feel sorry for, Oskar as one feels sympathy for Böll's victimized Fähmels. Oskar, like his drum, is a device, an artifice designed to expose.

At first glance, Oskar's relationship to his historical milieu seems exceedingly difficult to define: the grotesque dwarf with blue eyes is both abhorrent to the Nazis and an Aryan.[19] But he is intended as a kind of magnifying glass to be moved about in front of each historic episode; Oskar the artifice assumes whatever role can best reveal that event's import. Perhaps the only consistency one can expect of Oskar is continual contradiction. The contradictory roles do vary, however, between two extremes: support for or opposition to the Third Reich. In one situation, he is their collaborator, in another, a saboteur. As soon as he has played one role, he rejects it. He claims that he is neither a resistance fighter nor an artist of the "inner emigration"; he plays a large number of roles, but he cannot be defined by any one of them.

As a figure of fantastic contrivance, Oskar defies real historical categories; the strange gnome with a toy drum hanging from

---

19.   Ann Mason, "Günter Grass and the Artist in History," *Contemporary Literature* (Summer, 1973), pp. 347-348.

his neck does not appear as a serious representative of any historical action. His author has made him so thoroughly and parodically
aware of all the clichés created before and during the Nazi years
that he himself resists identification with any one category of
behavior. As Ann Mason has argued, Oskar's "total selfconscious-
ness causes him to transcend all particular roles; he never acts simply but always plays at this or that sort of behavior." [20] Thus Oskar
remains mobile: he can reflect as well as criticize the art of politics
around him.

Grass has made Oskar especially conscious of the Nazis'
presumptuous exploitation of the idealist tradition. In the
identification of art and politics under Hitler, the fascist dictator
was seen as counterpart to the poet; both were visionaries, elevated
above their fellow men and the unpoetic restrictions of rational
thought. Here the Nazis combined and capitalized on both sides of
a tradition, extending back to the eighteenth century in Germany,
of ascribing more or less divine attributes to cultural as well as political heroes: the sacred heroes include Klopstock, Goethe, and
Wagner, in addition to Frederick the Great and Hindenburg. [21]
Thus Father Matzerath drunkenly seeks counsel from the living-
room portraits of Beethoven and Hitler, the artist and the statesman. Hitler claimed to be sacrosanct artist and statesman in one.
He was destined to deliver the only truly creative race. Therefore,
he argued publicly (and in contrast to his private disdain of the
German masses), the German people were above the rational and
moral restraints of ordinary life. Poet-statesmen would use their
artistic visions to cultivate a "chosen folk."

Oskar the artist is to be understood in relation to Hitler the
artist. Many of the Nazis liked to refer to themselves as creative,
as poets; the frustrated art student Hitler called himself an
"impeded artist." Both Hitler and Oskar became artists in rebellion
against the occupations of their petit bourgeois fathers. [22] Referring

---

20. Ibid., p. 350.

21. Henry Hatfield, "The Myth of Nazism," in *Myth and Mythmaking*, ed. Henry A.
Murray (New York: G. Braziller, 1960), p. 216.

to the political aims of his art, Hitler proudly called himself the "Trommler" who drums a new faith into the German people.[23] As Grass apparently intended, the tin drummer parodies Hitler, especially in the Dusters episode (as will be discussed later). The Minister of Propaganda in particular prided himself on his cultivated background and aesthetic sensibility. Glorifying himself and the German people, Goebbels maintains in his novel *Michael* that the German spirit is essentially Faustian.[24] In a parody of this appropriation of the idealist heritage, Oskar refers to the two souls in his one drum. Grass parodies what Mann laments: the Nazi misuse of German cultural traditions. Throughout the novel, the tin drummer will embody as well as deflate the Nazi myth; with his drum, he will mimic as well as counter the Nazi aesthetics of manipulation.

Appearing to approach his first Nazi rally with an unbiased perspective, Oskar considers the Nazis potential friends. The playful three-year-old is out for amusement, not partisan politics; he prefers the wit of the Nazi Löbsack to the deadly earnest heckling of the Communists or Socialists. Expecting that the hunchback Nazi represents his and Bebra's cause, Oskar innocently inspects the platform from which Löbsack speaks. "What is that, a rostrum?" inquires Oskar. First and foremost, he observes, a rostrum must be symmetrical: "From back to front: six swastika banners side by side; then a row of flags, pennants, standards; then a row of black-uniformed SS men with storm-straps under their chins; then two rows of SA, who clutched their belt buckles during the singing and speeches; then, seated, several rows of uniformed Party comrades." (Bt, 94-95) This rostrum evokes "then," "then," and "then," a sense of strength in order, of import in uniformity: confronting the viewer on every level are ordered, solid rows of identically ranked party members and dignitaries, enhanced by fluttering flags and

---

22. Hanspeter Brode, "Die Zeitgeschichte in der 'Blechtrommel' von Günter Grass: Entwurf eines textinternen Kommunikationsmodells," in *Günter Grass - Ein Materialienbuch*, ed. Rolf Geissler (Neuwied: Luchterhand, 1976), p. 91.

23. Quoted in Ann Mason, p. 354.

24. Mosse, p. 105.

banners. This mass of human beings appears like an instrumental superunit, ready to take wing on the symbols of inspiration waving behind them, on the "singing and speeches" chanted around them. They are even described like solid architecture: "The base of the rostrum was tapered by the Hitler Youth." (Bt, 95) To subvert the intention of the imposing image, Oskar insists on praising Löbsack's hump over the rostrum's symmetry. Disappointed when the district leader proves himself no different from the mass of brown uniformity behind him, Oskar becomes suspicious of this party and its symmetry: "The longer I looked at the rostrum, standing in front of it, the more suspicious I became of the symmetry that was insufficiently relieved by Löbsack's hump." (Bt, 95)

The next Sunday Oskar approaches the rostrum from behind. From this viewpoint, he studies the naked, ugly scaffolding, the platform denuded of its magic and solidifying decorations. To escape rebombardment of his senses, Oskar scrambles about under the rostrum until he finds an appropriate spot "to enjoy the acoustical delights of a political rally at his ease, without being distracted by flags or optically irritated by uniforms." (Bt, 96) Not only his eyes but also his offended drummer's ears dispose him to be critical of the party: "Of course my criticism was leveled above all at the drummers and the horn-blowers." (Bt, 95) From his undermining position below the platform, Oskar takes up the instrument of his counter-aesthetics. Gradually his dancing rhythm infects the official drummers and sets the audience's feet to waltzing on the meadow. Noting Löbsack's displeasure, Oskar pretends to repent and changes over to the Charleston, "Jimmy the Tiger." Significantly, Oskar's counter-rhythm culminates here in what the Nazis regarded as decadent urban music. As George Mosse explains, the National Socialists viewed modern dancing as harmful to its ideal of womanhood. The rhythms were thought to incite sexual promiscuity; the dancing amounted to an orgy. [25] Indeed, those lost in the Charleston spilling over into the adjoining park "found the jungle that Jimmy had promised: tigers moving on velvet paws and an ersatz primeval forest for the folk that was crowded on the

25. Ibid., p. 22.

meadow. Law and order were gone." (Bt, 98) What the rigid, earnest goose-steppers feared has occurred: Oskar has released the repressed "primitive" energies which could otherwise have driven strictly marching feet. Law and order have been subverted.

Perhaps no artist's instrument is better designed to counter Nazi aesthetics than the drum. A music of rhythm, drumming counters Nazi aesthetic manipulation with one of its own instruments. The rhythm of Nazi news and propaganda films and of their parades and celebrations, and the very frequency of these attacks on the senses manipulated the average citizen into feeling that the tempo of life had changed, that it had taken on a momentum, racing frantically toward a monumental climax. Oskar's beat resists this disengagement from natural rhythms, Grass seems to suggest, by reminding those still reachable of their natural, basic, playful urges. Soloists like Oskar and the "ballet master" Heinrich Fähmel withstand the imposed rhythms of rectilinear march music. A toy drum does not lend itself to the earnest pomposity of rigid military rhythms. At the end of this Sunday, the drum again appears to represent free and spontaneous music. But like any instrument of art, Oskar's drum not only creates but also registers the sounds of the world. On this particular evening, "a refreshing storm with a cloudburst offered a long performance of beautiful hail drumming. Oskar's exhausted drum was allowed to rest and listen." (Bt, 99) His drum listens to the "drum solo" of the hail storm, the natural rhythms of the rain.

Although he disrupted other political rallies, Oskar denies that he belongs to the resistance against Hitler. He asks the reader rather to see him as "nothing other than a somewhat eccentric person . . ., who for private, and what is more, aesthetic reasons, also following the advice of my teacher Bebra, rejected the color and cut of the uniforms, the rhythm and volume of the music normally played on rostrums, and therefore drummed up some protest on a mere child's toy." (Bt, 100) Oskar counters ideological aesthetics (from the Vegetarians, to Jehovah's Witnesses, to Nazis) with the private, directly sensual aesthetics of the child. He undercuts their proclamations with a mere toy: "Whatever they might have to sing, trumpet, worship and proclaim, my drum knew better." (Bt, 101)

The novel is full of these contrasts between simple playfulness and the pretentious rigidity of "evangelists." When Jan Bronski is shaking with fright at the impending Nazi take-over of the Polish post office, he "regresses" from *Skat* to childhood games: he begins to build a card house. "Building card houses" suggests Jan's and Poland's romanticism, but it also contrasts with Nazi architecture. Extremely airy, precariously sensitive to the slightest draft, this light little house stands no chance against the rush of air accompanying the Nazi army as it storms the small room: "They ripped open the door screaming 'Come out!' which stirred up a wind that made the card house collapse. They had no feeling for this kind of architecture. They swore by concrete. They built for eternity." (Bt, 199) Again a simple child's game makes fun of the aesthetics of monumentality.

Oskar compares the rear view of rally rostrums with that of church altars: everyone, he remarks, should see both denuded of their magic before gathering in front of them. To reveal the parallels between political and religious ideologies, Grass examines the Nazis' adoption of religious aesthetics as a method of indoctrination. Whereas Böll contrasts Nazism with genuine religion, Grass primarily exposes its quasi-religious appeal.

The chapter called "Faith, Hope, Love" explicitly examines the transfer of a people's religious disposition to politics. Faith, hope and love are all invested in the political affairs of the Third Reich. Hoping for a combination Santa Claus-Christ figure in Hitler, "A whole gullible nation believed in Santa Claus." (Bt, 165) This credulous folk realized only later that their savior was a lethal gasman. By then "the faith in the gasman had been declared the state religion." (Bt, 166) The early NSDAP sensed and exploited the need of those suffering most from economic and social crises to believe in security and salvation from their life of disappointments and resentments. Leader worship had a following before the Nazi take-over. As Bracher points out, "Long before 1933, a wealth of grotesque practices and religious fervor testified to the quasi-religious impact of the Leader propaganda, as for example, obituaries in which the name of Hitler was invoked in place of the name of the Lord." [26]

The Nazis deliberately cultivated belief in their ideology as a substitute religion. Mosse describes the Nazis' careful self-portrayal of this secular faith:

> However much the Nazis wanted to substitute their world view for Christianity, they were careful to keep the traditional forms intact. Even the language they used in their speeches often employed familiar Christian imagery. Hitler and Goebbels talked about the "miracle of belief" (now meaning the Nazi faith), appealed to "Providence," and were not loath to call *Mein Kampf* the "sacred book of National Socialism." Indeed, the Führer's closest companions were called his "apostles," while he himself was often referred to as the "saviour." [27]

In contrast to most of Grass's critics, Ann Mason has shrewdly discerned that if Hitler will assume the role of artistic-messianic leader, then Oskar will identify with Jesus. This identity is blasphemy, but it also has a more important function: it points up the grotesque misuse of religion and religious metaphor during the Third Reich. [28]

In defense of these so-called blasphemous passages, Grass himself links the Dusters' band led by Oskar-Jesus to the Nazi band of the SA. The youthful sect around Oskar, Grass states, reflects in miniature the ideological cult of anti-Semitism: "The barbarism of the SA during the Crystal Night corresponds to the aggressive disposition of the youthful Dusters band later. Only thus, in relationship to unleashed force, can the deconstruction of the St. Mary's altar in the Church of the Sacred Heart be understood." [29] Just as

---

26. Bracher, p. 148.

27. Mosse, p. 235.

28. Mason, p. 353.

29. Günter Grass, "Günter Grass über seine Werke," in *Autor, Werk und Kritik* I, ed. Gudrun Uhlig (Munich: Hueber, 1969), p. 94.

the Nazis used their authority to exercise power unrestrained, the Dusters allow their aggressive and destructive desires full rein. In particular, their desire to dismantle the altar results in demystification of the religious symbol as well as a parody of the National Socialists. The Nazis arrogated religious images and rituals to the religion of the savior-gasman; as their analogue, the Dusters destroy the original Catholic images and appropriate them for their own use.

Like their new leader, Oskar, the Dusters disclaim any political or ideological affiliation. In their opposition to the ruling authorities, they are not to be classified. Viewed on the one hand as resistance fighters, some of them are also dutiful members of the Nazi Air Force Auxiliary. Not bound to any real historical-political category, they aid their Jesus-leader as a mobile artifice. The whole band simultaneously embodies and nullifies the Nazi myth of German society.

Prior to Oskar's "coming," this little group of rebels had been obliged to use the same weapons as the Nazis -- munitions stolen, in fact, from official supplies. Oskar-Jesus offers his followers a miracle instead and orders them to bury their old weapons: "'Our weapons are of a different kind!'" (Bt, 308) The Ministry of Propaganda also offered its faithful followers miracles and tried to encourage belief in the final victory. With his glass-shattering voice, Oskar claims to outdo the Nazis and parodies their propaganda: "There was a good deal of talk in those days about secret weapons and final victory. We, the Dusters, discussed neither, but we had the secret weapon." (Bt, 307)

Like many Nazi officials, Oskar's entourage takes advantage of their new power to avenge themselves on personal enemies. The Nazis marked Jewish windows for smashing; Oskar describes how he shattered "unwillingly but upon request the kitchen windows of the apartment of a teacher that the boys wanted to avenge themselves on." (Bt, 308) Anticipating the ultimate counter-drama, these performances parodically parallel Nazi activities: "In mid-December Rundstedt opened his offensive in the Ardennes, and we completed preparations for our major coup." (Bt, 312)

Their final coup parodies the pageantry of the Christmas Mass and imitative Nazi festivities. Having established an identification of Hitler with the Christ of Christmas, Oskar chooses, as the climactic episode in his counter-scenario, to produce a Christmas play. Seated on the virgin's lap, from which Jesus had already been sawed off, Oskar with his magnetic blue eyes fits into the spiritual scene; he notes ironically, "The virgin pointed her finger at Oskar, the drummer. I had indeed taken the place of Christ." (Bt, 315) This image of Oskar sitting with half-dismantled, hollow-cast Catholic statues, spotlighted by the boys' flashlights, demystifies the magic imagery and rituals of Catholicism and, by implication, of pseudo savior-gasmen. In a counter-ritual, Oskar slowly begins drumming out the chanting rhythms of the Christmas Mass for his apostle-henchmen. The band of criminals complete their confession of faith. Oskar, like Hitler, has utilized the ritual and pomp of Catholicism to play at being the savior. It can be no accident that Grass focuses on the aesthetic elements of Catholic imagery, as he explains its inclusion in his works about this epoch: "The author was concerned to portray this playful, colorful, half-heathen, half-Christian world and to place it in relationship to the epoch of National Socialism." [30]

In the ensuing surreal trial of the Dusters, Grass indicates that psycho-sexual needs motivate the bands of official as well as self-appointed vigilantes. As quoted earlier, Grass sees the aggressive disposition of the SA reflected in his Dusters. Grass's word here, *Aggressionslust*, has psycho-sexual connotations. In the trial scene of the Dusters, each member of the band is seduced by Luzie Rennwand to spring from a diving board into a waterless swimming pool -- in other words, to indict himself through suicide. Although each young man is able to resist the cries of the judges' chorus to spring, his sexual-aggressive urge is nonetheless aroused at the sight of Luzie: "Then he plunged furiously at the triangle, but missed it nonetheless." (Bt, 318) Only Oskar is not seduced to prove his masculinity although she tempts him also: "'Dive, sweet Jesus, dive,' whispered the prematurely developed witness Luzie

---

30.   Ibid., p. 93.

Rennwand. She was sitting on Satan's lap, which brought out her virginity still more. He awoke her appetite by handing her a hot dog. She bit into it with pleasure and remained nonetheless chaste. 'Dive, sweet Jesus!' she chewed, offering me her triangle, still intact." (Bt, 319) Oskar, however, "disdaining the ecstasy of the plunge," resists the temptation to dive for her and is acquitted of the crimes of the Dusters.

The real indictment in this strange swimming pool scene is directed against the source of the Dusters' and the SA's acts of belligerence: unsatisfied and then misdirected sexuality. Grass seems to agree with the Reichian view that a totally satisfied sexual being feels less desire for hostile aggression against others. As in *Billiards at Half-Past Nine*, psycho-social needs and wounded masculine pride predispose particular individuals to the fanaticism and ritualistic behavior encouraged by Nazi propaganda. The natural playfulness and sensuality of Oskar's counter-rhythms in the rostrum scene imply the same alternative behavior to Nazi rigidity as this exposure of the Dusters' adolescent belligerence. Emphasis on bodily primal needs throughout the novel has provoked many accusations of "pornography" in Grass's work. But Grass's concern with such sexual and sensual activity constitutes part of his aesthetics, and it is not intended by any means to serve a titillating purpose.

Like Böll, Grass also focuses on the fanatical rituals that comprised the Nazi cult of athletics. As in the Dusters' black mass, Catholic icons become analogues to Nazi "icons." Naively wandering about in the Church of the Sacred Heart, the three-year-old Oskar suddenly sees an athletic feat in Christ's "ability" to hang on the cross: "What muscles the man had! This athlete with the figure of a decathlon winner." (Bt, 112) If the Nazis can turn their athletes into objects of worship, Oskar will perceive Christ as a track hero. Oskar then proceeds to worship the muscular athlete with all the fervor that his contemporaries were spending on their idolized Aryan heroes: "Believe me, that I prayed: my sweet gymnast, I called him, athlete of athletes, world's champion hanger on the cross by inch-thick nails. And he never even twitched!" (Bt, 112) Jesus appears to be the winner in this event. Culminating his parody of Nazi veneration of sports heroes, however, Oskar kneels before his decathlon winner, "and tried to associate words like 'blessed' or 'afflicted' with Jesse Owens and Rudolf Harbig and last year's Berlin Olympics; but I was not always successful, for I had to say that Jesus had been unfair to the two thieves. So I disqualified him." (Bt, 113) Jesus has not competed fairly against the two thieves: Jesus may have drawn on "outside help." Such preposterous efforts to dismiss the winner of what is, after all, "his event" perhaps parody the Nazis' absurd efforts to disqualify the black athlete Jesse Owens.

Throughout the novel Oskar parodies many types of artists. He primarily mocks the Nazi artists of propaganda by unmasking their particular myths and clichés. He exposes their art from both sides of his ambiguous political identity: by disrupting their rally as well as by imitating them with the theater company on the front. He continues in the postwar period to drum a parodic beat of its manias. As a jazz musician in the Onion Cellar, he makes fun of the postwar confessional ritual of intellectuals; they need onions to induce the mournful flow of tears for the past. And as a recording star, the dwarf drums the nostalgic music that returns the Adenauer electorate to what it wants: childhood. From beginning to end, Oskar's art is destructive, as he says it is. His voice destroys directly what his drum destroys (by exposure) indirectly. Indeed, he must proffer destruction in order to survive: "Oskar's voice, even more than his drum, was eternally fresh proof of my existence; for as long as I sang glass to pieces, I existed." (Bt, 300) In other words: I destroy, therefore I am. Constantly in danger of Nazi arrest as an undesirable, abnormal dwarf, Oskar resists their "normal" world and its oppression by destroying it and thereby asserting his own "abnormal" perspective.

Oskar's detonating drum and voice represent Grass's aesthetics opposing the Nazis'. Like Böll's "aesthetics of the humane," Grass's formulas for art evolve at least in part out of opposition to the Nazis. Whereas they "aestheticized" politics, Grass "politicizes" art in the sense that he confronts propagandized illusions with the reality they distort. When Benjamin referred to communists politicizing art, he thought of the work of Eisenstein and Brecht, for instance. While Grass politicizes art, he does not of course follow the ideological example of those artists; he attempts, rather, to contrast the illusions of ideology with the realities of power. Grass exhorts the writer to explore a many-sided reality, not to select its most comfortable, visible, or "proper" aspects: "Reality, as the raw material of the writer, cannot be divided; only he who captures all of it and doesn't spare its shadowy sides deserves to be called a writer." [31] Grass uses his art to remind his readers of the realities which Nazi artfulness tried to blot out.

As noted earlier, Grass's evident concern for sexual and primal needs constitutes part of this aesthetics. The "shadowy sides" of reality, he says, cannot be omitted: "As obvious as it is, it should nonetheless be repeated: the sexual realm also, with its high and low points, in all its stale commonness, is part of this reality." [32] Both the rally sabotage and the Dusters' indictment point to authoritarian repression of sexuality, the rigid bodies strutting the parade beat and the aggressive brutality of vigilante bands. Repeatedly Grass contrasts the sexual psychology of these repressed adolescents of all ages with natural, spontaneous rhythms, the playful sensuality often linked with children. Thus, the allegedly three-year-old Oskar questions in his naiveté the rituals and imagery accepted by all those around him. The "truth" of the psycho-sexual reality constitutes in part "beauty" for Grass.

Since *The Tin Drum* appeared, shocked moralists and some literary critics have attacked or quarreled passionately about the sexual significance of innumerable passages in the novel. In response, Grass maintains that such taboo areas are realms of reality at least as significant as the sanctioned. Thus, not only sexual psychology but also sexuality "in all its stale commonness is a part of this reality." As shown through the numerous sexual activities of Agnes with Bronski, or Oskar with Maria, primary needs take precedence over the distant battles of Pearl Harbor and Stalingrad. The opposition of private to public concerns is intended not only to

---

31. Günter Grass, in Uhlig, p. 93.

32. Ibid., p. 93.

expose privatism (as was emphasized in the last chapter) but also to uncover the unheroic realities of daily life under the Nazis. This is also reality, Grass is saying, in contrast to the images in the cinema news reports and the grand heroic rhetoric projected over the radio. Clearly, the extramarital antics defy the Nazis' projected image of women as only wholesome reproducers for the Reich. Many of the sexual involvements of Agnes and Maria provide the only excitement available to them in the boring, oppressive mustiness of petit bourgeois daily life. (The cell leader Alfred Matzerath, in contrast to the women and Jan Bronski, found his escape from this drab environment elsewhere, of course.) The social implications of sexuality can disclose much about the human environment. These descriptions of daily sexuality are no more pornographic than the church episodes are simply blasphemous.

For such reasons, Grass defends his "blasphemy" as pertinent to the reality of his epoch: "In the same way, the relationship of contemporaries in an epoch to religion and to the reigning as well as suppressed ideologies belongs to the reality that should be portrayed." [33] Thus Grass's celebrated sensory awareness serves his graphic depiction of a many-sided reality, undercutting the ideological and aesthetic manipulaton of the Nazis.

Just as Oskar suggests knowledge as a deterrent to investing such faith, hope, and love in Nazism, Grass appeals to his readers' intellects through his method of exposure. He counters the ecstasy and hysteria intended in Nazi ritual with a child's common sense; the mystical unity and collective will engendered by their propaganda with a heretical, eternally unaffiliated individualism; and their illusory art of indoctrination with anti-illusionist views from the rear. In short, he confronts their entire substitute reality with a demystified and far more inclusive one. Politicizing his art against "aestheticized" politics, Grass presents the psychological, social and political realities that artful Nazis conjured away.

---

33.   Ibid., p. 93.

Oskar, the unaffiliated artifice, is moved about to magnify the grotesque dimensions of various social and political scenes across the years. Yet even major critics like Michael Hamburger have apparently confused the narrator with the author and chided Grass for his amoral or immoral novel. [34] The narrator's seemingly amoral indifference to taboo, however, illuminates realities hidden to the more conventionally "moral" human beings of his society. As the fantastic contrivance of Grass's imagination, Oskar can still serve a moral purpose and even disclose his creator's moral standards. Grass's moral perspective emerges especially in the "Moritat"-tones of the "Faith, Hope, Love" chapter, with its sober attacks on the mass murder of the Jews. Oskar verges on pathos as he protests against the ideology which required the liquidation of one "race" to fill the material and spiritual needs of the other: "I don't know, oh, I don't know, for example, what they fill sausage casings with, whose guts are necessary in order to fill them . . . and never will we learn who had to be reduced to silence so that sausage casings could be filled." (Bt, 166-167)

In an interview with Heinz Ludwig Arnold in 1970, Grass was asked to identify the sources of the moral attitude behind his novels. As a nonpracticing Catholic, Grass links himself more widely than the Catholic Böll to various European moral traditions. Grass speaks in this interview of his origins in Christianity and the utopian goals of *The Communist Manifesto* and the Enlightenment: "And against these we measure reality, historical, social, also ecclesiastical reality." [35] Whereas Böll portrays with his Fähmels a direct moral opposition to the Nazis' "aesthetics of the inhumane," Grass suggests indirectly, through a seemingly amoral approach, his own moral posture.

---

34. Michael Hamburger, *From Prophecy to Exorcism* (London: Longmans, 1968), pp. 153-154.

35. Heinz Ludwig Arnold, "Gespräch mit Günter Grass," *Text und Kritik* 1/1a (Günter Grass issue, October, 1971), pp. 7-8.

Indicted Aesthetics

The general mood of political self-scrutiny in the wake of Nazism induced many artists to re-examine the relationships between art and politics. If only through their writing, several postwar writers have endeavored to act in a more responsible political and social manner than was common among their predecessors before 1933. Grass, Böll, and others of the Group 47 have devoted their literary efforts to a critique of the past partly in order to prevent its recurrence. As one of the predecessors, Mann felt some personal responsibility for the earlier social and political role of the artist.

Because of his famous response to Bonn University's withdrawal of his honorary doctorate in 1936, Mann was highly regarded as an anti-Nazi. He nonetheless accepted some responsibility for the intellectual climate in which Nazism developed. One who shares in the life of the German spirit, Karl Jaspers argued, feels not tangible guilt, but something analogous to co-responsibility.[36] Like his successors later, Mann had begun in the 1920s to insist upon the social and political responsibilities of the artist for the survival of a humane and democratic order. In this connection he was to indict the baleful political effects of large parts of the German cultural past and present when he dealt with Nazi aesthetics.

All three novelists detect the artist in Hitler. Outside of *Doctor Faustus* Mann reveals the same sensitivity to the Führer's art of manipulation as Grass and Böll were to show. In *Mario and the Magician* (1929), Mann depicts the hypnotist who artfully bends the will of the Italian crowd to succumb to his own. In his 1939 essay "Brother Hitler" he grimly acknowledges the artist, and therefore brother, he sees in Hitler. But Mann also recognizes in Hitler another artful magician, Richard Wagner: "Wagnerian, on a degraded level, is the whole thing. One noticed it long ago and knows the well-founded, even if a bit presumptuous, admiration

---

36. Karl Jaspers, *The Question of German Guilt*, trans. E. B. Ashton (New York: Capricorn Books, 1961), p. 79.

that the political miracle-worker owes the artistic magician of Europe, whom Gottfried Keller already called a 'hairdresser and charlatan.'" [37] Mann refers here to the numerous Wagnerian performances in Third Reich opera houses, as well as to their adaptations in the political arena. He sees Wagnerian theater in the illusory, fairy-tale character of Nazi propaganda, and in the political producers' hypnotic inducement of mystic mass unity. The Nazis' "aestheticized" politics is "art uncontrolled by the mind, art as black magic." [38]

In the Hitler essay, Mann also discerns the psychological manipulation intended in the Führer's art of rhetoric which possesses "an unspeakably inferior, but effective power of persuasion over the masses. With this hysterically and theatrically disposed tool he bores into the wound of the people and agitates them with announcements of their insulted greatness, stunning them with promises." [39] Detecting Hitler's intent to vitiate any individual critical will, Mann exclaims, "How a man like this must hate any analysis!" [40] Likewise, the author has the devil say to Adrian: "If the devil hates anything, if anything in the whole world is contrary to him, it is analytical criticism. What he wants and dispenses is exactly the triumphant transcendence of that: a resplendent thoughtlessness!" To which Adrian responds: "Charlatan!" (DF, 316) References to the Nazi art of indoctrination are, however, few in *Doctor Faustus*. Why has Mann nearly abandoned portrayal of the art which propagated the mass hysteria and irrationalism that are central to his novel of this epoch, especially after he devoted parts of essays and a whole novella to the art of the "charlatan"?

Part of the answer can be found in the piece, "Brother Hitler," itself. The artistic temperament of this disagreeable brother

---

37. Thomas Mann, "Bruder Hitler," in *Schriften zur Politik* (Frankfurt am Main: Suhrkamp, 1970), p. 138.

38. Ibid., p. 142.

39. Ibid., p. 137.

40. Ibid., p. 141.

interests Mann more than the artist Hitler in action. Mann asserts that "readiness to identify oneself with the despicable" is more honest and productive than unmitigated hatred; he proceeds to describe the artistic disposition of the disgruntled outcast Hitler: "artistic genius . . . In a certain shameful way all the qualities are there: the difficultness, laziness . . . the stubbornly executed need to justify and prove oneself; the drive to overwhelm and to submit; the dream of seeing a world overcome by anxiety, love, admiration, and shame at the feet of the one once despised . . ." [41] In his attempt to understand, not just condemn, Hitler, Mann in effect discovers himself in the frustrated art student. Out of this admirable soul-searching effort to avoid displacing the responsibility on "the others," the author extends his "self-prosecution of the *Bürger*" to one of the artist.

To be sure, Mann does partly exempt himself: he sees the concerns of his youthful art perverted and debased by the Nazi political artists. He refers, for example, to the social-religious fanaticism of the monk in his novella *Fiorenza*, "who proclaimed 'the wonder of release from inhibitions.'" These and other ideas became the "clamor of the streets" twenty years later, Mann maintains. Thus he asks, "Who can be surprised that I wanted to disclaim them, when they had gone to the political dogs and romped about on a niveau that only professors infatuated with primitiveness and literary lackeys of anti-intellectualism did not scorn?" [42] Similarly, it is the debasement (*Verhunzung*) of Wagnerian aesthetics that Mann emphasizes in his analysis of their political adaption by Hitler. Mann is repelled by the low niveau of the Nazis, by their distortion of more elevated aesthetic ideas: the aesthetic aversion of this author to Nazism is not without an element of patrician disdain.

Mann does not content himself, however, with disdainful repudiation of the "clamor of the streets." Perhaps guilt feelings about his pre-1918 anti-democratic stance motivate Mann's need for

---

41.   Ibid., pp. 138-139.

42.   Ibid., pp. 140-141.

a confrontation with his own as well as his country's past. Refusing to perceive himself only as the exile, and thus "the good Germany," he indicates the self-critical method behind *Doctor Faustus* in his 1945 speech, "Germany and the Germans": "One *is* connected with the German fate and German guilt, when one is born a German. Truths that one tries to say about one's people can only be the product of self-examination." [43] This German attempts, then, to characterize what he has in common with his folk, their fate, and their guilt, without regard for differences distinguishing separate social groups. From such personal reckoning evolves a novel about Germany's political present and cultural past which attempts to demonstrate that "the bad Germany is the good one gone astray, the good one in a disaster, in a guilty downfall." [44] In contrast to *Mario and the Magician*, Mann is less specifically interested in the Nazis practicing the art of politics. Now the cultural traditions themselves, not the manipulation for which they were used, must be examined. In his novel of the epoch, his question about art and politics has become larger: how did the land of Beethoven and Mozart also support a Hitler?

To come to terms with the artist in himself and his traditions, Mann creates a modern composer whose life and music will prophesy in cultural terms the political holocaust to come. Adrian represents the "late" modern artist, and the expressionist in particular, toward the end of his career. Because he incorporates a line of artists extending back into the nineteenth century, he seems to exemplify their ultimate conclusion. Various aspects of the art, personalities, and lives of Nietzsche, Beethoven, and more modern composers -- Schönberg, Mahler, and Hugo Wolf -- merge in the figure of Leverkühn. [45] Adrian's music illustrates the return in some twentieth-century art to the archaic and primitive as a kind of private and isolated myth-making. Such art defines for itself no

43. Thomas Mann, "Deutschland und die Deutschen," in *Schriften zur Politik* (Frankfurt am Main: Suhrkamp, 1970), p. 164.

44. Ibid., p. 181.

45. Henry Hatfield, *Thomas Mann* (New York: Knopf, 1962), pp. 131-132.

real contemporary social function, according to Hans Mayer; rather "It is sufficient to itself, monologic in Gottfried Benn's sense."[46] These artists overlook the potentially dangerous social and political effects of their art. In his late works, Leverkühn parallels the expressionist's escape from the bourgeois world of de-vitalized tradition, the breakthrough to the primitive by way of sovereign mastery of the most extreme formalism.[47] In *Doctor Faustus* Mann implicitly accuses expressionists both for their irrationalism and their formal introversion, the social aloofness of their solitary art.

The expressionist solution to the modern artist's dilemma appears to Adrian in his hallucinated dialogue with the devil. This conversation in the novel can be located in the year 1911, one of the most important for expressionism. In their discussion about the apparent sterility of old musical conventions, Adrian suggests: "One could heighten the play by playing with forms out of which, obviously, life has disappeared." In response the devil formulates the crucial problem: "I know, I know. Parody. It could be fun if it were not so terribly melancholy in its aristocratic nihilism. Would you promise yourself much pleasure and greatness from such tricks?" To which Adrian angrily answers "No." (DF, 322) The other way out is the plunge into the so-called archaic and primitive, into expressionism. As Reinhard Baumgart has argued, however, this eruption and celebration of the irrational need not appear so suspicious as it does here in a pact with the devil.[48] Many expressionists directed their art against fascist and militarist tendencies in their society; their introverted art forms represent not so much a disregard for social or political problems as a stage in the development of a more socially responsible art in a rapidly changing world. While the author lets his composer choose a solution akin to that of the suspect expressionists, Mann himself pursued both answers. He

---

46. Hans Mayer, *Von Lessing bis Thomas Mann* (Pfullingen: Neske, 1959), p. 400.

47. André von Gronicka, "Thomas Mann's 'Doktor Faustus,'" *Germanic Review* 23, 3 (1948), p. 212.

48. "Diskussion zu Thomas Mann," *Sprache im technischen Zeitalter* 5, no. 17/18 (1966), p. 78.

chose in 1911 the form of parody in *Felix Krull*. In the same year, the writer also turned in *Death in Venice* to Aschenbach, another artist who succumbed to the beckoning devil of dissolution. This novella is of course no invitation for the reader to follow Aschenbach. But Mann appears in *Doctor Faustus* to have linked his own youthful fascination with irrationalism to the expressionist *Schrei* and both to the cultural origins of Nazism.

Ultimately, Mann mistrusts expressionist modern art, but he certainly sympathizes with and understands the contemporary artist's plight as part of a larger social crisis. Leverkühn grasps at drastic means to re-vitalize his art only because the culture and society surrounding him so thoroughly lack any sense of creative purpose. The musty decay enveloping the lives of the Rodde sisters and others in the environment illustrates the extent of the problem. Mann, along with his composer, dislikes this sterile bourgeois culture, but he cannot condone Leverkühn's art. However much Mann himself as an artist explores the darker underside of life, he always, as in the narrative tone of *Death in Venice*, maintains a grip of responsible control. Leverkühn, in contrast, indulges in a primitive barbarism in his music that makes Zeitblom shudder. The howling glissandos of the "Apocalipsis cum figuris," for example, can be heard as celebrating and encouraging barbarism. And it is not only a squeamish, old-fashioned humanist who is frightened by Leverkühn's music; not only the narrator but the novel itself criticizes these compositons: Leverkühn's expressionist art is about and inspired by hell, in league with the devil.

In connecting Leverkühn's music to the expressionists in particular, Mann singles them out for the damaging social impact of their art; but they appear to culminate a long tradition of outsider-artists and intellectuals who are seen as almost equally culpable in their lack of social responsibility. Even if Adrian's art does not encourage barbarism, it creates in its esoteric isolation "nothing in defense *against* the arising barbarism. Thus, it becomes guilty and complicitous, just as Zeitblom in passivity becomes complicitous."[49]

---

49. Hans Mayer, *Thomas Mann: Werk und Entwicklung* (Berlin: Volk und Welt, 1950), p. 389.

The unpolitical German inwardness decried by Mann in "Germany and the Germans" describes this isolated artist as well as his humanist friend. Since music for Mann is more associated with political backwardness and thoughtlessness than are the verbal arts, Adrian's music echoes in Zeitblom's ears as he listens aghast to the theoretical adherents of irrationalism in the Kridwiss-Kreis. Though more politicized than the solitary composer, these "intellectuals" are here linked with him in their social irresponsibility. They are the "professors infatuated with primitiveness and the literary lackeys of anti-intellectualism" Mann flays in "Brother Hitler" who contribute to the political degradation of the author's earlier views. He even looks as far back into the past as Luther for evidence of an isolated intellectual tradition: he stresses that theologian's refusal to extend his religious ideas into politics during the peasant revolts. Not surprisingly, Mann's speeches and essays in two decades of coming to terms with the Third Reich continually return to the social responsibility of the artist or intellectual.

Mann's re-evaluation of Nietzsche is part of this new emphasis. In the same year that Mann completed what has been called his Nietzsche-novel, he gave a speech called "Nietzsche's Philosophy in the Light of Our Experience." Without accepting any simply causal relationship of Nietzsche's philosophy to fascism, Mann nonetheless had grown far more critical of the thinker he had praised in his youth. Sympathetic to Nietzsche's historical position, Mann does see the philosopher's aestheticist revolt against the backdrop of bourgeois moralism. Nietzsche's glorification of the barbaric, however, derives from his aesthetic intoxication; in the light of fascism we must now reckon with this connection between aestheticism and barbarism. Without any concern for the political uses to which his thoughts might be put, the philosopher renounced *Geist* and morality in the name of beautiful, courageous, and reckless living. The same could be said of Adrian Leverkühn within his world of music.

Whereas Nietzsche's defense of instinct against reason was necessary at the time, Mann asserts that it remains eternally necessary to defend life in the name of *Geist* or morality. In response to Hitler, one must side with Christianity against Nietzsche's critique.

This indictment of the (Nietzschean) artist leads to Mann's moral imperative that the artist be socially responsible. Numerous speeches in the thirties and forties resound with this dictum for the artist: "Ultimately, aestheticism in whose name the free spirits rejected bourgeois morality, belongs itself to the bourgeois age; to transcend this means to step out of an aesthetic epoch into a moral and social one."[50] This statement from 1947 brings us to the threshhold of Heinrich Böll's lectures stressing the congruence of moral and aesthetic concerns. Although Leverkühn's art would seem to belong only to the aestheticist revolt against the bourgeois age, it also dialectically contains the seeds of its transcendence: Leverkühn's rejection of an anachronistic morality derives from a yearning for a more contemporary, social morality.

Leverkühn's art of revocation thus anticipates Robert Fähmel's art of demolition. Whereas Oskar's destruction is through exposure, Robert and Adrian destroy in their individual ways out of despair and cold anger at the inhumanity of the world in which each lives. Robert's demolitions are part of his answer to Nazi aesthetics. In anticipation of Nazism, Adrian's art, particularly his last composition, annuls traditions of noble, humane aspirations. Defying and parodying past conventions, Adrian's aesthetics counter the present sterility of his cultural heritage and his stultifying bourgeois environment. In his desperate efforts to "break through," to create a new music, Adrian opposes reverence for the past. His art, like Robert's, is carefully calculated to nullify any semblance of previous civilization and humanity still present in their worlds.

As it is for the demolition expert Fähmel, the quintessence of Adrian's aesthetics is a game. Like the billiards game, the composer's "magic square" encapsulates the design of his art as a whole. The exacting computation characteristic of Robert's formulas also distinguishes Adrian's musical designs. For both of them, formulas capture the essense of their experience; the discipline of

---

50. Thomas Mann, "Nietzsches Philosophie im Lichte unserer Erfahrung," in *Gesammelte Werke*, IX (Oldenburg: Fischer, 1960), pp. 710-711.

the formulaic structure facilitates the explosive expression of their deepest emotions. Adrian's twelve-tonal "For I die as an evil and good Christian" establishes the essential structure which releases the composer's subjectivity. For both, the final symbolic expression is *Klage*, a grievous lament. Like Fähmel's revenge for the deaths of his dear ones, Adrian's resolve to annul Beethoven's Ninth Symphony is originally prompted by the death of Echo. Coldly rational in their methods of expressing grief, both artists protect, secure, and project their feelings through their games and their art. The composer as well as the potential architect determine to deprive their society of its cultural monuments. To their culture's inhumanity, they proffer a monument of rubble and an ode to sorrow to replace the ode to joy.

The esoteric magic quadrate is the game of a modern representative of "high" culture, however, and billiards is that of an unassuming "little man." Unlike the haughty prophetic composer, Böll's artist is a simple guardian of moral, Christian little folk. Whereas Robert acts for the common people, Mann's arrogant, Nietzschean composer, in his rejection of bourgeois Christianity, only potentially points the way to the genuinely moral and socially responsible artist. In the meantime, he has also helped to clear the ground for others to establish a political religion; he has overlooked the social implications of his art. The source of such political irresponsibility is seen in the apolitical past of German idealism.

But Mann portrays the hideous culmination of the German idealist tradition from an ultimately idealist perspective. Although he criticizes the socially irresponsible artist, he does so more in spiritual than in social or political terms. Leverkühn's revocation of the Ninth Symphony orchestrates Doctor Faust's descent into hell, which culminates in a lament instead of a joyous chorus. The composer and symphony which once embodied the humanist and idealist yearning of German culture are appropriately replaced by music about and inspired by hell. The artist in league with the devil is the reverse side of the artist as prophet: both suggest the spiritualizing effects of idealism. The artist figure as the opposite extreme of the holy seer represents "the good Germany gone astray."

Mann's outlook is so colored by German idealism that he focuses almost exclusively on its culpability. Throughout the years of the Third Reich, it is the seeming paradox of the "good" and "bad" Germany that Mann repeatedly attempts to resolve for himself. An artist as sensitive as he to the liberating, humane aspects of Beethoven's music found the existence of excellent Beethoven concerts in Nazi Germany difficult to understand: "For what stupidity did it require to hear *Fidelio* in Himmler's Germany without covering one's face with one's hands and rushing out of the room!" He made this particular statement at least twice: before the war, in New York in 1938, and again in 1945. [51] His incredulity took much time and thought to still. Apparently expecting an audience to be aware of the contradiction between the opera and contemporary political circumstances, Mann indicts the spiritualized and apolitical idealism of German cultural life. He thus analyzes the German inward tradition and alleged "high" cultural prefigurations of Nazism to clarify the seeming paradox: it is particularly the land of Beethoven which becomes that of Hitler.

In *Doctor Faustus*, Zeitblom also tries to resolve the paradox when he queries: "Was not this regime in word and deed the distorted, vulgarized, and besmirched realization of a sensibility and notion of world affairs that one must recognize as characteristic and genuine -- that the Christian, humane person shrinks to see stamped on the features of our greatest, mightiest embodiments of Germanness?" (DF, 639) Not only modern, asocial art is implicated, but the whole German idealist tradition. Indeed, the "good" Germany seems in retrospect to explain the bad. As Erich Kahler wrote, in an essay which the novelist in turn praised: "The nation whose power of abstraction is the highest, whose spirituality is the most perfectly and perilously detached, the nation of Kant, Schiller, Hölderlin, plunges ahead of the rest into a subanimal condition." [52]

---

51. Thomas Mann, "Rede zum New Yorker 'Deutschen Tag' in Deutsches Volksecho," in *Sinn und Form* (Sonderheft Thomas Mann) (1965), p. 344. and Thomas Mann, "Warum ich nicht nach Deutschland zurückgehe," *Gesammelte Werke*, XII (Oldenburg: Fischer, 1960), p. 958.

52. Erich Kahler, *The Orbit of Thomas Mann* (Princeton: Princeton University Press, 1969), pp. 42-43.

Though often simplified and less sophisticated, Zeitblom's distaste for the crude and common Nazis corresponds to his author's, as examined in the previous chapter. Much of the anger that fuels Mann's analysis of the Nazi debasement of German culture arises out of this aesthetic aversion. His sense of beauty and culture were offended. But as heir to and admirer of the German cultural traditions he saw dialectically reversed, the writer could see that what was so debased contained the serious flaws of political irresponsibility and irrationalism to begin with. That the land of Beethoven could become the land of Hitler, Mann shows, was partly the result of the political aloofness of German intellectuals, and partly the result, first seen in Nietzsche and Wagner, of the progressive degradation of Germany's classical culture. [53]

Mann liked to view himself, and be viewed, historically; this is apparent in his very conception of the novel. Mann's choice to focus on the cultural background prior to Nazism was in keeping with his laudable "self-prosecution" and, of course, with his historical view of his own artistic life. But such a focus was also common in the intellectual and academic approach to Nazism in the immediate postwar period. Intellectual historians of liberal persuasion in these years followed an implicitly idealist view of Nazism as they concentrated on the responsibility of the German intellectual heritage for the calamities of the 1930s and 1940s. Thus, like Mann (though without his more personal reasons), they focused on the thoughts, attitudes, and decisions of the cultural elite, just as political historians were examining the political elite. From our current vantage we can perceive a major shift in the historical contexts of 1947, when *Faustus* appeared, and 1959, the date in which the other two novels were published. After the mid-1950s it became more common to study the mundane and immediate social sources of Nazi support, and to subject the workings of the Nazi terrorist state to

---

53. Mann's perspective here is similar to a number of postwar treatments of German intellectual history, but particularly Georg Lukács, *Die Zerstörung der Vernunft* (Berlin: Aufbau, 1954). Lukács was of course a great admirer of Mann.

the closer analysis which was impossible in the first years of emotional denunciation.[54] Less concerned with elevated ideas, Grass and Böll, like their contemporaries in the historical profession, examine the implementation of Nazi policy, the social appeal of this art of indoctrination.

Through Leverkühn, Mann portrays the role of the cultural elite; through their artists, Böll laments and Grass pokes fun at the manipulability of mass hysteria. The eldest writer describes in tragic tones his country's fall into damnation. Böll's melancholy inflections register the daily sensory-psychological battering of pounding drums and marching feet. Grass's humorous accents are the mark of one less scarred by prolonged experience in uniform, detached enough to satirize the system that was drumming in a new faith. The *Faustus*-composer, the irreconcilable demolition expert, and the grotesque tin drummer fittingly express as artists each writer's experience of art and politics under the swastika.

---

54. Geoffrey Barraclough, "Article II on the Liberals and German History," *New York Review of Books*, November 2, 1972, pp. 32-35.

CHAPTER THREE

Ideology and the Form of the Novel

Approaches to Ideology

Parades, political festivities, and manipulated mass media made up the artful politics of persuasion in the Third Reich. Such "art" propagandized Nazi ideology. But the ideology itself -- not only the media but also the message -- concerns our three novelists. The Nazi world-view engages their attention either as a pattern of ideas reflecting the reality of an age or as a deluded consciousness distorting reality. Both concepts may define the word "ideology"; they differ but are related to one another. Both meanings can characterize National Socialism; the two approaches to Nazi ideology were available to Mann, Grass, and Böll as they attempted to give form to their experience of Nazi society and its doctrine.

In his essay "The Concept of Ideology," the philosopher and social critic George Lichtheim distinguishes between the two meanings of ideology. Both Marx and Weber used the word in each sense. First, the term can refer to what a culture thinks about itself; such thought reflects something of the social realities. Fascism contained a coherent attitude; in the end, it even gave rise to a politial and social doctrine that attracted people from social strata who were having difficulties in the modern age, and to that extent accurately reflected certain "realities." [1] For example, the Nazi ideal of a unified German *Volk* appealed to the communitarian longings of some who were painfully aware of the growing size and anonymity of modern, and particularly urban, society. In their apotheosis

---

1. George Lichtheim, *The Concept of Ideology and Other Essays* (New York: Random House, 1967), p. 235.

of the German peasant and their selectively announced attack on big business, the Nazi leaders offered a "revolution" to the anti-modernists and the "little people" threatened by the march of modernization and industrialization in the twentieth century. On another level, the Nazi glorification of crowd passion mirrored the revolt against positivism in the high cultural atmosphere. This analysis of Nazi ideology is seen in Mann's approach. He studied what Lichtheim calls the consciousness of an epoch, the intellectual reflex of determinate social processes. Although in Mann's view National Socialism debased this consciousness, the official ideology might nonetheless serve as an accurate guide to that society's particular reality, just because it was reflected in the doctrine. With this approach to ideology, there is no question of "unmasking" anyone or anything.

Second, the term can signify the deceived consciousness of persons unaware of their biases. Thinking may be ideological in the sense of distorting, rather than reflecting, the reality it represents.[2] Here ideology refers to the conscious (as in the Ministry of Propaganda) or unconscious (as with many followers) misinterpretation of reality in the interest of certain groups. When Böll and Grass expose the manipulative techniques of a Nazi midsummer night's festival or local political rally, they unmask both the conscious and unconscious distortions of reality, the aims of the party ideologues as well as the needs of their less calculating faithful followers.

The two meanings of ideology can be related to one another. An ideology can, even as a misinterpretation of reality, reflect the real ideas of an epoch. Whereas Mann criticizes the ideas themselves as morally culpable, Grass and Böll reveal how the ideas distort reality. To focus on the consciousness of the epoch is to imply that National Socialism represented the entire society; to attack deluded consciousness, however, is to aim at an ideology reflecting the interests of particular groups, albeit the ones in power. Mann rarely distinguishes among social groups when he mentions the

---

2.   Ibid., p. 31.

Germans and the Nazi holocaust, in speeches and essays as well as in *Doctor Faustus*. In contrast, Grass lines up Nazism alongside other ideologies: Marxism, Catholicism, vegetarianism, each representing the vested interests of a particular group. Likewise, Böll portrays the interaction and conflicts between the buffalos and the lambs. For both Grass and Böll, Nazi ideology appears less monolithic than in *Doctor Faustus*. Unlike Mann in 1943-47, they were not writing under the threat of an ideology which tolerated no divergent expression.

Certainly Mann's fascination with the interplay of ideas and history also differentiates his approach to ideology from those of Böll and Grass. Less convinced than Mann that ideas shape history, the other two novelists portray the manipulated consciousness of a Matzerath or a Nettlinger, who are much less rooted in German intellectual life than the Kridwiss-Kreis. Each writer's response to Nazi ideology shapes his novel. Mann attempts to encompass the consciousness of his epoch, as well as its historical sources, and thus creates the "novel to end all novels" in the traditional self-contained form stretched to the breaking point. Grass and Böll, less ambitious, try merely to unmask the ideological distortions of contemporary reality, which reflect the interests of the ruling and supporting groups. They do not attempt to contain a whole world; on the contrary, they pointedly indicate that impossibility. Their open forms leave their readers to complete that world for themselves. It is as if they have carried Mann's indictment of German idealist traditions to its conclusion: idealism and its self-contained art forms are not able to represent modern, and particularly fascist, reality. The open novels of Grass and Böll evolve out of their anti-ideological stance.

The German classical-idealist culture of Goethe and Schiller fostered a still prevailing definition of "symbol." The Goethean notion that a symbol both "is" and "signifies," that the particular can contain within it the general, parallels the conception of the self-enclosed work of art. Much controversy reigns in the critical literature on *Doctor Faustus* as to the relationship between Faustus-Leverkühn and Nazi Germany. Is Adrian's life a symbol, allegory, or analogue? I will argue that Mann enlarged the

Goethean symbol, just as he expanded the self-contained novel. In contrast, Böll's signification of lambs and buffalos helps to enclose an otherwise open novel. But the symbol of the most open work, the drummer, remains open and variable.

Some critics have also stressed that *Doctor Faustus* actually interprets itself. To a greater and lesser degree, so do *Billiards at Half-Past Nine* and *The Tin Drum*. The three games discussed in the previous chapter provide a self-commentary of each novel, its form and intentions. In the microcosm of the games emerge small reflections of the closed and open forms.

Consciousness Enclosed vs. Deluded Consciousness Laid Open

In the *Story of a Novel*, Mann speaks of his predisposition "to see all life as a cultural product and in the form of mythical clichés. I tend to prefer the quotation over 'self-dependent' fiction." (EDF, 784) This statement reveals at once the author's perspective on the epoch he will treat in his novel as well as the form the work will assume. The tendency to see life generally in terms of the mythical and conceptually typical leads to an approach to Nazi ideology focusing on its ideas, and the culture of which they seem to be a product. Several Mann scholars, like Fritz Kaufmann, Henry Hatfield, André von Gronicka, Joseph Frank, and Erich Kahler, have examined at length the novelist's views on the intellectual roots of Nazism. Suffice it here to review briefly some of these sources in order to discern the core of Mann's analysis of his epoch's consciousness. For it is this response to Nazi ideology which encourages his expansion of the self-contained novel.

If any one word can capture the essence of Mann's exposé of Nazism, it is irrationalism.[3] Hitler rose to power in a culture permeated by philosophies of the anti-rational. Certainly far too many intellectuals of this period were either ready to hail Hitler as their leader or at least responsible for the dangerous cult of the irrational; Mann depicts them in the Kridwiss-Kreis. His suspicions about the current course of his country's history are confirmed by an observation about the past: the inward German soul found its most appropriate and fruitful expression in music, seemingly the least rational of the arts. Mann even sees this trend of irrationalism extending back as far as Luther and the preceding Middle Ages.

---

3.   It is revealing that Mann read Peter Viereck's *Metapolitics: From the Romantics to Hitler* (New York: Knopf, 1941) and wrote a letter to the author praising highly his critical history of German irrationalism. The letter is contained in the 1965 edition of Viereck's book (New York: Capricorn) on pp. 356-364.

Luther in the novel is an Erastian who holds that the church must accede in all secular matters to authorities, a Christian view which abetted the disastrous German separation of spiritual and political realms. But Mann stresses even more a daemonic irrationalism in Luther's views. Professor Kumpf, the comic personification of Luther, re-plays with variations the famous anecdote about the Father of the Reformation hurling an ink-bottle at the devil: "'Look, there he stands in the corner,'" cries the theology professor Kumpf in 1905, "'the mockingbird, the malcontent, the sad, sour spirit, and cannot stand to see us merry in God with feasting and song! But he shall not find any fault with us, the arch-villain, with his sly, fiery arrows! *Apage!*' he thundered, seized a roll and flung it into the dark corner." (DF, 132) *Lutherdeutsch* also becomes the language of the devil and of Adrian, already destined to come under his power. Finally, the Faust-chapbook, from which Mann draws more than from Goethe, originally represented Lutheran opposition to Renaissance humanism. As a warning against the hubris of trusting human reason, the chapbook could encourage the regressive folk-fanaticism seen as characteristic of the Middle Ages.

At times Mann appears to view fascism as a relapse into the hysteria, blind faith, and absolute authoritarianism of the medieval period. The theme in the novel of "reaction as progress," the reactionary revolution of National Socialism, reflects his notion of fascism as medieval barbarism. Barbaric fanaticism and Germany's provincialism stem from this period and appear to have returned under Hitler. Zeitblom's description of Kaisersaschern (as Mann's of Lübeck in "Germany and the Germans") illustrates the author's view of fascism as archaic and reactionary in its irrationalism: "But something was still in the air from the spiritual constitution of people of the last decades of the fifteenth century: the hysteria of the declining Middle Ages, something of a latent spiritual epidemic. . . . Our time itself tends . . . to return to those earlier epochs; it enthusiastically re-enacts symbolic deeds that are sinister and fly in the face of the spirit of the modern age: deeds like book-burnings and other things of which I prefer not to speak." (DF, 52) From this perspective, the mystical, mass hysteria of the *Volk* constantly impends: it hangs "in the air" and is ever ready to erupt given the

02563

Consciousness Enclosed vs. Deluded Consciousness Laid Open 101

right encouragement, despite the presumed progress of civilization into the modern age.

Mann has expressed this fear, referring to Freud's emphasis on the power of the unconscious. Whereas the irrationalists are fundamentally right in declaring reason to be weaker, Mann argues, they are eternally wrong if they glory in the frailty of the intellect and try to destroy its already precarious control.[4] From Mann's viewpoint, potential hysteria is omnipresent, ready to repeat itself. He often makes no historical distinctions between the irrationalism of the Middle Ages, the pre-Nazi cult of instinct among the intelligentsia, and the impassioned faces cheering Hitler. Nazism appears as the inevitable repetition of an irrationalism extending back beyond Luther.

In Mann's view then, as Henry Hatfield has concluded, "German culture and German tradition are polluted, retroactively as it were, by Nazism."[5] Indeed, Mann does seem to run the risk of perceiving all of German history as a prehistory of fascism.[6] In some very serious, unparodied passages, Zeitblom confirms this sense of necessity when he speaks of the tragic "fate" or "destiny" of the German nation under Hitler. Writing of his painful exile from Nazi Germany, the author echoes his narrator in a famous letter to Walter von Molo in 1945: "That everything happened the way it has is not my doing. Not by any means! It is a result of the character and destiny of the German people . . ."[7] It may have been an understandable feeling of helplessness which drove Mann to this fatalistic and monolithic approach to the "character of the German people." Certainly, too, the monstrous scale of the crimes perpetrated

---

4. Thomas Mann, "Die Stellung Freuds in der modernen Geistesgeschichte," *Gesammelte Werke,* X (Oldenburg: Fisher, 1960), pp. 256-280.

5. Henry Hatfield, *Thomas Mann* (New York: Knopf, 1962), p. 140.

6. Inge Diersen, *Untersuchungen zu Thomas Mann* (Berlin: Rütten & Loening, 1965), p. 313.

7. Thomas Mann, "Warum ich nicht nach Deutschland zurückgehe," *Gesammelte Werke,* XII (Oldenburg: Fischer, 1960), p. 956.

by the Nazis may have seemed to call for explanations implicating all of German history: an attempt to make the incredible credible. Later historians were in a better position to dispute the view of inevitability. Bracher maintains, for example, that the possibility of democratic development remained throughout; the events of 1848, 1870, 1914, 1918, and 1933 were decisive crossroads, when this possibility eventually became ruled out. [8]

Mann's sense of the overwhelming inescapability of Nazism caused him to stress irrationalism's ever-present threat to engulf us. Whereas the generalized horror at historical inevitability holds sway in the novel, Mann also perceived certain contemporary causes of the unleashing of the daemonic. Leverkühn's efforts at liberation from hollow bourgeois cultural forms reflect the efforts of much of the German bourgeois intelligentsia to overcome a sense of a modern dessicated and alienated existence. [9] The decline of Christian, liberal, and classical humanist values by the early twentieth century created a vacuum of meaning into which circles like the Nietzschean Kridwiss-Kreis interjected an irrationalist philosophy, giving their otherwise empty lives a dynamic and vital quality. Likewise, in *The Revolution of Nihilism* (1937), an early interpretation of Nazism, the conservative and former Nazi Hermann Rauschning viewed the movement's irrational appeal in terms of a violent cult of unfocused dynamic and destructive action. [10] Although such analysis of irrationalism is a culturally focused explanation of the social crisis which helped to give rise to the Third Reich, it applies to more of the population than the elite intelligentsia -- it includes deep layers of the educated middle class -- thus making the Kridwiss-Kreis seem more representative. *Doctor Faustus* does emphasize this defensible approach to fascism. But the extensive search throughout for intellectual precursors of

---

8.   Bracher, p. 27.

9.   Erhard Bahr, "Metaphysische Zeitdiagnose: Kasack, Langgässer und Thomas Mann," *Gegenwartsliteratur und Drittes Reich*, ed. Hans Wagener (Stuttgart: Reclam, 1977), p. 151.

10.   Hermann Rauschning, *The Revolution of Nihilism*, trans. E. W. Dickes (New York: Longmans, Green, & Co., 1939).

Nazism (the massive secondary literature on this aspect of the novel suggests how predominant it is) and the prevalent view of Nazism as Germany's doomed destiny tend to subordinate this theory: it becomes an explanation for the current eruption of irrationalism that German history already predestined.

It has also been argued that Adorno and Mann's long discussions about *Doctor Faustus* left their mark on Mann's theory of fascism: that a critique of modern technological society, suggested in Adorno's *Philosophy of Modern Music* and developed more fully with Max Horkheimer in *Dialectic of Enlightenment*, informs Mann's analysis of fascist irrationalism. [11] Adorno and Horkheimer theorized that instrumental and technocratic rationality in capitalist society led to the domination of nature and the repression of instincts; the repressed then returned in barbaric forms such as Nazism. Hence fascism was seen not merely as regressive but as "modern archaic." [12] Mann's descriptions of Leverkühn's compositions do show Adorno's musicological influence and occasionally the social analysis which underpinned the musicology. For example, Adrian says his twelve-tonal system unites the archaic with the modern and revolutionary, and Zeitblom observes that the rationalism Adrian calls for in imposing this system has also something superstitious and daemonic about it, "the kind of thing we have in games of chance, fortune-telling with cards. . . . Your system seems to me more calculated to dissolve human reason in magic." (DF, 258) Leverkühn's music thus anticipates the manner in which the Nazis rationally calculated the dissolution of rationality.

---

11. See, e.g., Bahr, "Metaphysische Zeitdiagnose: Kasack, Langgässer und Thomas Mann," pp. 151-152, and Franz Futterknecht, *Das Dritte Reich im Deutschen Roman der Nachkriegszeit. Untersuchungen zur Faschismustheorie und Faschismusbewältigung* (Bonn: Bouvier, 1976), pp. 38-110; and Agnes Schlee, *Waudlungen musikalischer Strukturen im Werke Thomas Manns* (Frankfurt am Main: Peter Lang, 1981), pp. 148-179.

12. Theodor Adorno and Max Horkheimer, *Dialectic of Enlightenment* (New York: Herder and Herder, 1972).

But the social implications of Leverkühn's music are relatively few and remain on a highly symbolic level instead of resonating in other spheres of the novel. Symbolically, the evolving life and music of Leverkühn might illustrate the vengeful return of repressed nature, except that no instance of initial repression or its social causes are evident. Mann's Aschenbach in *Death in Venice*, who obviously represses instinct in the name of productivity, exemplifies the Adorno-Horkheimer theory (prior to its development) more clearly than does Leverkühn, whose coldness seems inherent from birth, and not the result of a repressive work ethic. Leverkühn's music does reverberate symbolically in the Kridwiss-Kreis, but these irrationalists condemn reason as such, without distinguishing its instrumental or technocratic versions. Furthermore, modern technology and productivity, the social basis that Adorno and Horkheimer designate for music like Leverkühn's twelve-tonal "domination of nature," are hardly visible in the rest of the novel, in the salons and social gatherings Mann portrays. [13]

While Mann was eclectic enough to assimilate portions of the neo-Marxist philosopher's ideas, he still emphasizes mainly the need for rational control and constructive channeling of the id, in a manner similar to the liberal Freud. Although Zeitblom's humanistic reason may seem obsolete in contest with the Sorelian irrationalists, Mann apparently saw nothing in its stead to rely on. Indeed, the tone and language of the narrator become increasingly eloquent in the last third of the novel and seem to suggest the views of the novel itself. Zeitblom's humanism appears, then, still to have some merit as a viewpoint from which we are to judge these ill-fated historic events. Perhaps Mann hoped that the best values of this outlook, such as, for instance, the humane rationality of Zeitblom's

---

13. Mann declined to review Adorno and Horkheimer's *Dialectic of Enlightenment* for the *New York Times* and asked his son Golo to write about the book instead, saying "I understand nothing of it." (See Katia Mann, *Meine ungeschriebenen Memoiren,* ed. Elisabeth Plessen and Michael Mann [Frankfurt: Fischer, 1974], p. 149.) Although Mann may have exaggerated, his comment should give pause to anyone who claims Mann truly integrated Adorno and Horkheimer's social analysis or philosophy of history into *Doctor Faustus.* ʼ

sober judgments, could be rescued for the future, once Germany's demons had danced themselves out.

Mann's sense of Nazism as a fated historical development permeates the entire novel's structure down to the daily life of Leverkühn. The archaic, provincial, and anti-rational character of the epoch's general consciousness is linked to the particular: the story of a modern composer. His music, predetermined from the start, is always that of the medieval-like town described earlier, "music from Kaisersaschern." The shape and style of Adrian's story and of the whole novel around it bear witness to the inescapability of a cultural and national "terminal age." Nearly every detail or event is linked to another and laden with significance. Mann employs every stylistic device in his repertoire including some experimental ones to weave a grand tapestry of episodes and ideas appropriate to this terminal era: a totally enclosed world.

Georg Lukács, whose analyses of Mann's own work the author always admired, was a great advocate of the closed work of art. According to Lukács, "The goal for all great art is to provide a picture of reality in which the contradiction between appearance and reality, the particular and the general, the immediate and the conceptual, etc., is so resolved that the two converge into a spontaneous integrity in the direct impression of the work of art and provide a sense of an inseparable integrity." [14]

Mann's novel in 1947 does not entirely conform to this traditionalist theory. As indicated in the *Mittelstand* chapter, Mann, along with the other novelists, is aware of the limitations of the nineteenth-century realism linked to this closed form. Just as such realistic elements are parodied, so are other aspects of the traditional novel. Precisely Mann's emphasis on a "terminal age of art" indicates his awareness of the problems of the modern novel. In *Doctor Faustus* itself, Zeitblom recapitulates Adrian's suspicions of the closed work of art: "And now the question arises . . . whether

---

14. Georg Lukács, "Art and Objective Truth," in *Writer and Critic and Other Essays*, trans. Arthur D. Kahn (New York: Grosset & Dunlap, 1971), p. 34.

the work as such, that self-sufficient and harmoniously self-enclosed form, still stands in any legitimate relationship to the complete uncertainty, ambiguity, and discordance of our social circumstances; whether or not all illusion, even and precisely the most beautiful, today has become a lie." (DF, 241) And certainly Mann did not go on naively writing in the old manner like Zweig, Feuchtwanger or Zuckmayer. At least one critic has announced that with *Doctor Faustus* the traditional boundaries of the novel are broken. Devices such as the montage technique or the several levels of the novel would not be possible in the closed novel. [15] Inserting crude reality through montage or proffering a narrator allegedly unequal to his task would appear to violate the novel's self-containment. But it is precisely these techniques which augment the authenticity of this novel's closed world, which expand and thus sustain its "inseparable integrity." The seeming disorder, as Fritz Kaufmann observes, is carefully arranged; the novel is self-contained, to the highest degree. [16] As a terminal book, *Doctor Faustus* is a final apotheosis of the traditional narrative form.

The complex tri-level structure of the novel does not dissolve its boundaries but strengthens them. Hans Mayer has designated three levels: the life of Leverkühn; the interpretation by Zeitblom of this life, including its relationship to historical events; and the interpretation of this interpretation (where the hand of the author is felt, as for instance through parody of the narrator). [17] Whether or not the story of a modern composer might be appropriate as narrative fiction concerning Nazism, without the narration of Zeitblom this tale would link only implicitly to that historical period. And without the parody of the narrator, the whole structure of significant, related details and events which he "unintentionally" reveals would dissolve. Although the author is able to correct the

---

15. Hans Poser, "Thomas Manns 'Doktor Faustus,'" in *Möglichkeiten des modernen deutschen Romans*, ed. Rolf Geissler (Berlin: Moritz Diesterweg, 1965), p. 31.

16. Fritz Kaufmann, *The World as Will and Representation* (Boston: Beacon Press, 1957), p. 203.

17. Hans Mayer, *Literatur der Übergangszeit* (Berlin: Volk und Welt, 1949), p. 168.

other narrative levels, and hence in the end remains omniscient to some degree, the multi-perspective approach is better able than traditional realism to deal with a subject as complex as the epoch culminating in National Socialism. In short, the second two levels seem necessary to make the particular general.

In his interpretation of the life of Leverkühn, the ostensibly clumsy biographer gradually creates the sense of integrated predetermination which permeates all levels of the novel. Unlike Oskar, whom the reader rarely can trust, Zeitblom, precisely through his "mistakes" and anticipatory remarks, unintentionally conveys a perspective of the fictive events that the reader can trust. The outcome of nearly every episode is foretold pages ahead -- merely mentioned briefly, subtly leaving for the reader a trace of the future. With the introduction of the figure Schwerdtfeger into the novel, for example, Zeitblom characterizes him, gives others' opinions about the violinist, and then slips in: "For my part I had nothing against Schwerdtfeger; indeed, I like him sincerely, and his early, tragic death, which for me was cloaked with an especially uncanny horror, shook me to the depths of my soul." (DF, 265) Such details are not intended as any kind of Brechtian signpost, to encourage the reader to contemplate the "how" and "why"; rather, they prepare the reader for the interpretation which will be given in the novel itself. If readers were permitted to become engrossed in an immediate, particular plot, they would overlook the general, the conceptual that Lukács speaks of.

"Parody as pretext" characterizes Leverkühn's early work and indicates a function of the parody of the novel's narrator. As the bungling pedant, Zeitblom can naively muse "I do not know why this double time-reckoning captures my attention, and why I feel called upon to point it out," (DF, 335) in order to introduce long, often essayistic passages on the Second World War. Exclaiming at every turn "Oh, I write terribly!" Zeitblom can proceed to explain Adrian's music in connection with the impending national doom. Parody of Zeitblom, the blundering biographer, provides a pretext for tying the specific to the general.

Without parody, too, the author lets key concepts become established as linked. Already in the first chapter, "loneliness" characterizes Germany and then Leverkühn. Long before the pact with the devil in the middle of the novel, Adrian's predisposition to sacrifice intellect to instinct is evident: the environment of Kaisersaschern and his father's pastime of "elementa speculieren" are two of the many early indications. The innumerable incidents of such implicit interpretation of the novel have led more than one critic to remark with some exasperation that the novel suffers from overprecision in its inextricably integrated form. No event remains just that before it freezes into a significant kind of symbol. [18] Only when an elaborate framework of conceptual interconnections has been established, can Zeitblom abandon his lengthy asides and analyses for what would otherwise be termed free, naive narration. Over and over again the schoolmaster has maintained that he is no novelist, particularly not an omniscient author, that this is no novel, but a biography, only to vitiate his protest in the next paragraph. Zeitblom pays in effect many tributes to the problems of the modern novel in order finally to be able to ignore them. With the intricate conceptual "grand design" securely anchored in the reader's mind, the narrative gains full momentum. For about the last two hundred pages, the reader is engaged in a dramatic, emotional account of Adrian's life and the people related to it. The Rodde sisters, Schwerdtfeger, Echo, Adrian: all are then permitted to enact their pre-ordained tragic roles. Each tragedy on each time plane has been anticipated and appears inevitable: "My tale is hastening to its end -- like all else today. Everything presses and rushes to its end, the world stands under the sign of the end -- at least it does for us Germans. Our 'thousand-year' history refuted, reduced *ad absurdum*, fatally failed . . . transforms into a journey to hell lit by dancing, roaring flames." (DF, 599)

Even the experimental devices of montage and quotation augment the novel's self-contained design. As Mann emphasizes repeatedly in the *Story of a Novel*, insertion of reports from the

---

18.   Frank Trommler, "Epische Rhetorik in Thomas Manns 'Doktor Faustus,'" *Zeitschrift für deutsche Philologie* 89 (1970), pp. 240-258.

world wars or quotation of episodes from Nietzsche's life are important means to realize the fictive.[19] They are incorporated to make
the world of the novel appear more real, legitimate and able to
stand on its own. Not intended to refer readers to that extra-
literary reality or to encourage them to reflect on Nazism or
Nietzsche independently of the perspective in the novel, these devices are meant to keep readers within the universe of the novel,
and even to enrich this world for them. More consistently avant-
grade writers like Brecht or Döblin use such techniques to alienate
readers and to fragment any experience of an enclosed world.
Mann's montage and quotation do not destroy but strengthen the
authenticity of the "inseparable integrity."

The narrator's emotional tones also prevail upon readers to
view this self-contained world from his perspective. The earnest
pathos of Zeitblom's voice is meant by the end to move one deeply.[20] Any irony left in the novel here is no longer playful, but a
means to make the unbearable bearable.[21] In deadly serious tones,
Zeitblom angrily curses the Nazis and despairs over the consequences of this war: "No stopping them! My soul, do not think it
through! Do not venture to measure what it would mean if in our
extreme, uniquely horrible situation the dam should break, as it is
on the verge of doing, and there were then no stopping the bound-
less hatred that we have inculcated among the peoples all around
us!" (DF, 448) Zeitblom's voice in its torment and pathos rings in
the reader's ears.

---

19. Cf. Helmut Jendreiek, *Thomas Mann: Der demokratische Roman* (Düsseldorf:
    Bagel, 1977), pp. 412-491, who argues that these techniques attempt to break
    through the aesthetic isolation and fictionality of Mann's art to encourage
    democratic, socially responsible attitudes.

20. Herbert Lehnert, "Satirische Botschaft an den Leser: Das Ende des Jugendstils,"
    in *Gestaltungsgeschichte und Gesellschaftsgeschichte*, ed. Helmut Kreuzer and
    Käte Hamburger (Stuttgart: Metzler, 1969), p. 509.

21. Henry Hatfield, "Der Zauberer und die Verzweiflung," *Wirkendes Wort* vol. 12,
    no. 2 (1962), 93-94.

Numerous narrative elements combine, then, to define the reader's perspective, to form what Lukács called the inseparable integrity of the self-contained work of art. Mann's perception of Nazi ideology as the fated culmination of German history structures an inextricably integrated novel. Within this enclosed totality, the unfolding of the culture of irrationalism could interrelate with the particular life of an artist, become comprehensible, resolved.

Any kind of cathartic resolution is viewed by an advocate of the open work of art as undesirable. Rather, the reader is to be left to complete the perspectives and attitudes which the artist has left open and incomplete. Writers of the open novel imply that modern society is too opaque to be made comprehensible, especially within a single, enclosed piece of art; they emphasize that complexity through their choice of narrative mode. They may, for instance, narrate a series of unintegrated episodes from confusing, often multiple perspectives. Not aspiring to capture the macrocosm, these novelists consider it impossible to express the universal in the individual.

Whereas the open work of art reappears often, particularly in the twentieth century, it becomes a preferred form among post-World War II writers as a direct response to their experience of Nazi ideology. Volker Wehdeking has studied the origins of West German literary activity in the American POW camps; he has linked these writers' revulsion against Nazi, and apparently any, ideology to their ideals of literary style. Seeking emancipation from ideological tendentiousness, they reduce authorial guidance; combating blind pathos, they stress exact, concrete description and avoid cathartic resolution. Among these prisoners of war were the founders of the Group 47, Hans Werner Richter and Alfred Andersch. They wrote semi-documentaries; they tried to confront the reader with uninterrupted, and therefore unideological, immediate experience. Grass, Böll, and others continued to hold similar political and literary values. The Group 47, Richter describes in his *Almanach*, shared an antipathy for all organizations, for every form of normative collective action with a general line, flag, and program. This generation did not wish to lose its individual freedom again. [22] And as Wehdeking has pointed out, "The total suspicion of ideology of the early postwar period continues in the fifties; the taboo on emotion remains, moreover, an important aesthetic principle of German writers." [23]

It was not only writers, of course, who were repelled by ideology after the experiences of Nazism and Stalinism. Changes within the Social Democratic Party (SPD) reflect a more widespread similar attitude. In the fifties, SPD-leader Ernst Schumacher began encouraging the recruitment of middle class members who knew little of Marxist traditions and less of working class life. [24] This trend culminated in the "Bad Godesberg Programm" in 1959 which explicitly abandoned Marxist doctrine in order to gain middle class voters (who had no doubt been opposed to more than the ideological aspect of Marxism). Grass's own suspicion of ideology was clearly a commonly held view among politicians and intellectuals who themselves subscribed to a Social Democratic or "liberal" point of view. Although Grass's active engagement in the "Es-Pe-De" in 1965 came after his first novel, his sympathies for this party began much earlier. The character of his later political activity stemmed in part from his opposition to ideologues and the blind pathos they encourage. In a speech to a young voter who felt inclined to choose the NPD (National Democratic Party of Germany), Grass warned that the idealism of this generation could be misused, just as that of his own was exploited. [25] His aversion to such idealism determined his own political opinions, which emphasize gradual reform at a "snail-like" pace. Likewise, his political language is earnest, often slightly dull, free from emotional, idealist exhortation. He thinks political campaigning should "go without saying" (should be

---

22. Hans Werner Richter, *Almanach der Gruppe 47* (Reinbek: Rowohlt, 1962), p. 10.

23. Volker Christian Wehdeking, *Der Nullpunkt* (Stuttgart: Metzler, 1971), p. 142.

24. David Childs, *Germany since 1918* (New York: Harper & Row, 1971), p. 154.

25. Günter Grass, "Rede an einen jungen Wähler, der sich versucht fühlt, die NPD zu wählen," in *Über das Selbstverständliche* (Berlin: Deutscher Taschenbuch Verlag, 1968), p. 90.

"selbstverständlich"), unlike the idealist theorists he disdains who remain above the "stinking reality" of politics. [26]

Out of this aversion to idealism and ideologies which exploit it, Grass's generation continues to prefer the open work of art espoused by the Group 47. Aware of the Nazis' exploitation of the classical idealist tradition, these writers turn against that tradition: they depose the self-enclosed, harmonious work of art and refuse to see themselves as secular prophets. [27] Thus, *The Tin Drum* is a reaction against the self-contained novel of Mann, one of the last of those prophets. Grass's open work rejects every expectation of the reader to be led by a recognizable intention, a comprehensible structure. [28] D. J. Enright's comparison of the two writers indicates how much confused frustration such a loose structure as that of *The Tin Drum* has wrought on some critics: "Something approaching Thomas Mann's meticulousness, his exhaustiveness, is deployed in the service of what turns out to be a dirty joke or a slapstick anecdote. . . . The author *is* committed -- but to what?" [29]

Indeed, the general shape of Grass's novel rejects the inclusive scheme of works which aspired toward a total image of society. As Peter Demetz observes: "Grass's realism (he likes the term himself) explodes in twisted shapes; articulating through the organization of his narratives his distrust of harmony, coherence, translucence, and his generation's fierce opposition to a graceful classicism that clearly failed, Grass mobilized his counterstrategies of disproportion, ugly incompatibility, and willed obscurity." [30] Instead of leading his reader by the hand, the writer creates an eccentric dwarf for his narrator, who gladly and deliberately contradicts himself. Not

---

26. Günter Grass, "Über das Selbstverständliche," in *Über das Selbstverständliche*, p. 81.

27. Herbert Lehnert, "Satirische Botschaft," p. 514.

28. Ibid., p. 508.

29. D. J. Enright, *Poets and Conspirators* (London: Chatto and Windus, 1966), p. 191.

30. Peter Demetz, *Postwar German Literature* (New York: Pegasus, 1970), p. 226.

integrated into a meaningful whole, episodes appear to be related only at the narrator's whim. The author's defiance of linear, interrelated developments can be pursued down to the details of his syntax: one sudden idea generates the next fancy in a freely associative manner; sentences remain incomplete. In reaction against the elevated language of classicism, Grass uses idiomatic and even obscure dialectical terms, like "Bulve" for potato.

Grass's anti-classical novel is, in addition, an anti-*Wilhelm Meister*. Although *Doctor Faustus* has also been viewed as a reversal of the *Bildungsroman*, every episode along the way in Leverkühn's life is nonetheless heavy-laden with significance as part of the unified whole. His artistic career parallels national cultural developments. Oskar is no such passive mirror implying integral connections between the life of one individual and his society. To be sure, harmony between the isolated artist Leverkühn and his society is impossible. [31] The harmony exists rather in the representativeness of his isolation, his provincialism. Leverkühn is educated into daemonic isolation instead of concord with his society. Although such harmony is the self-proclaimed aim of the traditional *Bildungsroman*, Adrian's marginality is actually the more logical result. German "educational novels" are products of the inward tradition; they focus on the hero's problematic process of integration and only bring Wilhelm Meister and "Green Henry" to the potential point of union with society. These works end where that reality would begin. Thus, *Doctor Faustus* is a terminal testimony to the traditional *Bildungsroman* as seen in the light of contemporary experience.

Whereas Adrian is destined to develop toward daemonic isolation, Oskar is destined to develop hardly at all. Unlike Adrian, Oskar changes little in any linear manner; he only plays at development. At various points in the novel, Bebra as a parodic variation of the familiar guide figure appears to counsel Oskar. On Bebra's advice, Oskar takes on different roles which indicate no process of

---

31. Jürgen Scharfschwerdt, *Thomas Mann und der deutsche Bildungsroman* (Stuttgart: Kohlhammer, 1967), p. 240.

personal integration into society. From rally saboteur, to the Dusters' leader, to the postwar jazz musician, Oskar's roles serve to
highlight historical episodes. In this anti-developmental novel,
such episodic separable vignettes reflect a scattered disunity of
experiences, not a linear development even of a consistent political
attitude, let alone a maturing individual. Not a grand revocation
which upholds through negation an old form, *The Tin Drum* rejects
the imposition of any order onto disharmony and incoherence.
Mann's damned hero, growing, advancing inevitably toward the
diabolic, is replaced by an unclassifiable anti-hero who willfully
stunts his growth.

Such wayward disintegration of traditional forms is meant to
disorient readers. It encourages them, for instance, to question set
systems of ideas -- should one expect or even desire a process of lone
individual growth and subsequent integration into the larger
society? A writer suspicious of all ideological perspectives will
carefully avoid possessing or offering any of his own. Aware that
many readers in the postwar Biedermeier of the fifties would prefer
to read a more morally informed account about what should have
been, not what was, Grass refuses them this comfortable, definitive
viewpoint. Approaching ideology as a deluded consciousness, the
novelist attempts to unmask the real interests of the groups whom
that world-view serves. Essentially the psycho-sexual and social
needs of the *Kleinbürgertum*, as analyzed in the previous two
chapters, come thus to the fore. Grass unsparingly exposes "what
was," what little normal folk were capable of. It is unsettling for
readers to view everything de-mystified with no alternative, unify-
ing perspective.

Oskar aims to debunk every belief that is infused with passion. The author's understandable opposition to blinding ideologies
often leads him, however, to compare movements and groups which,
in spite of shared similarities, deserve distinction from one another.
Most frequently, communism, Catholicism, and Nazism appear all
too indistinguishable. Just as Nazi ideology is exposed as a pseudo-
religion, Oskar makes fun of the "faith" of his communist friends

Klepp and Herbert Truczinski: "I heard Herbert sigh, appealing to God, Marx and Engels and cursing them in the same breath." (Bt, 148)

Several narrative devices throughout foster the desired skeptical attitude in readers. Every so often Oskar reminds one that he is currently in an insane asylum. The reader then remembers the narrator's undependability and emerges from any unreflective absorption in a particular episode. Oskar's constant alternation between "I" and "he" jostles readers between sympathy and distance, denying them a consistent viewpoint on an inconsistent reality. The narrator's free associations, corrections of previous narration, and satirical self-commentary, like "quickly now, a little pathos" -- all these devices too undermine traditional story-telling. This general technique of interruption encourages critical reserve and distrust in the reader; such skepticism is the "ideal" of the anti-ideologist. Although Zeitblom also launches into asides, corrects and anticipates his narrative, and converses with the reader about the structure of his "biography," all of his "interruptions" gradually converge into a reliable conceptual perspective for the reader. Mann's techniques foster comprehension of an epoch's consciousness; Grass's urge skepticism toward deluded consciousness.

Even small details of Grass's syntax and word-play dissolve readers' habitual expectations, requiring an active, critical attitude. Grass lines up nouns together futuristically (acknowledging his debt to Döblin), and avoids possessive and demonstrative pronouns as well as definite articles. [32] Thus, objects appear to dominate in his novels; things seem to take on a life of their own, free of any integrating perspective. Grass also likes to dissect language. While Oskar is waiting for Agnes in church, he ponders the various incompatible and yet compatible uses of the word "cross": "There is also the Greek cross, not to mention the Latin, or Passion cross. . . . I have seen the patty cross, the anchor cross, and the cloverleaf cross overlapping in relief. The Moline cross is handsome. The

---

32. Klaus Wagenbach, quoted in *Autor, Werk und Kritik I*, ed. Gudrun Uhlig (Munich: Hueber, 1969), p. 70.

Maltese cross is coveted, the hooked cross, or swastika, is forbidden." (Bt, 113) Such playing with words relieves the word "cross" of its religious and ideological appeal.

As discussed in the previous chapter, Grass is neither as nihilistic nor as amoral as his loose novelistic form appears to suggest. Placed strategically at the end of Book One, the author's most direct moral condemnation of Nazism is channeled into a strict structure that departs drastically from the freely associative form of the book.

Grass earmarks this chapter in particular as depicting the ideology of National Socialism, especially its anti-Semitism: "In *The Tin Drum* chapter 'Faith, Hope, Love,' the prevailing ideology, namely National Socialism, strikes in its most aggressive way at the Jewish minority and its religion." [33] In fugue-like form, the narrator tells and then retells with slight variations the story of one man's brutality, which has socio-psychological causes. The musician Meyn's shifting and precarious social status sensitizes him to social rebuff and requires the numbing balm of drink. When he is injured by Schugger Leo's horrified rejection of him and frustrated without the liquor he had sworn off to become an "orderly" SA-member, Meyn makes a scapegoat of his cats and slaughters them. Contrapuntally interwoven scenes of the Crystal Night implicitly parallel Meyn's deed with the SA's attack on its scapegoat. Meyn's private act of aggression is then explicitly compared with the nation-wide brutality: "Even his conspicuous bravery on the night of November 8, which later became known as the Crystal Night, . . . could not halt his expulsion from the Mounted SA. For inhuman cruelty to animals he was denounced and stricken from the membership list." (Bt, 163) Whereas Meyn's violence against the cats must be punished, the aggressions of the SA are of course officially sanctioned. With this grotesque tale Grass highlights the moral hideousness and deadly results of Nazi ideology.

---

33.   Günter Grass, "Günter Grass über seine Werke," *Autor, Werk und Kritik* I, ed. Gudrun Uhlig (Munich, 1969), pp. 93-94.

The religious faith in Nazi ideology is described as the faith, hope and love tranferred from Christianity to Nazism. Oskar compares the hope invested in Hitler with a small child's naive belief in Santa Claus; he imitates the child's excitement: "He's coming! He's coming? Who came then? The Christ child, the savior? Or did the heavenly gasman come, with the gas meter under his arm that always goes ticktock?" (Bt, 165) This metaphor for Hitler, the heavenly gasman, incorporates two aspects of Nazi reality: the gas man provides fuel for the followers' basic daily needs as well as for the asphyxiation of human beings. He appeals to them as their savior by appearing to fulfill their real material needs: "And he said: I am the savior of this world, without me, you can't cook." (Bt, 165) Like Christmas with its spiritual and material sides, he proffers religious and material sustenance: "Spirit and gas, so that credulous souls found it easy amid the dense blue air to look upon all those gasmen in front of the department stores as Santa Clauses and Christ children in all sizes and at all prices. So they believed in the gas company as their only salvation." (Bt, 165) Later they learn that the gas they have been sold is meant primarily as fuel for mass murder, not to cook their food.

Such thoughtless and naive faith, rather than a deep belief in the need to liquidate the Jewish "race," did indeed motivate most of Hitler's followers, aside from the fanatics of the SS. Historian George Mosse has written: "The majority of those who collaborated with national socialism were Nazis only in a vague sort of way. They believed in Nazi ideology only because they thought it pointed the way to a better life; they thought little about what Hitler had written in *Mein Kampf.* Order would be kept, security assured, and the state of the nation would improve." [34] Against this vague sort of belief, the narrator pits one slight weapon: "Only knowledge and ignorance are subject to times and limits." (Bt, 166) Information and knowledge are the "hope" of the opponents of ideology.

---

34. George Mosse, *The Culture of Western Europe* (Chicago: Rand McNally & Co., 1965), p. 370.

Fused together in this chapter are several devices which manage to evoke the unspeakable horror of the impending holocaust without dramatizing it to a cathartic resolution. Gathering speed intermittently, the fugal narration advances forward implacably. The repeated invitation to fairy tales, "once upon a time," insinuates the childishly vague perceptions of unwitting followers, as it introduces and re-introduces this narrative of atrocities. Thus the most barbarous realities are presented as tales which turn out to be horror stories. But they cannot be resolved with a satisfying shudder; rather, the serious brooding mood suggested in the fugal repetitions, the sober, almost documentary tone throughout, render the horror more palpable. Similarly, the grotesque contradictions in Meyn's story are allowed simply to speak for themselves in "New Sobriety" (*Neue Sachlichkeit*) fashion. Finally, the narrative, in the face of the impending disaster it has evoked, trails off with repetitions of "I don't know" and "once upon a time" in a coda which restates all the fugal themes. Even in this passage of the novel where strict structure is most evident and the pathos of moral condemnation most apparent, the anti-ideological author refuses to orchestrate a climactic or cathartic conclusion.

Grass will not induce unequivocal moral judgments with such force again. Strewn, however, throughout the novel are hints of Oskar's guilt -- for the deaths of his mother or either of his "fathers," for example, or for his leadership of the Dusters gang. In each case, the degree or kind of guilt is difficult to determine, as the numerous critical arguments over this issue suggest. His patricides can be seen as understandable revenge against the "political failure of a whole generation" [35] or as a reflection of the moral deformity around him: this deformed creature betrays his fellow human beings just as the ruling powers of his time encouraged people to do. [36] Oskar as artifice lends himself to either a rebellious or

---

35. Juergen Rothenberg, *Günter Grass: Das Chaos in verbesserter Ausführung: Zeitgeschichte als Thema und Aufgabe des Prosawerks* (Heidelberg: Carl Winter, 1976), p. 17.

36. Hanspeter Brode, "Die Zeitgeschichte in der 'Blechtrommel' von Günter Grass. Entwurf eines textinternen Kommunikationsmodells," in *Günter Grass - Ein Materialienbuch*, ed. Rolf Geissler (Neuwied: Luchterhand, 1976), p. 90.

complicitous role. Since the deaths of both Bronski and Matzerath fit their characters so appropriately, some critics would exempt Oskar from responsibility here altogether.[37] Such an array of mutually nearly exclusive but plausible interpretations indicates Grass's success in presenting the difficulty of passing judgment on Oskar. Maintaining the neutral narrative perspective which has proven so disquieting to many readers, the anti-ideologist refuses to provide all-encompassing or categoric answers to the thorny questions of metaphysical, collective, or individual guilt in this epoch.[38] He prefers to stimulate readers to puzzle over their own answers to these questions.

The Tin Drum was conceived as a protest against the widespread postwar tendency to repress guilt; it skillfully presents a narrator who finds himself unable to ignore his own guilt. Maria is more successful than Oskar at avoiding guilt and may well represent the assumed reader of the text: she is "a well-acclimated person" who flees from her memories into the consumer realm, where she chatters about refrigerators and such.[39] Grass stresses the "motor of guilt" that propels the narration of his first three works: "All three first-person narrators in all three books write out of guilt: out of repressed guilt, out of ironized guilt. . ."[40] The repeated emphasis on the child's game, "The Black Cook," underscores the repressed guilt in Oskar. He begins writing with "unschuldiges Papier" (connoting innocent as well as white paper) and then "desecrates" these pages with his story. He allegedly writes to free himself from guilt. In the end, Grass has not excused the irresponsible imp for his deeds; even an artifice such as Oskar does not escape judgment. The smaller the gap becomes between

37.   Volker Neuhaus, *Günter Grass* (Stuttgart: Metzler, 1979), p. 64.

38.   Lester Caltvedt makes a similar point in "Oskar's account of himself: narrative 'guilt' and the relationship of fiction to history in *Die Blechtrommel*," *Seminar* vol. 14, no. 4 (1978), p. 293.

39.   Hanspeter Brode, "Die Zeitgeschichte in der 'Blechtrommel' von Günter Grass," p. 104.

40.   Heinz Ludwig Arnold, "Gespräch mit Günter Grass," *Text und Kritik* 1/1a (Günter Grass issue, October, 1971), p. 10.

the past that Oskar describes and the present in which he lives, the more his fear of the Black Cook grows. Writing his narrative has not freed him but reminded him of his responsibility. The Black Cook who pursues him is part of a game which emphasizes not only the difficulty of determining degrees of guilt, but also the inclusion of all individuals present. In the game, one child blindfolded turns around in the middle of a circle of other children and points a finger, reciting all the while: "You are guilty and you are guilty and you are most of all." Never neatly resolved, the guilt that hounds Oskar points its finger at the reader too.

The Black Cook suggests an "appropriate parody-image of the demonization of guilt and responsibility,"[41] especially with its reference to the child's game. Grass consciously opposes the tendency of some earlier postwar literature to focus on metaphysical dimensions of guilt (he emphasized the parody of Oskar's transcendent vs. earthly strivings even more in an earlier version of the manuscript). Grass parodies not only Goethe but also Mann's *Doctor Faustus* with its metaphysical interpretation of history. Yet Mann's novel must have been important to Grass in helping him to carve out his own perspective: he commented in a 1975 survey by *Die Zeit* that *Doctor Faustus* is "his favorite book."[42] Mann's novel must have stimulated Grass's confrontation with idealist cultural traditions and philosophy of history. Like his mentor Döblin, Grass resists efforts to impose meaningful constructions onto what he sees

---

41.   Michael Hollington, *Günter Grass: The Writer in a Pluralist Society* (London: Boyars, 1980), p. 35; cf. Georg Just, *Darstellung und Appell in der 'Blechtrommel' von Günter Grass; Darstellungsaesthetik vs. Wirkungsaesthetik* (Frankfurt am Main: Athenäum, 1972), p. 208f., whose emphasis on meaningless, daemonic forces exemplifies the confusion that can result from an ahistorical approach to this novel.

42.   Silke Jendrowiak, "Die sogenannte 'Urtrommel': unerwartete Einblicke in die Genese der *Blechtrommel* von Günter Grass," *Monatshefte* 71 (1979), pp. 182-183; Silke Jendrowiak, *Günter Grass und die "Hybris" des Kleinbürgers: "Die Blechtrommel"* - *Bruch mit der Tradition einer irrationalistischen Kunst- und Wirklichkeitsinterpretation* (Heidelberg: Winter, 1979), pp. 230-231.

as the absurd developments of history. [43] Grass attempts in *The Tin Drum* to define himself against Mann's novel and the heritage it represents.

With his half-open novel, and his less than total suspicion of all ideologies, Böll falls somewhere between the older Mann and the younger Grass. Unlike Grass, who was born ten years later, Böll's formative years (he was born in 1917) preceded the final discrediting of German idealist traditions which Grass experienced in the late 1940s. According to Hans Mayer, Böll's generation resembles some expressionists in the sharp antithesis it sees "between power and the mind (*Geist*), between social realities and intellectual engagement. That whole generation of burned children maintains a profound mistrust of power, but also a secret self-condemnation for one's mind, which can presume too much and likewise want to become powerful." [44] The dilemma of this age-group of writers is between the idealist traditions of Mann and the perspective of Grass. In his profound mistrust of the powerful, of the "others" who make history, Böll continues the traditions of inwardness without the elevated cultural conceptions of Mann. While Grass pursues what he called "democratic trifles," actively engaged in practical politics, Böll usually maintains a more non-partisan, sometimes provocative, position.

In the Frankfurt lectures of 1963-64, Böll himself views his experiences as inducing a more or less withdrawn and resigned suspicion of ideology: his student listeners need to learn, he says, "what is difficult for one who has experienced an empire, a republic, a dictatorship, an interregnum, and a second republic before he was thirty. What is difficult is to believe in states." [45] He believes that

---

43. Hanspeter Brode, *Die Zeitgeschichte im erzählenden Werk von Günter Grass: Versuch einer Deutung der "Blechtrommel" und der "Danziger Trilogie"* (Frankfurt am Main: Peter Lang, 1977), pp. 86-87.

44. Hans Mayer, *Deutsche Literatur seit Thomas Mann* (Reinbek: Rowohlt, 1967), p. 64.

45. Heinrich Böll, *Frankfurter Vorlesungen* (Munich: Deutscher Taschenbuch Verlag, 1968), p. 86.

his generation's "literature of ruins," designed to expose the devastating realities of the war and postwar period, stems from mistrust of the "blind man's bluff writers" who always support the prevailing ideological world-view. Böll resists ideological infiltration of his perspective to keep it pure; he prescribes: "The eye of the writer should be humane and incorruptible." [46]

Böll's opposition to ideology is less aggressive and all-inclusive than that of Grass. Whereas Grass assails communist ideology as a secular religion much like Nazism, Böll can refer to himself as an "impeded Communist," saying that his observations of Nazism, Stalinism, and the cold war prevented him from becoming one. [47] Actually, Böll often seeks to disregard the ideological aspect of events. His literary transformation of the original historical event behind the conception of *Billiards at Half-Past Nine* illustrates the author's studied attempt to avoid the issue of political ideology in the modern age.

Discussing the inception of this novel with Horst Bienek, Böll reveals: "The first cell of this novel is the second half of the chapter on the baseball game. And this cell developed out of an historical incident. In 1934, I think it was, Göring ordered here in Cologne the hatchet execution of four young Communists." [48] In the novel, Böll divests the youths of their ideological commitment. Yet these figures assume religious contours: "The theme was then transformed in many ways when I saw the altar in Ghent of the Van Eyck brothers in the middle of which stands the lamb of God." [49] Although Böll thus side-steps the issue of political commitment, his viewpoint is nonetheless ideological in a religious sense:

---

46. Heinrich Böll, "Bekenntnis zur Trümmerliteratur," in *Erzählungen, Hörspiele, Aufsätze* (Berlin: Kiepenheuer & Witsch, 1964), p. 342.

47. Heinrich Böll, "Interview mit mir selbst," quoted in Albrecht Becket, *Mensch, Gesellschaft, Kirche bei Heinrich Böll* (Osnabruck: Fromm, 1966), p. 11.

48. Horst Bienek, *Werkstattgespräche mit Schriftstellern* (Munich: Deutscher Taschenbuch Verlag, 1962), p. 173.

49. Ibid., p. 173.

he interprets events through the perspective of a coherent and internally consistent Christian world-view. His "humane and incorruptible" eye thus creates a mixture of anti- and pro-ideological perspectives.

It is this religious outlook which opposes Nazi ideology and thus gradually provides the exemplary perspective from which the reader is to view events. The novel is told from the viewpoint of genuinely Christian simple folk, untainted by the political ideology inspiring the bravado of those marching by outside. Goebbels' novel *Michael* exemplifies such pseudo-heroics when it rejects the Sermon on the Mount as a source of only despair and shame, not consolation. [50] In direct contrast, Böll's narrators frequently praise the Christian humility called for in that Sermon. The priest Enders, according to Robert, would take care of the "lambs," but the postwar church authorities hide him in an isolated village: "They give him only rams; he is suspicious because he so often makes the Sermon on the Mount the subject of his sermons; perhaps one day someone will discover that it's only an interpolation and they'll cross it out." (Bil, 229) Böll emphasizes that one who preaches humility in this society is considered subversive.

Such Christian interpretation of events, which tends to enclose the novel around itself, is most apparent in the symbolism of lambs and buffalos, to which we shall return. Several other aspects of the narrative perspective, however, contribute to the openness of this work. The unannounced changes in point of view, for example, confuse many readers. At times one does not know who is telling the story, or when it is taking place. Without the identifiable perspective of a named character, readers are forced to puzzle about whose vision is guiding theirs. The reader also experiences the same events told from differing viewpoints. The history of the last fifty years is portrayed not through a linear narrative of facts and dates, but in individual states of consciousness which come alive in separable vignettes out of the past. Time appears as if behind a veil, filtered through different characters' memories. Thus the reader is

---

50. Mosse, *Nazi Culture*, p. 104.

called upon to decipher alone the hazy maze of remembered history. The concrete, realistic description in such passages does not create the comprehensive macrocosm of nineteenth-century realist novels. The author has refused to impose either a single integrating narrator or a linear chronological development upon the complex memories of the Nazi past.

Interior monologue is an appropriate narrative mode to reveal these conflicts of conscience and painful memories. As the least social form, the monologues prevailing in the first chapters suggest a social reality too opaque and vast to be comprehended. Thus, the reader views history from the isolated and unindoctrinated viewpoints of unassuming "little people."

As in *The Tin Drum*, the overall loose structure of the novel extends down to details of syntax and niveau of language. Instead of the ordered, hypotactic syntax of Mann, parataxis and the free associations of memory reign here. Phrases prevail; sentences remain uncompleted. Like Grass, Böll usually prefers colloquial language. Mann appears to be the last major representative of traditional literary language. In contrast to his commanding and elevated phrases, common prose expresses the modest viewpoints of Böll's demure, uncorrupted outsiders.

But intimations of a more sovereign perspective accumulate in both narrative style and ideological outlook. A very literary style, exemplified by words like "züngelnd" and "emporwanden," occasionally interrupts and transcends the spoken language of the narrators. [51] The lamb and buffalo significations, along with other leitmotifs, indicate also a more lofty level of meaning than the simple perspectives and language suggest. With the resolution, finally, of gnawing questions from the past, Böll's open novel appears to close with decisive verdicts. As Walter Sokel has observed, the point of view in Böll's earlier novels of victims and witnesses tends to become in his later works that of the accuser and judge. [52] The

---

51. Manfred Durzak, *Der deutsche Roman der Gegenwart* (Stuttgart: Kohlhammer, 1971), p. 103.

perspective of the avenging judge forms the nucleus of *Billiards at Half-Past Nine.* Politically anti-ideological viewpoints are integrated into a religiously ideological view. Only in Grass's exceptional "Faith, Hope, Love" chapter does Oskar induce so directly the correct moral attitudes which Böll's "incorruptible and humane" narrators come to exemplify. Examination of Böll's symbols will illuminate more fully the effect of such "completion" of an otherwise open-ended novel.

"Symbols" for an Epoch

If traditional realism is no longer equal to the complexity of twentieth-century society, then the classical symbol suffices no better. The attempts of Böll and Mann to capture an epoch in extended forms of symbols have generally received more suspicious scrutiny than praise from critics.

Perhaps most startling about Böll's symbols is their unannounced, unprepared appearance. Several lambs seem to exist, who have sworn never to partake of the sacrament of the buffalo. As soon as Robert hears of the group, without further question he becomes one of their shepherds. Unknown to each other, various figures in the novel possess the nickname "Lamb of God." Hugo, Edith, Schrella, and Ruth all unknowingly belong to the same unorganized group the existence of which seems self-evident. Gradually, the history of the last fifty years is subsumed under the conflict between the lambs and the buffalos. The symbols themselves, even more than the characterization of the novel figures, seem often to organize members of society into two groups: good and evil. In addition, the division extends in an ahistorical manner from Wilhelmian Germany to the postwar Federal Republic. It is as if the open work of art encourages Böll to insert the general

---

52. Walter Sokel, "Perspective and Dualism in the Novels of Böll," in *The Contemporary Novel*, ed. Robert Heitner (Austin: University of Texas Press, 1967), p. 22.

significations, which are for him explanatory devices, without establishing their intrinsic evolution out of the fictive or real history. The self-evident character of the division is underscored when it is thus unsubstantiated.

The separation of humanity into lambs and buffalos appears unquestionable, part of eternal good and evil. Böll's essentially pessimistic view derives from a Christian dualism. Specifically Christian is the presentation of the good as persecuted and oppressed, while the evil flourish in worldly success and prosperity -- as the emphasized Sermon on the Mount suggests. In the novel, the opposition of the two camps reaches far beyond Nazism and anti-Nazism. Walter Sokel writes: "It is ultimately not a political, but a moral, spiritual, and religious dualism, which is founded on Christianity but has a Manichean element in it. The Nazis' persecution of their victims is seen as a variant of the age-old battle between good and evil, light and darkness, holy grace and unholy power."[53] Böll's symbols thus structure into the novel an all-encompassing dualism.

An interwoven design of leitmotifs augments the impression of a symbolically created totality. Klaus Jeziorkowski has observed that the lambs are characterized primarily by two leitmotifs from the Bible and literature. "Shepherd my Lambs," which originates in the Bible, complements a homage by Hölderlin to inwardness: "Compassionate, the eternal heart remains firm after all." The religious

---

53. Ibid., p. 20. Cf. Linda Hill, "The Avoidance of Dualism in Heinrich Böll's Novels," in *Germanic Review* 56 (1981), pp. 151-156. Although the buffalos are heterogeneous, as Hill points out, they are, nonetheless, still evil, simply in different ways, which does not, therefore, detract from the essential dualism of the novel. If we are, e.g., to judge the meaning of Nettlinger's name from his behavior, the "nett" does not suggest that he is a genuinely nice, helpful buffalo, but that he is "nice" in an ironic sense, or at the very best, "ingratiating." When Böll asserted in an interview ("Drei Tage im März, in *Werke*, X, ed. Bernd Balzer [Cologne: Kiepenheuer & Witsch, 1977-78], p. 424) that he considers "the dualistic system that is constantly preached" to be untenable, he did not disclaim his own dualism but a dualism which is generally, conventionally believed in and preached by our religious and social institutions. He shows in *Billiards at Half-Past Nine*, e.g., that Nazis who laid claim to respectability denounced those actually more respectable than themselves.

and secular spiritual traditions thus associated with the lambs are juxtaposed with the nationalist, militaristic, or fascist origins of the following leitmotifs for the buffalos: "Must have a weapon," "The weary bones are trembling," "Wild geese rush through the night," and "Forward with hurrah and Hindenburg." The biblical warning, "Their right hand is full of bribes," is also attached to the buffalos, suggesting their inveterate corruption.[54] Supplementing the symbols, the leitmotifs identify and remind the reader of the eternal dualism.

Böll's buffalo symbol is historically apt in implying that Nazism was a beastly secular religion. The mass of Hitler's supporters believed in him as if they had partaken of a sacrament. Johanna Fähmel recognizes the economic miseries which stimulated faith in this religion when she describes the followers' fear of anything less than an infinite promise: "You know also that sacraments have the horrible quality of not being subject to the finite. And they were hungry, and the bread was not multiplied for them, nor the fish. The *Host of the Lamb* did not still their hunger, but that of the *Buffalo* offered plenty of nourishment." (Bil, 123)

The buffalo image of stupidity and crude strength accurately characterizes some Nazis themselves. It can suggest the "banality of evil"; "büffeln" connotes the dutiful toil of Eichmann and those like him.[55] Böll only occasionally refers to these beasts as wolves probably because the more common biblical opposition of the wolf to the lamb would imply more individual cunning than the dangerous torpor of the buffalo does. Buffalo herds which dumbly trample everything recall the massive parades of marching Nazis. Particularly the link of the buffalos with Hindenburg provides the symbol with concrete, historical precision. The destruction of parliamentary democracy was in part the work of the conservative and

---

54. Klaus Jeziorkowski, *Rhythmus und Figur* (Bad Homberg: Gehlen, 1968), pp. 160-161.

55. Therese Poser, "Heinrich Böll - 'Billard um halb zehn,'" in *Möglichkeiten des modernen deutschen Romans*, ed. Rolf Geissler (Berlin: Moritz Diesterweg, 1965), p. 242.

military elites. Thus the central figure during the pre-Nazi period of 1930-1933 was Hindenburg, not Hitler.

In his treatment of the Federal Republic, Böll's universalizing buffalo symbol is less apt; it tends to conflate Nazism and the Bonn democracy. Certainly, the growth of the NPD and the zealous restoration of one-time Nazis to important posts in the fifties justifies some concern. Furthermore, the re-militarization of the Bonn republic for the cold war inflamed many pacifists and anti-fascists in the fifties, who, like Böll, perceived in rearmament a kind of renascent fascism. While Böll was writing this novel the SPD lost the test vote on rearmament. As the final public celebration in the novel shows, the author emphasizes the military character of the buffalos. But rearmament, the NPD, and restoration of former Nazis did not constitute a revival of the Third Reich.

The description of Otto's "transformation" into a buffalo shows how Böll's eternal dualism can obscure reasons for becoming a Nazi. Characterizing Otto accurately as a petty official like Himmler, Robert implies a socio-historical explanation for this metamorphosis. But only the inevitability of evil can explain why one member of the Fähmel family of lambs can become a buffalo. Neither social class nor family environment can elucidate for the Fähmels a kind of mystical process which is out of their control: "And Otto was suddenly no longer Otto: a horrible miracle had taken place: he was Otto and he wasn't anymore. . . . Otto was now only Otto's husk which quickly received a new content; he had not only tasted the *Host of the Buffalo*, he was inoculated with it." (Bil, 109)

The lamb symbol seems to be less grounded historically and politically than that of the buffalo. Not linked to any historical figures, as the buffalos are to Hindenburg, the lambs also represent no organized political group. They oppose the buffalos for unpolitical, chiefly moral reasons, unlike the source of their inspiration, the communist youths of Cologne. Certainly the religious opposition to Hitler would indicate that such isolated resistance groups and individuals as the Fähmels and Schrellas did exist. But subsuming the resistance under this moral opposition disguises the political and ideological character of opponents on the left and right.

As the tender, meek servants of the Lord that such biblical imagery suggests, the lambs and their shepherd figures, like Robert, exemplify predominantly a truly Christian way of life. They identify themselves in biblical terminology. In his imagination, Father Fähmel recalls, he was "David, the little one with the slingshot, and Daniel, the little one in the lion's den." (Bil, 89) Edith is referred to as the Lord's messenger, Mother Fähmel as a "tool of the Lord," particularly in her assassination attempt. They apply Christian teachings to their everyday lives, often in sharp contrast to Church institutional practices. Mother Fähmel, for example, receives for her own privileged family butter and honey from the abbot of Saint Anthony's during the wars. Unlike the abbot, she distributes such rare luxuries among the poor. The lambs criticize the Church's betrayal of Christian values, for the Church seems to have drawn the greedy buffalos into its fold instead of protecting the charitable lambs. Hugo, for example, asks: "What did Christ die for? How does his death help me? How does it help me when they pray every morning, when they receive communion every Sunday, and when the huge crucifixes hang in their kitchens, over the tables where they eat potatoes with roast and gravy or sauerkraut with bacon? It doesn't." (Bil, 54) Alone and undefended, the lambs embody a truly Christian consciousness; the buffalos and their institutions represent the beastly false consciousness.

These symbols put a religious construction on politics and history and thus close off a nearly open-ended novel. The monologues of isolated individuals display their political powerlessness as they struggle to come to terms with the past; but enclosing their consciousness within the religious dimensions of the lamb symbol labels them as exemplary, indeed blessed. History, when laid open in interior monologues, appears episodically disconnected and relative to an individual point of view; the symbols, however, interpret and explain events as part of the universal battle between good and evil. Whereas Grass's readers may puzzle over shades-of-gray degrees of Oskar's guilt, Böll's black and white symbols define clearly how each participant in history is to be judged. Böll's non-political, religious approach to Nazi ideology, the false secular religion, structures the dualistic enclosure of the novel.

Whereas Böll's symbols enclose an epoch otherwise relatively uncontained, Mann's handling of the Faust myth symbolically consummates the self-contained novel. In his essay "Freud and the Future," Mann asserts, "Myth is the legitimation of life; only through it and in it life finds its self-awareness, its justification and consecration."[56] Myth in the largest, neutral sense of the word could be used to depict the self-awareness of the pre-Nazi period. Mann's mythical symbol is informed primarily by the Faust legend from the 1587 chapbook, in addition to several religious, cultural, and literary "mythical" figures. The contours of Christ, Faust, various writers and composers merge in the Leverkühn-*Gestalt*; he consciously quotes from figures like Nietzsche and Shakespeare. Such a personified synthesis of well-known cultural symbols exemplifies Mann's conception of a mythical portrayal of life. But his emphasis here on an unoriginal and borrowed mythology (in both the Freud essay and in *Doctor Faustus*) is also to suggest the cultural sterility which faces the modern age. In this he is quite successful.

Mann's numerous quotations multiply the implications of this Faust symbol, just as they make the fictive self-contained world in his novel appear more real. No single mythic figure alone could represent this epoch; Christ, Luther, Nietzsche, and Mahler, among others, all contribute to the realization of Faustus-Leverkühn. These synthesized, specific aspects of Adrian's life and person bear from the beginning the mythical stamp of general significance. As symbolic artifice, Leverkühn both "is" and "signifies."

Just as other figures in the narrative become a significant part of a whole almost before they appear, Adrian's characteristics of coldness or provincialism acquire a general significance almost before the reader experiences them specifically. The same

---

56.   Thomas Mann, "Freud und die Zukunft," *Gesammelte Werke*, IX (Oldenburg: Fischer, 1960), p. 496.

"incompetent" narrator who sketches and then underlines the grand design of the novel also universalizes the particulars of each "signifier." In short, the same narrative devices and "quoting" techniques augment and thus secure both the self-contained novel and its major symbol. The seemingly fated eruption into irrationalism that is established in the narrative design finds its symbol in a Faustian pact with the devil. The emphasis on the general significance of Leverkühn's life suggests a symbol that approaches allegory. [57]

Such a synthesized artifice resembles in some ways Grass's many-faced Oskar: Adrian and Oskar both are modern artists who are completely and parodically aware of all the clichéd categories of art and artists. Adrian plays at being the seduced Nietzsche at the outset of his artistic career and consciously closes his "sane" life in a transformed repetition of the original Faust legend. He is an artifice and is constantly making himself into one.

The differences between the artists that Oskar and Adrian recall suggest their diverging functions as artifices. Whereas Oskar plays at being a contemporary artist of the resistance, as well as a Nazi army entertainer, Adrian re-plays parts of the lives of pre-Nazi legendary cultural heroes. As an embodiment of the immediate reality, the gnome of an artist takes on grotesque dimensions. Because Adrian represents in part the "high" refined culture prior to Nazism, he takes on the more normal dimensions of the artistic outsider but as a mythical, nearly unreal representative. These dimensions of the archetypal individual culminate in Adrian's final Christ-like appearance. Whereas Oskar can only make fun of the tragic and metaphysical proportions of the Christ and Faust figures which the Nazis appropriated to their own myth, Adrian assumes

---

57. Since Leverkühn's life story both "is" and "signifies," and thus preserves basic elements of the traditional symbol, I would not abandon this term for allegory, as have other critics, notably Gisbert Ter-Nedden, "Allegorie und Geschichte: Zeit-und Sozialkritik als Formproblem des deutschen Romans der Gegenwart," in *Positionen des Erzählens*, ed. H. L. Arnold and Theo Buck (Munich: Beck, 1976), p. 100, and Erhard Bahr, "Metaphysische Zeitdiagnose: Kasack, Langgässer und Thomas Mann," p. 149.

these two roles seriously. Adrian embodies on the higher cultural level what the Nazis, in Mann's view, debased. In sharp contrast to Grass's artifice, Leverkühn was to be, according to the author, "an ideal figure; a 'hero of our times'; a person who bears the suffering of the epoch." (EDF, 739) As an ideal martyr, an unreal embodiment of the afflictions of the age, Adrian must remain a relatively inanimate artifice: "A prohibition was to be held to here," wrote Mann, "-- or at least a commandment to be obeyed: to exercise the greatest caution in any external animation, which would immediately threaten the spiritual case and its symbolic value and representativeness with degradation and banality." (EDF, 740) Oskar's unreal aspects facilitate his mobility; Adrian's artificial aura prevents him from descending to the imp's banal level and sustains his symbolic value as a tragic reflection of pre-Nazi German culture.

Another similarity between these artificial symbols further reveals their differences. Both Oskar and Adrian have highly unusual, fantastic gifts. As Hans Mayer has stated, both are artists on the far side of language. [58] It is as if no common, human language could be found for these artists to express and symbolize the reality of their epoch. Hell, too, according to the devil, is beyond words: "Actually one cannot talk about it at all because words cannot identify what actually happens." With implicit reference to Gestapo cellars and concentration camp atrocities, the devil says of the horrors practiced in hell: "It is done, it happens and, in fact, without being called to account by words: in sound-proof cellars, deep below God's hearing, that is, in eternity." (DF, 326-327). Music, as a nonverbal art, has long been associated for Mann with the cult of the irrational. In league with the devil, Adrian will attempt to give expression to an apocalypse through his music, which in retrospect will appear as a prophecy of his country's impending hell. By contrast, Oskar's drumming and glass-shattering songs expose, in their own fantastic way, atrocities of the Third Reich as more banal.

---

58.   Hans Mayer, "Günter Grass and Thomas Mann: Aspects of the Novel," in *Steppenwolf and Everyman*, trans. Jack Zipes (New York: Thomas F. Crowell Co., 1971), p. 196.

Critics have debated not only the nomenclature but also the validity of Mann's symbol. Perhaps the novel's most legitimate claim to general significance lies in its symbolization of the "late" intellectual or artist of any nation.[59] This artist desires not the fantastic trips of Faust of old but a rich life in a psychic, creative sense. In the *Story of a Novel*, the author himself links his composer's crisis with the modern cultural one: "the proximity of sterility, the inborn despair, pre-disposed to a pact with the devil." (EDF, 723) As analyzed earlier in this chapter, the sterility of traditional values by the onset of the twentieth century also predisposed much of the educated middle classes to seek a sense of vitality and meaning in the same irrationalist philosophies embraced by the pre-fascist Kridwiss-Kreis. Leverkühn's desperate pact with the devil may symbolize the German bourgeoisie's effort to also "break through" at any cost. Any yet this culturally focused symbolization of fascism has its drawbacks.

The consequences of Leverkühn's indulgence in primitive barbarism in his music, however lamentable, are far less horrific than six million dead Jews. The hubris of artistic genius would seem to be in a different category from ruthless political ambitions. One major critic of Mann has nonetheless argued: "The tragic significance of the disdainful genius in Leverkühn consists in anticipating through dictatorial strictness of the grandiose yet reckless musical constructions the law of the lawless, the brutal totalitarian control and the regimentation of the mob."[60] But should this "freedom through constraint" in Leverkühn's music be related so directly to political lawlessness under law? Does the cold pride of an atonal composer really compare with the cold arrogance of mass murderers? Such discrepancies do detract from the symbol's validity.[61]

---

59. Henry Hatfield, "Two Notes on *Doktor Faustus*," *Modern Language Forum* 34 (March/June, 1949), p. 17.

60. Fritz Kaufmann, *The World as Will and Representation* (Boston: Beacon Press, 1957), p. 203.

61. Henry Hatfield, "Can one sell one's soul?" in *Great Moral Dilemmas in Literature, Past and Present*, ed. Robert MacIver (New York: Harper, 1956), p. 94.

In addition, this cultural symbol cannot represent all of German society, nor would it need to; but Mann frequently suggests that it does. The ideas and daemonic despair of Leverkühn or the Kridwiss-Kreis do not shape history to the degree that Mann's total focus on them would imply. Zeitblom characterizes all Germans, for example, as susceptible to Nazism because they "all too willingly live according to theory." (DF, 638) As in the novel, in "Germany and the Germans" Mann overgeneralizes from an important tendency among German intellectuals when he attempts to describe the relationship of *the* German to the world: "Abstract and mystical, that is, musical, is the relationship of the German to the world -- the relationship of a daemonically tinged professor, awkward and yet motivated by an arrogant attitude of feeling superior to the world in his profundity." [62]

But Mann himself invests Nazism with such profundity. Adrian's symbolic pact with the devil demonizes, in effect, Nazi Germany; its destruction is then literally apocalyptic, described as a "descent into hell" invoking the "Last Judgment." Mann often referred to his novel of the epoch as a "book of the devil" (*Teufelsbuch*). It appeared more meaningful to be the victims of demons and monsters than of ordinary, respectable little men. [63] In contrast, Grass exposes the utter senselessness of so much suffering and destruction. The degrees of de-demonization in *The Tin Drum* and *Billiards at Half-Past Nine* correspond to the openness of these novels.

To be sure, Mann's concept of the Nazi as a debased version of the arrogant artistic genius has some historical validity. Certainly a number of disgruntled outsiders in the twenties, less pathological but similar to "Brother Hitler," could be considered a lower form of the outsider-artist. These paranoids, sadists, and ne'er-do-wells felt their talents finally recognized in the NSDAP. For them the Nazi

---

62. Thomas Mann, "Deutschland und die Deutschen," in *Schriften zur Politik* (Frankfurt am Main: Suhrkamp, 1970), p. 167.

63. Michael Hamburger, *From Prophecy to Exorcism* (London: Longmans, 1968), p. 142.

claims of the Jewish influence in German life explained their past failures. With their own kind of hubris, these fanatics considered themselves justly disdainful geniuses. Very few of the participants in the Third Reich were seriously alienated from the "real" world, however, let alone clinically abnormal. The minority of frustrated outsiders also tended to be eliminated from 1933 on. The real executors of the Third Reich were "other-directed," not mad or alienated but "banal" in their evil, the "normal" representatives of a pathological society.[64] Alfred Matzerath or Nettlinger are their literary relatives. Mann, on the other hand, personally observed the growth of the Nazi party mainly before 1933, while the fanatics were more highly visible, though even then a minority. Thus, the proud confidence of the composer finds its debased form in the arrogance of these self-proclaimed geniuses. Their reach for a realization of their submerged talents could be seen as a degraded form of Adrian's breakthrough. The theories of the more "spiritual" German in the *Observations of an Unpolitical Man* have become in the mouths of such disgruntled outsiders the "clamor of the streets."

Critics have also argued that an artist's fate is something much too individual to symbolize a nation's destiny.[65] Although Mann does personify Germany in order to correlate the two, he seems to have several understandable reasons for doing so. Subject to personal attacks and threats to his life from Hitler and Goebbels, the novelist experienced his tireless opposition to Nazi Germany partly in terms of his person against theirs. Commenting in his diary on Germany's final defeat, Mann reflected: "After the fall of France five years ago, Goebbels announced my death. . . . To survive meant to win. I had fought and bestowed ridicule and curses on the slanderers of humanity by living: so it is personally also a victory." (EDF, 758) Perhaps, too, a writer needs the friend and the enemy;

---

64. David Schoenbaum, *Hitler's Social Revolution* (Garden City, New York: Doubleday & Co., 1967), p. 287.

65. E. M. Butler, *The Fortunes of Faust* (London: Cambridge University Press, 1952), p. 336.

he needs personalities, not anonymous figures and groups.[66] In addition, personification of a country so dehumanized resists its *Gleichschaltung*. Thus, Germany does often appear individualized in the novel. The last paragraph of the novel underscores the tie between a personified Germany and a damned Faust figure: "Germany, its cheeks reddened from the hectic, was reeling then at the height of its dissolute triumphs, about to win the world by virtue of the one contract that it intended to keep, which it had signed with its blood." (DF, 676) An individual's fate representing a nation's destiny does evoke a strong emotional response in the reader which an anonymous mass would not.

We mourn not only Adrian's fate, but also the deaths of related characters, especially Echo; the grief for individuals merges with that for Nazi Germany. As Zeitblom exclaims: "Everything is hastening toward its end." (DF, 627) This symbolic personification of the nation's fate culminates in an emotional catharsis which is sadly resolved by Zeitblom: "A lonely man folds his hands and says: may God be merciful to your poor soul, my friend, my fatherland." (DF, 676) Only if the reader accepts the all-encompassing symbolic framework which links the personal to the general, which traces this catastrophe through the irrationalism of the Wilhelmian period back to the hysteria of the late Middle Ages, is this catharsis totally satisfying.

From the start, the Faust figure and the nation it symbolizes have been destined for a long since established doom. Just as Adrian's pact with the devil only consummates what was fated since Kaisersaschern, so too Nazi Germany's daemonic dissolution culminates the irrationalism reappearing since the late Middle Ages. For Adrian, as for Germany, there is no turning back. Mann's metaphysical perspective precludes alternative possibilities and resembles a Wagnerian orchestration of the end of the world.[67]

---

66. Walter Jens, *Moderne Literatur, Moderne Wirklichkeit* (Pfullingen: Neske, 1958), p. 28.

67. "Diskussion zu Thomas Mann," *Sprache im technischen Zeitalter* vol. 5, no. 17/18 (1966), p. 75.

Doctor Faustus is a critique of the romanticism and irrationalism allegedly reigning in Nazi Germany from an ultimately romantic outlook. [68] Since all opposition to the Nazis' rise to power had been in vain, Mann sadly interprets fascism as diabolically inevitable.

Not that Mann was devoid of all hope. Implicit in the novel, and more explicit in the essay on Nietzsche, is the view that once irrationalism has run its course, reason may again perhaps prevail. There is, for example, a kind of rationalism in the moral pathos of the old humanist narrator who condemns Nietzschean and Nazi irrationalism. Mann too argues against Nietzsche in an essay and asserts his belief in a higher judgmental authority: "And if it is not morals, then it is simply the spirit *(Geist)* of human beings, humanity itself as criticism, irony, and freedom, bound together with the judgmental word." [69] Against the anti-rational ideology of Nazism, as symbolized in his Faustian artist, the writer desperately pits humane rational judgment.

Although Nazism is measured against basic ethical standards of Christianity in all three novels, Mann and Grass do not utilize religious perspectives as Böll does to oppose political ideology. Rather, they call on a more secular rationalist posture to subdue the hysterical shrill of Nazi propaganda. But they do so differently: where Grass seeks to encourage sober, practical common sense against mass hysteria, Mann draws on an aesthetic of harmony and balance.

At pains to defend himself for *The Observations of an Unpolitical Man* and for the supposed sudden changes in his political views since 1918, Mann argued already in 1922 that his current "support

---

68.   Klaus Bock. *Geschichtsbegriff und Geschichtsbild bei Thomas Mann* (diss., Kiel, 1959), pp. 23-24. Similar arguments are made by T. E. Apter, *The Devil's Advocate* (London: Macmillan, 1978), pp. 138-157 and Paul Gerhard Klussmann, "Thomas Manns *Doktor Faustus* als Zeitroman," in *Thomas Mann Symposium - Bochum, 1975*, ed. Klussmann and Fechner (Kastellaum: A. Henn, 1978), p. 98.

69.   Thomas Mann, "Nietzsches Philosophie im Lichte unserer Erfahrung," *Gesammelte Werke*, IX (Oldenburg: Fischer, 1960), p. 695.

for the Republic continues today the sensibility of the *Observations* exactly and without interruption, and his [current] values are unmistakably, undeniably those of that book: German humanity."[70] Kurt Sontheimer and others who have studied Mann's political views have confirmed the novelist's assertion.[71] Whereas earlier Mann aimed his humanist barbs, inspired all along by the model of Goethean balance, against the banal positivists of the democratic and socialist Left, by the 1920s Mann perceived the threat to humanity hovering in the opposite camp. Seeing his fears confirmed as the instigators of mass hysteria in the NSDAP grew in strength, the writer redoubled his efforts to stave off the anti-rational cult. In other words, Mann defends against either extreme in the struggle to preserve humanity. Through all these shifts, he remained committed to an ideal of *Humanität* which he defined as the mean between the two polarities of German cultural history, "between romanticism and the Enlightenment, between mysticism and reason."[72] The balance of *Humanität* which reason had threatened to destroy must now be championed by reason.

Humanität is an aesthetic concept: the "mean" of balance and harmony in a culture creates a pleasing ambience which fosters development of our many-sided potential; cultural overemphasis of any one tendency in a human being's disposition causes imbalanced, ugly discrepancies.[73] The humanist narrator's more universal religion of Catholicism, for example, counters the provincial and isolated Lutheranism of Leverkühn and the nation he symbolizes.

---

70. Thomas Mann, "Von deutscher Republik," *Schriften zur Politik* (Frankfurt am Main): Fischer, 1970), pp. 24-25.

71. Kurt Sontheimer, *Thomas Mann und die Deutschen* (Frankfurt am Main: Fischer, 1965); Klaus Bohnen, "Argumentationsverfahren und politische Kritik bei Thomas Mann," in *Gedenkschrift für Thomas Mann, 1875-1975*, ed. Rolf Wiecker (Copenhagen: Text & Kontext, 1975), pp. 173-182.

72. Thomas Mann, "Von deutscher Republik," p. 44.

73. Bock, *Geschichtsbegriff*, pp. 23-24.

Grass's rationalism is of a different kind. Appearing to be as suspicious of balance and symmetry as his dwarf is, Grass focuses on the grotesque incompatibilities evident in the Third Reich, without proffering the balanced resolution of Mann's self-contained novel. Less attached to the high culture which Mann endeavors to preserve, the younger writer focuses little on a cultured, sophisticated form of reason. He thus stresses less the espoused, irrational aims of Nazi ideology and more the practical functions of that ideology in distancing the "little people" from their more immediate needs. Both explicitly in the "Faith, Hope, Love" chapter and implicitly through his narrator, Grass emphasizes "reasonableness" -- common sense or matter-of-fact thinking -- more than reason. Through the open, unresolved form of his novel, he merely exposes the emotional exploitation of Nazi ideology -- offering no answers, but suggesting his reasonable stance. Oskar's matter-of-fact thinking about frantic, ideological rituals complements the skepticism induced in the reader by the open-ended form. The three-year-old's simple common sense, like his related spontaneity and natural playfulness, resists and unmasks the drunken fanaticism on all the rostrums.

Oskar's apparently naive, unsocialized common sense derives from a humanistic anarchism, the base of Grass's satirical assault on the Nazis and their fellow-travelers. [74] The free spirit of Oskar is anarchic in the sense that it is anti-authoritarian. Always relying on his own common sense, Oskar persistently resists any parental, political, or religious authority. Since such skeptical, matter-of-fact thinking protects Oskar from being led astray into some blindly ideological movement, the author seems to imply that the common sense in every child could help rescue humanity. Instead of a harmony of the mystical and rational sides of German culture, Grass's less lofty vision of a humane society appears to require simple reasonableness and expressive awareness of basic needs. Mann opposes fascism by stressing the precarious and vitally necessary binding of the instinctual into a wider harmony governed by humanistic reason (as opposed to merely technical intellect). In contrast, Grass

---

74.   John Mander, "Variations on a Tin Drum," *Encounter* vol. 19, no. 5 (1962), p. 82.

implies that if given direct expression, the instincts will not be open to the kind of manipulation and odious misdirection which results from such a "return of the repressed." Such free and naive expression of psychosexual desires facilitates matter-of-fact thinking rather than distorted, rigid, and compensatory responses to daily problems.

Yet such solutions are only intermittently implied in *The Tin Drum*; the dwarf is never consistently or directly a model of resistance to ideological manipulation. Just as Grass declines the self-enclosed fictive world, which would integrate the whole epoch, he creates a narrator who deliberately defies symbolic classification. In contrast to Böll's more static symbols, what Oskar signifies changes constantly and evolves anew out of each historical scene: Böll's significations are transcendent, Grass's historically immanent.[75] As both what the Nazis were and what they rejected, the blue-eyed dwarf is a variable, open symbol for his age. Similarly, Oskar symbolically reflects and rejects postwar German society. In 1945 Oskar begins to grow halfway toward normality; his physical deformity then mirrors concretely the moral obtuseness of the average, "normal" citizen claiming a good conscience.[76] But he also satirizes their "inability to mourn" and seeks refuge from their "normality" in the abnormality of the asylum.

Böll's categories -- the banal Nettlingers, for instance, as beastly "others" -- and Mann's choice of the possessed artist as symbolic representative -- allow readers to disassociate themselves from the evils described. Oskar, by alternately representing and resisting his age, does not remain a fixed and distant "other"; Grass's

---

75. Rainer Nägele, *Heinrich Böll. Eine Einführung in das Werk und in die Forschung* (Frankfurt am Main: Athenäum Fischer, 1976), p. 29; cf. Hanspeter Brode, "Die Zeitgeschichte in der 'Blechtrommel' von Günter Grass. Entwurf eines textinternen Kommunikationsmodells," in *Günter Grass - Ein Materialienbuch*, ed. Rolf Geissler (Neuwied: Luchterhand, 1976), p. 110, who over-allegorizes Oskar as solely representative of Nazism in the first two books.

76. Hanspeter Brode, "Die Zeitgeschichte in der 'Blechtrommel' von Günter Grass," p. 90.

chameleon-like symbol refuses any ultimate or categoric character to explain and judge inhumanity. Because this inhumanity is not labeled as beastly or daemonic, the banality of evil becomes most accessible here as it simply speaks for itself.

Self-Interpretation of the Novels

Various arts are suggested in the titles to the three novels; each is a major key to the work, especially its formal response to the question of ideology. As Leverkühn's last composition, "The Lamentation of Doctor Faustus" summarizes and epitomizes his own musical endeavors as well as the entire novel. Similarly, the billiards game and the toy tin drum disclose the form and intent of the works of which they are a part. The games which these fictive artists play denote those of their creators.

Adrian speaks of and plays with a magic square in several of his last compositions. This game's function in his final cantata suggests a code for the whole structure of *Doctor Faustus*: the magic square and the twelve-tonal system are metaphors for the form of the novel. By definition, the magic quadrate requires that a group of numbers be arranged in a square in such a way that they add up to the same sum, vertically, horizontally, and diagonally. In Mann's notion of the atonal composition, the same notes, in a predetermined order, are varied both vertically and horizontally. There can be no free note. The magic number seven also works in conjunction with the square. Henry Hatfield has designated seven themes in the novel, each functioning on seven levels. For example, the themes of break-through, or salvation vs. damnation, operate on the levels of the Faust legend or politics. The most important chapters are the most abundantly "orchestrated": all levels and themes occur. [77] Like the composer's last cantata, *Doctor Faustus* itself is a magic square; in both compositions, the free note no longer exists.

---

77. For the thorough analysis of which this paragraph is only a brief summary, see Henry Hatfield, "The Magic Square," *Euphorion* vol. 62, no. 3/4 (1968), pp. 415-420.

In accordance with this twelve-tonal technique, then, the first chapters designate already these major themes and levels to be repeated in all their variations for the remainder of the novel. Parody prevails in Leverkühn's earlier work and in the first two-thirds of the novel. The extremely strict form and pre-organized material in "The Lamentation of Doctor Faustus" facilitate the composer's submission to total expressive subjectivity: the cantata is without parody, milder and more melancholy than what has preceded in Leverkühn's *oeuvre*. Zeitblom describes this genuinely expressive music as the "birth of freedom out of constraint," as the "release of expression." (DF, 644) Likewise, Zeitblom's narration becomes liberated: direct, linear, and expressively melancholy only after his elaborate design of pre-organized themes has been firmly established.

The dialectics of this artistic liberation have in the novel broader cultural and social implicatons. Perhaps both art and Germany may be redeemed. As Jack Stein has written: "The 'Weheklag' is art which has won its way back from the isolation of the art-conscious 'cultured' public, to the cult, to the service of the *Gemeinschaft*, an art which, in the directness and immediacy of its expression, can speak to mankind on intimate terms despite its technical complexity." [78] Like his composer, Mann also sees the drawbacks of art confined to an isolated inward sphere. In predestining his Faust to damnation, with little hope of mercy, the author seems to revoke the Goethean Faust of idealist culture, as Leverkühn annuls the noble and high ideals of the Ninth Symphony. After fascism, mercy for Germany's Faust appears less likely. Yet Leverkühn's yearning for a community "auf du and du" recalls the similar hopes at the end of *Faust II*, and his attainment of a subjective "freedom through constraint" seems like a modern version of Goethean classicism. The values of classical humanism still inform Mann's visions of the ideal, however much he may question their current validity.

---

78. Jack M. Stein, "Adrian Leverkühn as a Composer," *Germanic Review* vol. 25, no. 4 (1950), p. 274.

Mann's own hope for his country's redemption despite its seeming damnation also finds immediate expression in Zeitblom's most direct and intimate address to readers (the intimate *ihr* for "you" is used) describing the conclusion of Adrian's work: "Listen to the end, listen with me: one group of instruments after another retires, and what remains, as the work fades in the air, is the high G of a cello. . . . Then nothing more -- silence and night. But the tone which vibrates in the silence, the tone which is no more, which only the soul still hears, and which was the last voice of mourning, is no longer that note. It changes its meaning; it abides as a light in the night." (DF, 651) Like the close of this composition, the end of this chapter, along with many of the last pages, is genuinely expressive and deeply moving. Mann too speaks finally to his audience on intimate terms in spite of the novel's technical complexity.

The game of the architect Robert Fähmel facilitates in its own way also a liberation from isolation; like the cantata, it parallels in its development the structure of the whole novel. In the beginning monologues, each individual alone sifts through memories of the past mixed with scenes from the present. As the geometric constellations on the billiards table graphically represent, formulaic gestures, figures, and designs secure Robert's memories, keeping them intact and available for abstract reflections upon relationships between past and present. In the end, Robert's private ritual commemorating the past becomes a game played with a partner in the "permanent present." Once Robert and his fellow lambs have mourned and assimilated their recollections from the last fifty years, they move out of their isolation into the present.

Resembling the form of the novel, Robert's mode of remembering implies a model for readers as well. Robert's people are repelled by those who can repress the Nazi past, those who appear to think that time heals all. Mother Fähmel exclaims, aghast at the rigidly respectable faces of those about her, "What is a human being without sorrow?" (Bil, 212) Alexander and Margarete Mitscherlich's *The Inability to Mourn* underscores Johanna's observation that few have even mourned, let alone come to terms with any sense of responsibility for their past under Hitler. [79] Böll's characters urge us: remember the past and do not reconcile yourself to its vestiges in the present.

The artful designs and movements of the billiards game represent Robert's way of translating this message into action. He applies the same principles of statics and dynamics with the balls and cue that he follows as a demolition expert. Robert explains to Hugo why he still, even after the defeat of Nazism, cannot take up his profession as an architect: he cannot erect buildings which testify to a balance of strength, an equilibrium of forces. Instead, he destroys supporting structures, emphasizes the imbalance in this society's edifices and, by extension, its existing social structures. Just as the billiards cue destroys every balanced configuration, Robert and his people behave adversely, resist collusion with those who so comfortably "forget." The constant tension in the narration between past and present is resolved not in easy negation but through integration of memories of the past into the present. And those who remember remain irreconcilable, "out of balance" with their society.

In all three novels, the narration evolves out of the memories of the narrators. But it is only for those two writers who include the post-Nazi period that the issue of "forgetting" the Third Reich becomes so important. For Böll and Grass, the games that their artists play help to chronicle the past. Like the sober demolition expert who recalls the past while bent over the billiards table, Oskar consults his drum whenever he wants to find his way back to personal or historical events: "If I didn't have my drum, which, when handled adroitly and patiently, remembers all the incidentals that I need to get the essential down on paper, . . . I'd be a poor bastard without proof of his grandparents." (Bt, 17) Even when Oskar tries to forget some incident in which he is implicated, his drum resists. Wishing to destroy the last witness to his "Judas deed," his betrayal of Jan Bronski to the Home Guard, Oskar works very hard to demolish his drum; finally "the accusations of the lacquered and

---

79. Alexander and Margarete Mitscherlich, *Die Unfähigkeit zu trauern* (Munich: Piper, 1967).

red-inflamed conscience hanging around my neck began to carry less conviction: the lacquer cracked and peeled; the tin grew thin and fragile." (BT 211) The drum's colors recall also Poland and thus Nazi aggression. The devastation of the drum is in the end to no avail: Oskar's sense of guilt will still pursue him.

Thus the instrument of this narrative, the toy drum, appears to resist directly adult distortion of nearly every reality it witnesses. Only Oskar's hope of receiving a drum on his third birthday comforts him when he confronts the prospect of entering the misbegotten petit bourgeois world of his parents. He needs the drum to protect himself from this "normal" world running amok politically which soon will tolerate no vulnerable, abnormal creatures. Deciding between his father and mother's plans for him at birth, the newborn child observes a moth drumming on the sixty-watt bulb: "The moth chattered away, as if in a hurry to unburden itself of its knowledge, . . . as though this dialogue between moth and bulb were in any case the moth's last confession." (Bt, 36) Taking the brown, powdery moth for his master, Oskar embraces the natural rhythms of a less than impressive or beautiful creature (it is no butterfly), and rejects the musty, distorting confines of his father's milieu. The confessional tone to the moth's drumming is also not lost on this master's disciple. Throughout the novel, the drum of narration serves intermittently as Oskar's conscience, reminding him of an irresponsible past he would rather forget.

The drum, like the variable symbol Oskar, resists ideological distortions, not only directly, as regarding the repression of guilt, but also indirectly. Satirically simulating aggressive military or ritualistic rhythms, the drum punctures political illusions of the Third Reich. After the war, the drum in the Onion Cellar renders satirically the litany of the postwar confessional mania and reveals the inability to mourn genuinely. The role of this instrument of art in the novel parallels the potential function of the novel for its reading public. Grass's game is to expose and subvert the imposed tempo with natural rhythms: to release finally the appropriate grief and sense of responsibility that Oskar and his readers have tried to repress.

The cantata, the billiards game, and the tin drum each provide a "self-interpretation of the novel." Each self-commentary summarizes the formal direction of the novel. The pre-determined, technically complex cantata with its expressive lament reflects the entire structure of *Doctor Faustus* in miniature. In contrast to Mann's recondite, conceptual approach to Nazi ideology, the architect's simple game represents the lambs' model memory which keeps them morally irreconcilable to the beastly faith which still prevails. The aim of Oskar's drumming changes constantly and thus reflects less directly than the other games the target of its author, as befits an open-ended novel. Yet the toy tin drum upholds, if only by implication, unmanipulated natural rhythms against the distorting cadences of every confused adult consciousness. The magic square carefully orchestrates the reader's response that the billiards game or the drumming merely suggest; but all three games try to release in the reader the emotions necessary in confrontation with Nazism: guilt, outrage, grief, and the unmitigated pain at inhumanity.

The closing passages of these novels accentuate again the shape of each work as a result of the author's approach to Nazi ideology. Zeitblom's description of Germany's descent into hell reproduces Leverkühn's Faustian lament: "Today, entwined in demons, one eye covered by a hand, the other staring into horrors, it plunges from despair to despair. When will it reach the bottom of the abyss?" (DF, 676) Although Zeitblom questions, his tone reveals the fateful meaning he recognizes in the daemonic catastrophe. He then resolves his despairing questions with the melancholy hope for mercy for his friend and fatherland. The novel seems to close with an "amen." Although both Mann and Böll perceived the Nazi catastrophe as fated, Böll's less resolved ending evokes none of the emotional catharsis of a Faustian tragedy. Heinrich Fähmel, finding his abbey commemorated in the form of a sweet anniversary cake, seems to join in the café's unintended mockery of his work when he "cut off the spire of the Abbey first, and passed the plate to Robert." (Bil, 237) This conciliatory, rounding-off gesture resembles the end of many comedies; the characters seem to shrug their shoulders at the audience, as if to say, "What else can we do?" Böll's humane little folk thus smile at their own powerlessness, while they assert, nonetheless, their incorruptibility. In contrast to Mann's conclusion, the repeated queries at the end of Grass's novel receive no clear or final answer. As Oskar says, referring to the Black Cook still on his tail, "Don't ask Oskar who she is! He has no more words." (Bt, 493) The narrative which can have no resolution, no comforting completion, simply breaks off abruptly. A kind of gallows humor pervades Oskar's last words: "Is the Black Cook there? Yes! Yes! Yes!" (Bt, 493) The reader is left with this discomforting thought: is the guilt to be assigned? Yes, yes, yes!

To encompass the consciousness of his epoch, Mann rewrites the Faust myth within an elaborate, self-contained narrative design. Böll lays open a politically unideological consciousness intended as exemplary; he encloses confusing, unorganized narrative with definitive, all-encompassing symbols. Grass's protagonist is neither exemplary nor even reliable; he defies every ideology and any definitive, coherent perspective. The consciousness which Mann encloses Grass exposes. The shape of each work attests to its creator's confrontation with Nazi ideology.

Epilogue:
The Continuing Confrontation

Through the 1960s *Doctor Faustus*, *The Tin Drum*, and *Billiards at Half-Past Nine* continue to stand out as the most successful postwar novels on the Nazi epoch. Novels of the seventies on the whole leave behind the urge to encompass the Nazi era itself. They bring instead a new, more selective, personal and contemporary emphasis to the problem of Nazism, a development to be examined later in this epilogue with particular attention to Peter Handke's *A Sorrow Beyond Dreams* (1972), Uwe Johnson's *Anniversaries* (1970-73), and Christa Wolf's *Patterns of Childhood* (1976).

Prose literature on Nazism in the sixties reflects two wider literary directions of this decade: grotesque realism and the documentary. Both styles provide a means of coming to grips with an increasingly insecure grasp of reality, exacerbated by the heretofore unthinkable realities of Nazism. Grass's *The Tin Drum* seems to have stirred up in its wake a wave of grotesque, socially critical reckonings with the Third Reich, including *Soul of Wood* (1962) and *Landscape in Concrete* (1963) by Jakov Lind, and *The Giant Dwarfs* (1964) by Gisela Elsner. Grass's own *Dog Years* (1963) sustains this mode of realism, but unlike its predecessor, appears to billow out of control in its abundant material and unnecessarily complicated narrative structure. Labeled a "chronicle," *Dog Years* is also less fictive than *The Tin Drum*, in keeping with the documentary trend of the decade. The flood of documentary literature on Nazism carries on in the tradition of earlier postwar efforts to confess moral truth denuded of literary embellishments. From this perspective, it is impossible for fiction to portray a reality that has already outstripped our imagination. Alexander Kluge's *Battle Description* (1964) attempts to drive home documented truths that Nazi propaganda obscured; Peter Weiss's *The Investigation* (1965) and Rolf Hochhuth's *The Deputy* (1963) are famous documentary dramas of the same decade. Like Grass, Böll assimilated documentary techniques to his later novel on Nazism, *Group Portrait with Lady* (1971). This work brings into a more contemporary focus basically the same concept of Nazism developed in *Billiards at Half-Past Nine.* Primarily the same transhistoric dualism holds sway here as the explanation for the course of historic events: the good people are victimized by the evil, before, during, and after the Third Reich.

Siegfried Lenz's bestseller *The German Lesson* (1968) simultaneously looks back to the "classics" on Nazism of 1959 and forward to the novels of seventies. Narrated from an asylum, this novel describes provincial life in the thirties in traditional realist style, and seems to echo, nine years later, the novels of Grass and Böll. Distant from the mass festivities or bombing raids, however, the milieu in Lenz's book verges on the idyllic, even more so than the provincial setting that Böll portrays. Historical catastrophe and German guilt are thus neutralized and made more acceptable to readers.[1] The narrative structure, which focuses on the moral integrity of Siggi, suggests, however, that this is a novel as much about the effect of the parents' political errors on the younger generation as about art and politics during the Third Reich itself. Such concern for a fatherless, skeptical generation, which can no longer accept norms handed down to it, considering recent German history,[2] lends the novel its forward-looking face.

Grass's generation appears to be the last to reckon with the whole Nazi era itself as a primary purpose of its writing. Most writers who grapple with this period in its entirety were born in the late twenties or early thirties: Hochhuth, Kempowski, Lenz, Lind, Walser, to name a few. The war ended as these writers reached young adulthood. The issues of guilt and responsibility which they then confronted, for the first time relatively independent of their parents, here understandably stamped their thinking for much of their adult lives. In addition, they carry with them a keen sense of their accidental survival. Their generation and those

---

1.   Manfred Durzak, *Gespräche über den Roman* (Frankfurt am Main: Suhrkamp, 1976), pp. 207, 211.

2.   Ibid., pp. 212, 218-219.

before them were decimated by the war. As Grass said, he considers himself in effect to be writing for those who cannot.[3] Writers of his generation can feel a sense of responsibility to portray what others lived and might have written. For those born later or those writing from the distance of the seventies, personal introspection about the aftereffects of life under Nazism dominates. This more subjective perspective has roots in cultural historical developments in both West and East Germany.

The birth of the "new subjectivity" in the Federal Republic came for many writers with the death of the student movement. Especially its terrorist outgrowth generated public cries for "law and order" and the "Radikalenerlass," which could bar former student radicals from government-subsidized positions. This atmosphere encouraged the turn inward and away from more directly political activity and writing.[4] In a decade of economic recession, fears of unemployment and economic insecurity also motivated writers to withdraw from potentially subversive activity to reassess priorities or strategy. One should not claim a total newness for this subjectivity, however, if only because that would overlook the subjectivist component in the political counter-culture of the sixties and the social-political implications of personal self-examination in the seventies. In a review of the short novel (*Erzählung*) *A Sorrow Beyond Dreams*, Reinhard Baumgart comments aptly that Peter Handke, who unswervingly maintains his subjectivity, brings forth more reliable objective material than those whose political writing is a reflex of confused subjectivity.[5] His introspective novel can thus well be analyzed for its social and political implications. Still,

---

3.   Heinz Ludwig Arnold, "Gespräch mit Günter Grass," *Text und Kritik* 1/1a (October, 1971), p. 3.

4.   Helmut Kreuzer, "Neue Subjektivität. Zur Literatur der siebziger Jahre in der Bundesrepublik Deutschland," in *Deutsche Gegenwartsliteratur. Ausgangspositionen und aktuelle Entwicklungen*, ed. Manfred Durzak (Stuttgart: Reclam, 1981), p. 79.

5.   Quoted in Peter Beicken, "'Neue Subjektivität': zur Prosa der siebziger Jahre," in *Deutsche Literatur in der Bundesrepublik seit 1965*, ed. P. M. Lützeler and Egon Schwarz (Königstein/Ts.: Athenäum, 1980), p. 168.

few studies have ventured observations about the new subjectivity as a response to the political past. Most of these writers evince little direct interest in Nazism partly because they are too young to have felt much of its direct impact. Handke, who was born in 1942, reveals, however, in *A Sorrow Beyond Dreams* how that oppressive authoritarian past helped to rouse an intense desire to free subjectivity from imposed conventions. [6]

Though Uwe Johnson's *Anniversaries* is not a work of new subjectivity, it exemplifies a related tendency of novels in this decade toward the autobiographical. Autobiography and autobiographical novels flourished in West Germany during the seventies, even amongst writers of older generations: Frisch, Grass, and Lind, for example. This form integrates the documentary's claim to authenticity, so important in the sixties, with introspection about one's self, the hallmark of the seventies. Autobiographical writing which necessarily includes experiences of the Third Reich encourages unflinching commitment to "telling the truth" about those years, particularly their effect upon one's own individual development. Johnson, who was born in 1934, explores in his autobiographical novel vexing questions of personal identity that are intricately bound up with the Nazi past.

Socio-political developments in the German Democratic Republic fostered revealing literary documentation of the ideologically dominated postwar and construction period, but scarcely any works of permanence on Nazism were produced there until the seventies. [7] The numerous developmental novels (*Entwicklungsromane*) that appeared into the mid-sixties are full of black and white stereotypes: the other Germans were the Nazis, not anyone recognizable in the German Democratic Republic, as if modes of behavior that

---

6.   At least one other work of new subjectivity, Róland Lang's *Die Mansarde* (1979), delineates explicitly a personal struggle for liberation from the authoritarian world of the father.

7.   Frank Trommler, "Zur aktuellen Situation der DDR-Literatur," in *Deutsche Gegenwartsliteratur. Ausgangspositionen und aktuelle Entwicklungen*, ed. Manfred Durzak (Stuttgart: Reclam, 1981), pp. 579, 585.

predisposed Germans psychologically and intellectually to fascism had suddenly been eradicated under socialism.[8] Christa Wolf, who was born in 1929, cannot reconcile her childhood experiences with the officially sanctioned portraits. She cautiously expressed her concern about this didactic literature: "It disturbs me a little that many of our books about this time end with heroes who quickly transform themselves, with heroes who actually already during fascism come to quite significant and appropriate insights, politically and humanly."[9]

Such model heroes in the prescribed socialist realist mode, whom many saw as necessary during the construction of a new state, were less needed as the GDR passed into its consolidation phase in the mid-sixties. In this period, economic progress and the security of an independent state identity made possible a realism more socially critical and aesthetically self-reflexive: a literature of individual experience. When writers could compare their own erstwhile hopes with contemporary realities, a greater interest in developments of the past ensued. In addition, the completion of the construction phase shifted the major focus of discussion from the future, allowing more assessment of the past.[10] These cultural developments thus facilitated the personally introspective reckoning with the Nazi past that Wolf's *Patterns of Childhood* represents. That this cultural thaw is hesitant and intermittent, however, is suggested not only by critical reactions in the GDR to Wolf's book, but also by the expatriation of the dissident folk singer and poet Wolf Biermann in 1976. But then, Wolf's work was still published after her protest against Biermann's expulsion.

Handke's *A Sorrow Beyond Dreams*, Johnson's *Anniversaries*, and Wolf's *Patterns of Childhood* are highly autobiographical and introspective confrontations with the Nazi past that emerged out of the differing cultural backgrounds in West and East Germany. The

---

8.   Ibid., pp. 582-583.

9.   "Diskussion mit Christa Wolf," *Sinn und Form* vol. 28, no. 4 (1976), p. 861.

10.   Trommler, pp. 579, 580, 585.

subjects of the preceding three chapters are useful in examining the impact of Nazism on these works. In their continued confrontation with the Third Reich, the three writers scrutinize how the middle- and lower-middle-class milieu, the aesthetic manipulation of politics, and ideological deceptions leave imprints on an individual's attitudes and behavior. While novels of the seventies still include broad historical panoramas like Walter Kempowski's *Tadellöser & Wolff* (1971), a stronger trend is the individual, subjective outlook on the Nazi past, as seen in the novels of Handke, Wolf, and Johnson. As Wolf explains, the question is no longer "How could that happen?" but "How have we become what we are?" [11] The earlier novels of the epoch tried to answer the first question; let us now examine the three later works' answers to the second.

All three writers depict their literary personae studying the lower-middle- and middle-class milieu to discover "how they have become who they are." Whereas such focus on social context is not surprising in a writer of Wolf's ideological persuasions or Johnson's neorealist style, Handke, in his relentless pursuit of his own subjectivity, usually in his other works omits the mediating influence of society on his subjective consciousness. Yet his concentration in *A Sorrow Beyond Dreams* on the lower-middle-class milieu, which discouraged his mother from developing a strong self, discloses significant sources of Handke's subjectivism. His effort here to come to grips with his mother's "unhappiness without a wish" (the literal translation of the German title) attests ultimately to the negative formative influence of this environment on him.

Handke portrays the behavior and psychological development of his mother's family members as tied to socio-economic circumstances of the petite bourgeoisie. Generations of forefathers without possessions engender in the small property owner, Handke's grandfather, the understandable drive to survive by the only apparent means possible: saving. After the inflation of the twenties wipes out previous savings, he begins to save money again,

---

11. "Diskussion mit Christa Wolf," p. 876.

especially by stifling his own needs. (WU, 14-15)[12] This common plight of the petite bourgeoisie fosters habitual self-denial. To be born a female in such circumstances nearly guaranteed suppression of self to others' demands and conventions. (WU, 17) Handke's mother's lack of a sense of self-worth helps to explain her attraction to Nazism: "She had always wanted to be proud of something; because now everything that one did was somehow important, she became really proud, not of something specific, but generally proud, as an attitude and as expression of a finally attained experience of life." (WU, 24)

The kind of oppression his mother suffered is reflected in her milieu's language: the stagnant idiom of the convention-bound petite bourgeoisie. Significantly often it is literature by foreign writers, like Dostoevsky and Faulkner, which helps her later in life to express her genuine experience. Only by removing herself mentally from her native milieu can she temporarily free herself from confining codes to discover functions of language that have meaning to her personally. [13] The implicit criterion for individuality here is the ability to speak about oneself--to be able to assert "that's me." A minimal self-awareness at age fifty-one, however, can only bring the recognition of her life as the process that her son outlines: "She was; she became; she became nothing." (WU, 44) She commits suicide.

Although grappling with his own childhood is not the central aim of the story, Handke's attempt to come to grips with his mother's identity, or lack of it, calls his own into question. Her environment is after all in many ways also his; he is threatened

---

12.   Such notes in parentheses refer to the following editions of the works:
      Wunschloses Unglück (Salzburg, 1974), abbreviated WU
      Jahrestage (Frankfurt am Main, 1970-1973), abbreviated Jt
      Kindheitsmuster (Darmstadt, 1981), abbreviated Km
      All translations are my own.

13.   Cecile C. Zorach, "Freedom and remembrance: the language of biography in Peter Handke's *Wunschloses Unglück*," *German Quarterly* 52, (1979), pp. 490 & 492.

with her fate. The intense anxiety aroused by her death gives him
dreams in which "her feelings become so substantial that I experience them as a *Doppelgänger* and am identical with them." (WU, 48)
Ultimately he confronts her wordless despair, which can only be
overcome through suicide, with wordless anxiety, to which he
finally yields with "Later I will write about all this more exactly."
(WU, 105) [14] In recognizing his own momentary speechlessness and
his identification with his mother, he confronts the long-lasting
effects of her environment upon him. Handke's struggle for
authentic language to express his subjective experience is a battle
to free himself from the language of the convention-bound petite
bourgeoisie. Handke thus responds not so much to Nazism itself
here, but to the lack of genuine individuality in this milieu that the
Nazis so exploited.

A sign of the protagonist's unhappiness is the typical quality
of her life. Thus the writer-narrator not only imitates the
nineteenth-century realist style which portrays the typical (in
Lukács's sense), but also reflects upon that style in order to distance the reader from an outdated consciousness. This alienated
point of view shows how anachronistic the portrayed attitudes and
milieu have become. [15] The critical perspective on traditional realism that Grass and Mann achieve through parody Handke accom-
plishes through interspersed commentary on that style and the
social circumstances upon which it rests.

Like Handke, Wolf analyzes the ways in which her petit bourgeois family denied or could not articulate threatening, "inappropri-
ate" emotions. Subjecting snatches of memories from her childhood
to scrupulous scrutiny, she traces the growing split in her personality from the denial of feelings that began in her youth before the
Third Reich. Unlike Handke's mother, Wolf's protagonist possesses
throughout a remnant of her personal integrity to fall back upon,

---

14. Ursula Love, "'Als sei ich . . . ihr geschundenes Herz': Identifizierung und nega-
      tive Kreativität in Peter Handkes Erzählung *Wunschloses Unglück,*" *Seminar* 17,
      (1981), pp. 142 & 144.

15. Ibid., p. 137.

represented as the "du" of her inner dialogues. Nelly, however, the child described in the more distant third person, behaves according to parental and societal expectations. From the earliest instances of sibling rivalry, which Nelly's mother consistently misinterprets as Nelly's devotion to her younger brother, Nelly learns to enjoy unearned praise. (Km, 23-24) She will be ripe for similar denial of her real feelings to win the approval of her Nazi teacher, Juliane Strauch, and other local Nazi leaders. (Km, 178, 203, 210) Wolf laments the countless moments when her parents could barely speak about anything disturbing which appeared to be outside their control, from disastrous war crimes to her mother's miscarriage. (Km, 174-176) Like Handke's petit bourgeois family, these small shopkeepers concentrated instead on their struggle to survive. To protect the future generation from such verbal evasions, Wolf's narrator carefully elicits and answers her daughter's questions, instead of suppressing what children "should not hear."

Narrated in traditional realist style, the numerous vignettes out of Nelly's early life represent typical experiences, but the repeated interruptions of the author-narrator's "ich" distance us from that alienated third person perspective. From the beginning, we try to understand how the present person could have been the earlier one, the "ich" the "sie." In search of a subjectively genuine mode of narration, both Wolf and Handke react against the adapted language and behavior of their petit bourgeois families, which contributed to the strength of Nazism.

Johnson's *Anniversaries* rounds out our image of the *Mittelstand* developed here, not only because it presents members of the stratum higher in wealth and status (the provincial businessman's family Papenbrock), but also because it concentrates on moral decisions of involvement and thus points to potential resistance to Nazism, reminding us that *Mittelstand* support of Hitler was not monolithic. (Böll's "lambs" also express their moral protest against the Nazis.) In making decisions about where to live, the characters of this novel reveal a complex plurality of motives, partially anchored, to be sure, in their *Stand*, but not reducible to it.

The narrator's mother, Lisbeth Cresspahl, was sheltered in Mecklenburg by her solid middle-class family. She thus associates unemployment and poverty with England, which she comes to dislike, especially as she begins there her marriage of downward mobility to a carpenter. (Jt, 141-145, 148) Provincial attitudes developed in the small town of Jerichow also motivate her unease as a foreigner in an English urban environment where she no longer knows who lives behind each curtain. Once she forces her husband to return to Nazi Germany, however, her Christian scruples about Nazi anti-Semitism torture her, though she is unable to translate these religious convictions into useful political action. The contradictions in her character result from the contrast of values represented by her middle-class parents: her mother's religious principles and her father's unscrupulous opportunism. [16]

Foreseeing the coming war, her husband Heinrich would prefer to stay in England, but he follows his love back to Germany in 1933, not least of all out of his material desire for a house given them there. Once in Jerichow, he can ignore his principles as a one-time Social Democrat for the sake of his family's political and economic security: he applies for membership in the NSDAP. (Jt, 418) Even his war-time espionage for the British may stem from economic more than moral or political concerns (his motives are left ambiguous in the novel). Like the family of Wolf's book (they too were originally Social Democrats), Heinrich Cresspahl needs a stable and secure household, and this need enlarges his capacity for self-delusion: he talks himself into building a life in Nazi Germany, even though he perceives clearly enough the evils of that regime. The religious and political qualms that Lisbeth and Heinrich exhibit, however, reflect the two major sources of the active resistance to Hitler.

Their daughter Gesine, the narrator of the novel, studies their middle-class milieu in order to learn the truth about her family and herself. Yet she reveals a similar capacity for self-delusion.

16. Leslie L. Miller, "Uwe Johnson's *Jahrestage*: The Choice of Alternatives," *Seminar* vol. 10, no. 1 (1974), p. 60.

However opposed she is, for example, to the Vietnam War, her considerations of familial economic security curb her impulses to participate in demonstrations against it. In assuming she can thus go her own way, she simulates the anachronistic individualism of the *Mittelstand* that would only be appropriate if they could as individuals actually control their fate. Indeed, Gesine flees often in her memories to Heinrich Cresspahl's seemingly unalienated artisan existence and appears to seek refuge there from the disinfected, neon-lit world of her New York employment. [17] Her anti-modern nostalgia for the provincial idyll recalls the attitudes of Böll's *Kleinbürger*. They too could voice *Anniversaries'* main theme: "Where is the moral Switzerland that we can emigrate to?" (Jt, 382)

Whereas Johnson's other novels have been more avant-grade, *Anniversaries* comes close to the neorealism of the more traditional Böll. Like Böll, Johnson does not parody or reflect directly upon his own modified nineteenth-century style to suggest the anachronism of the style or the character's consciousness. Unlike Handke, who clearly stamps his mother's outlook as rooted in the nineteenth century, Johnson does not intend to portray Gesine's consciousness as out-dated. Although on one level the narration suggests a modern perspective, particularly in the insertion of documentary material from the sixties in New York, even these interruptions grow periodically less frequent. By 1933 in the story, for example, the longer passages on Jerichow absorb the reader more in the old-fashioned fictive world.

Just as they examine the influence of the middle-class milieu on the individual psyche, all three writers scrutinize Nazi aestheticization of politics for its immediate personal effects. Wolf and Handke examine the psychological scars; Johnson looks at the parallel creation of new ones. Although Handke, Wolf and Johnson

---

17. Bernd Neumann, *Utopie und Mimesis. Zum Verhältnis von Aesthetik, Gesellschaftsphilosophie und Politik in den Romanen Uwe Johnsons* (Kronberg: Athenäum, 1978), pp. 294, 296. We cannot, of course, know what the fourth volume will bring.

do not portray artists with counter-aesthetics, their narrators are all writers themselves, and as such can be expected to have aesthetic responses to the Nazi art of politics.

Handke reviews the effects of Nazi propaganda on his mother as well as himself. Her life takes on the new existential rhythm of the thirties: the repetition of new communal rituals lends festive significance to the most automatic and boring rural work. Communal bonds and a sense of pride bolster weak egos. (WU, 23-24) During the war Nazi propaganda has a decidedly different impact upon the mother than upon her young son, who was born in 1942. For the mother, the "war--victory announcements introduced by portentous music, pouring from the 'people's radio sets,' which gleamed mysteriously in dimly lit 'holy corners'--further enhanced a sense of self, because it 'increased the uncertainty of all cir- cumstances' (Clausewitz) and made the day-to-day happenings that had formerly been taken for granted seem excitingly fortuitous." (WU, 26) For the son, this experience of the war is a "childhood nightmare that would color his whole emotional development." (WU, 26-27) The victory announcements with imposing music impinge upon the child's ears, and the radio set in the sanctified corner gleams mysteriously at him. Such sensual bombardment at a sensi- tive age could help to explain Handke's later rejection of externally imposed aesthetic and social experiences.

Wolf too records the sense of self-importance created by com- munal festivities: "An elevated existence stood then before her." (Km, 177) Nelly leaves her first *Heimabend* treasuring a hitherto unknown feeling of comradeship, even though the evening of sing- ing simple songs also annoys her. Characteristically, Nelly strives repeatedly to overcome her inner resistance in order to become the admirable comrade the group leader expects her to be. (Km, 176- 177) Wolf's concentrated pursuit of her own subjectivity partly stems, like Handke's, from an aversion to Nazi aesthetic manipula- tion of individuals in mass politics: "Remaining is: an oversensi- tivity to mass exercises, roaring sport stadiums, halls clapping in time." (Km, 249)

Johnson first looks at the aestheticization of politics during his portrayal of the war years, especially when Gesine is propagandized at school. Gesine recalls the classroom wall in front of her where they had painted "in fat brown Gothic lettering":

You are the Germany of the future
and we want therefore
that you are to be
as this Germay of the future
one day should and must be. A. H. (Jt, 934)

The imposing position and lettering corresponded to the weighty message, which outweighed any other thinking: Gesine could not concentrate on her math lessons. As a child still, she contemplated the hypnotic rhythm of the verses she had learned at school, irritated that they returned to her mind unwished and without her believing in them. (Jt, 859) Unlike Handke and Wolf, Johnson stresses less the aftereffects of Nazi propaganda, however, and more the historical repetitions of school propaganda itself. He describes the Russian versions that Gesine received in 1947 (Jt, 1331) and the American lessons about the Vietnam War that Marie gets in 1967. (Jt, 312-313) He thus emphasizes the apparently unavoidable repetitions of history, no matter the differences in time, place, or ideology.

A postwar suspicion of ideology, evident in Grass and Böll, continues in these later works. Like Grass and Böll, all three writers study the confused ideological consciousness of their characters, but only Wolf and Handke expose that consciousness with open works of art. Instead of laying open ideological delusions for readers to examine from their own perspectives, Johnson describes them from Gesine's point of view. Her form of skepticism is then sealed and delivered as the guiding perspective; paradoxically, readers are not encouraged to develop their own skeptical points of view.

The highly autobiographical quality of all three works of the seventies encourages an anti-ideological orientation of the reader. Out of his own mistrust of ideologies, Grass created an unreliable narrator; perhaps even more skeptical, Wolf, Handke, and Johnson construct writer-narrators who are unsure of their knowledge and authority, who when narrating an episode find their own motives for its portrayal suspect. Such self-scrutiny moves beyond the self-reflexive gestures which have become nearly traditional in the modern novel: the autobiographical works of the seventies tend to differing degrees to dissolve the boundaries between author and narrator. They thus defy what has long been a dogma of literary criticism: that writer and narrator are distinct and not to be confused. [18] Narrators who are separate, full-fledged beings in their own right implicitly assert their authority over the story they tell (unless their truthfulness is deliberately undermined, as with Grass's Oskar) and carry the assurance that the story itself is worth telling. Authors who intrude, however, into their narrators and stories seem to have lost faith in the power of the story itself. Without the narrative personae who offer counsel through storytelling, authors lose their privileged voices. Without the aura of higher authority, such modest narratives are more open to reader inspection for their degrees of truth. Wolf's and Handke's writer-narrators more closely exemplify this phenomenon than Johnson's Gesine who, although an autobiographical figure, remains a separate fictive narrator. In this way too Johnson's work more nearly approximates the enclosed totality of the traditional novel.

Lent the fictive aura of higher authority, Gesine relates tales of Jerichow to her daughter and thus often resembles the story-teller of the old oral tradition. Marie's efforts to call Gesine's versions into question are repeatedly frustrated, showing that Gesine is the sole informed, if not all-knowing, narrator. [19] Her attempts to understand her family guide the reader's; Gesine pieces together for us the various socio-economic and psychological explanations for her parents' self-deluded behavior during the Third Reich. Her narrative of this enclosed world in Jerichow recalls the traditional novel:

---

18. Rainer Nägele, "Geschichten und Geschichte. Reflexionen zum westdeutschen Roman seit 1965," in *Deutsche Gegenwartsliteratur. Ausgangspositionen und aktuelle Entwicklungen*, ed. Manfred Durzak (Stuttgart: Reclam, 1981), p. 238.

19. Neumann, p. 304.

Anniversaries has often been compared with the nineteenth-century realist family novel, though Johnson's adaptation is psychologically enriched. [20]

Episodes from the past do not make up the entire novel. Gesine's present meditative life during the sixties in New York is supplemented by excerpts from her newspaper reading, which provide a grand summation of current world events. Similar to Mann's montage and quotations, these résumés and quotations from the *New York Times* augment the reality of the fictive characters; indeed, the constant intermittent newspaper reports come almost to dominate the narrative, so that the experiences, thoughts, and feelings of Gesine read like reports also. [21] Thus the montage technique enlarges and brings up to date the nonetheless enclosed world of the novel. Johnson himself said a novel is "just a world of its own," and he implicitly justified the large size of *Anniversaries* when he argued in a 1973 lecture: "There must be room for more things than go into a television screen." [22] In his desire for epic totality today, he defends the novel against the mass media, but he does so partly by including the mass media.

Indeed, Johnson often reproduces as inevitable an overwhelming experience of modern urban life: the numbing overload of detailed information and sensory impressions. Attempts at totality require discriminate selection of significant details, however; Johnson's voluminous work seems sometimes like an endless sum of too many details. [23] Much of its realism outside of the Jerichow episodes consists of Gesine's attentive reception and reflection of the news and related general facts. Her sponge-like consciousness absorbs and reproduces information; [24] she then intersperses the

---

20.   Mark Boulby, *Uwe Johnson* (New York: Ungar, 1974), p. 102.

21.   Heinrich Vormweg, "Uwe Johnson. Bestandsaufnahmen vom Lauf der Welt," in *Zeitkritische Romane des 20. Jahrhunderts: Die Gesellschaft in der Kritik der deutschen Literatur*, ed. Hans Wagener (Stuttgart: Reclam, 1975), p. 375.

22.   Quoted in Neumann, p. 305.

23.   Durzak, p. 461.

24.   Ibid., pp. 476-477; Vormweg, p. 377.

records with her own reflections. Although the passages of her inner dialogue and moral self-scrutiny resemble the psychological realism so prevalent in Handke and Wolf, here a mood of resignation to external events prevails. Such "storytelling" appears ultimately to counsel a passive, or at best contemplative and melancholy, attitude toward events.

The reflective narrative perspective that encloses the novel's fictive world seems to echo the balanced "objectivity" of the frequently quoted *New York Times*. Like the newspaper, Gesine seems to disclaim any ideological bias; she refuses to "take sides." As Bernd Neumann has remarked (significantly in Goethean phraseology); *Anniversaries'* kind of totality suggests that in journalistic reflection we have life. Gesine's apparent aim at "objectivity" orders all views and events in a way which neutralizes them. Reports of war crimes in Vietnam, for instance, are placed adjacent to those on Soviet trials of writers, as though reference to the latter exculpates the heinousness of the former. Thus an indecisive "on-the-one-hand" and "on-the-other-hand" gives an impression of breadth and epic totality. Of course it is possible to show injustice in both the capitalist and communist worlds. But Gesine's skepticism appears to arise from a political resignation that "seems to have unlearned any mode of partisanship in the face of the complexities and inhuman mechanics of 'political physics.'" [25] Such views inhibit rather than encourage action.

As noted earlier, Gesine, like her parents, can collude with political powers she objects to for the sake of her family's economic security. No matter how clearly both generations see through the prevailing ideologies of their times, they tend to fall back upon an out-dated individualism which hinders them from acting effectively. Gesine supports herself and her daughter, for example, with a job at a bank whose foreign transactions hurt Czechoslovakia, the nation to which she may next emigrate. Disappointed in her efforts to settle in a country which does not compromise her moral integrity, she retreats into private life. In her seclusion, she

---

25. Neumann, p. 294.

watches as present events recall atrocities of the past: Vietnam is seen as a kind of anniversary of World War II. Whereas this exaggerated parallel was often developed in the sixties to incite energetic action against the Vietnam War, Johnson's apparent embrace of Gesine's political understanding makes all such efforts seem futile. His derivation of her consciousness from that of her parents (who are shrewd, but often demoralized) suggests, in effect, that these "anniversaries" are unavoidable. The next generation also offers no great hope: Marie's growing capacity to make compromises and criticize politics could just as well lead her to repeat her mother's mistakes as to avoid them.[26] Johnson's apparent moral outrage is coupled with resigned acceptance of a repetition of history and thus recalls the uncomfortable sense of paralysis conveyed by Böll.

Handke carries the postwar suspicion of ideology a giant step further than Böll, Grass or Johnson. He repeatedly tries to destroy any definitive ideological views through constantly new literary means: "I expect literature to crush all world-views which appear conclusive."[27] In *A Sorrow Beyond Dreams* he targets both the underdeveloped consciousness of his mother, who sought in Nazism a sense of self, and the nineteenth-century creed of realism appropriate to the typical selfless episodes of her existence.

Handke even uses literary terminology in describing his mother's life and response to Nazism to suggest an intimate connection between ideology and literary style. Since the poverty of a petit bourgeois family has to be a "formally perfect squalor," and the woman bears more responsibility to keep up such appearances, gradually the daily effort to "save face" robs his mother's face of its soul. Handke observes that "formless squalor," however, might have

---

26.   Eva Schiffer, "Politisches Engagement oder Resignation? Weiteres zu Uwe Johnsons *Jahrestagen*," in *Der deutsche Roman und seine historischen und politischen Bedingungen*, ed. Wolfgang Paulsen (Bern: Francke, 1977), pp. 243-244 argues the opposite view.

27.   Peter Handke, "Ich bin ein Bewohner des Elfenbeinturms," *Prosa Gedichte Theaterstücke Hörspiel Aufsätze* (Frankfurt am Main: Suhrkamp, 1969), p. 264.

engendered a shameless "proletarian class consciousness," more appropriate to the social circumstances than the submissive consciousness of the status-seeking petite bourgeoisie. (WU, 61-62) As discussed earlier, Handke describes Nazism as imposing a form and totality of communal relatedness where none existed. (WU, 23-24) He revolts against all manner of prescribed formal perfection in life and literature.

Although his author-narrator considers himself at the beginning of the narrative as a "remembering and formulating machine" who wishes to turn his mother's suicide into a "case," (WU, 10-11) he does not achieve such detachment through writing. He cannot freeze her life in traditional realist expressions. On the contrary, writing about her only intensifies his consciousness of her painful existence. Handke's own mode of realism is to record the process in himself: in sympathetic identification with his mother's silent despair, his narrative finally dissolves into fragments. No viable form succeeds the "everywoman" biography. The unmitigated anguish of the mother, registered by the son in this fragmentary, open ending, can only encourage each reader to secure his or her own self-awareness from the devastation of a prescribed consciousness.

Handke champions an individuality that boldly resists ideological dictates and conventional authorities. His firm stance of individual protest defies the powers that be, unlike the individual resignation of Johnson's characters. Gesine records the struggles of the ideologically opposed world powers, only to withdraw in disappointment; she feels and is powerless, even as she holds out a slim hope for Dubzek's "socialism with a human face." Her resignation leaves the door open to political complicity with unjust authority. In contrast, Handke's narrator projects an articulate and powerful self-awareness, unlike his mother's manipulable state of mind, that makes resistance possible.

Although Wolf had sufficient exposure to Nazi propaganda to be skeptical of ideological doctrines in the GDR, the individuality she espouses is not the radical iconoclasm of Handke. Not questioning basic tenets and ideals of Marxist ideology, Wolf writes about the difficulty of saying "I myself" to her society and the hope of being able to do so. In *Patterns of Childhood* she therefore presents an individual experience of Nazism considered atypical in a country which has until recently denied much of its brown past; she sees fascism as unrecognized "radioactive material," with long-lasting effects upon the inhabitants of the contaminated environment. Although one may try to discuss fascism as a "phenomenon" separate from one's self or as the past of "the others," one has, in Wolf's view, a duty to explain it to the younger generation from a personally responsible perspective. Assuming as she does that the socio-economic roots of fascism are already understood, she concentrates more on its "radioactive" effects. [28]

Wolf arranges her work to enable the reader to reconstruct the "structure of my generation's relationships to the past." [29] The multi-level narration aims to uncover the remaining imprints of ideological deceptions upon an individual's attitudes and behavior. The reader pieces together Nelly's experiences of historical events from 1931 to 1947, the narrator's journey back to her now Polish home town in 1971, and the writing difficulties and concurrent world events at the time the work was written: 1972-1975. "Narrative levels," however, does not aptly describe these interwoven experiences over time because the term separates past and present in a far too discrete and linear manner. To represent the varied and "unbelievably entangled matting" (Km, 252) of past and present experience, the author-narrator intertwines strands of narrative sometimes with exact and clean boundaries, sometimes with an undifferentiated change in mid-sentence. Nowhere does Wolf relax long enough into the conjuring, "whispering imperfect" for such past episodes to become as independent as the more closed worlds of *Anniversaries*; Wolf more frequently interrupts and curbs the reader's absorption in linear plot development. Whereas Gesine mediates for us between clearly separate levels, which occasionally appear so separate as to have no obvious connections, Wolf's

---

28.   Hans Kaufmann, "Gespräch mit Christa Wolf," *Weimarer Beiträge* vol. 20, no. 6 (1974), pp. 99 & 103.

29.   Ibid., p. 103.

narrator forces us to work alongside her to untangle her subjective wicker-work. In both Wolf's and Johnsons's novels, the juxtaposition of past and present suggests the awful repetitions of history. While Gesine passes along to the reader her resignation, however, Wolf's narrator offers hope in a critically subjective vision of experience.

From the beginning of *Patterns of Childhood*, the writer-narrator draws the reader's attention to the highly reflective mode of her narrative by commenting on its significance, success, and alternative directions. Although these commentaries also contain pieces of stories, it is not the tales themselves but the narrator's reflective mode that dominates and directs the narrative. The reader observes her, like Handke's narrator, choosing her words ever so carefully to come closer to a subjectively perceived truth. She then scrutinizes and reviews each individual interpretation of large-scale history. As for Handke, writing for Wolf is not a process to describe an experience, but one which first produces experience in the act of writing. Whereas Johnson reports that he begins to write a story after he has thought it through from beginning to end,[30] Handke and Wolf cannot predict beforehand the direction their writing will take them. Perception of the new and different reality is the "subjective authenticity" Wolf aspires to. Seeing finished objects of art reduced to commodities, she justifies this open, subjective form as appropriate to socialist ideals: a writer is presumptuous to expect readers to be changed by reading a book if the process of writing it involved no change for the writer and was settled from the outset. Furthermore, Wolf maintains that her reflective style was especially necessary to approach a more adequate confrontation with the Nazi past;[31] such searching, personal scrutiny of her past had been impossible in the *Moscow Novella*, when she followed the dictates of socialist realism. The subject of Nazism thus necessitates the form: in order to pierce through her

---

30.   Bienek-Interview, quoted in *Über Uwe Johnson*, ed. Reinhard Baumgart (Frankfurt am Main: Suhrkamp, 1970), p. 172.

31.   Kaufmann, pp. 94-95, 99.

remaining ideological delusions, Wolf breaks the boundaries of the novel and writes a novel-essay.

Realizing her aim of subjective authenticity, Wolf seeks to discover through writing how much she knew as a child about the Nazi program of genocide, the most heinous effect of its world-view. Suppression and repression of knowledge about the death camps enabled many Nazi fellow-travelers like the Jordans to continue their vague faith in a better life under Hitler. A camp survivor confronts the evasions of that deluded consciousness when he asks, in what becomes a leitmotif of the book, "Where have you been all these years?" Gradually the author-narrator puts together bits of overheard conversation about "Russians dying like flies" in the nearby camp and recalls Nelly's efforts at the time to act deaf and ignorant as expected: she became a "model" child. ("Models of childhood" is an ironic implicit meaning of *Kindheitsmuster*.) Wolf asks about this process of cumulative amnesia in her generation and the aftereffects: "How many encapsulated caverns can a memory accept until it must stop functioning? How much energy and what kind of energy must it constantly produce to repeatedly reinforce these capsules whose walls might over time become rotten and cracked?" (Km, 69) Such intermittent images capture the processes of repression and adaptation in her consciousness that the writer-narrator tries with uncompromising honesty to reveal.

To confront the social amnesia on Nazism, writers often utilize documentary, objective materials, in ways which suggest their differing views on how literature can best make people remember. In a passage directly following the above quotation, Wolf's narrator defends literature against the claim that documents are superior and make literature superfluous. Unlike literature, which recreates human thought processes, documents cannot break open the walls to these "closed rooms in our memories." Yet Wolf, like Johnson, also studies documents: she reads in the museum old hometown newspapers from her youth. Both writers thus amplify the documentary aspect of their works even beyond that inherent to autobiography. Characteristically, Wolf, however, researches these documents out of mistrust of her own memory, to give her another angle on her experience in her unflinching self-examination;

Johnson's Gesine studies old newspapers to provide a coat for the "skeleton" of her narrative (Jt, 144): to augment the veracity of her stories, much in the same way as the *New York Times* functions in the contemporary narrative. In short, Wolf's documents open up further perspectives from which to scrutinize reality en route to a subjective authenticity; Johnson's enhance the reality of his enclosed worlds. In his relatively well-known contemporary novel on Nazism, *Tadellöser & Wolff,* Kempowski strives for a greater sense of objectivity than does Johnson: whereas Gesine still paints some of her pictures from the past in idyllic hues, Kempowski's narrative of the same period assumes tones of a sociological inventory. Both Kempowski and Johnson in their voluminous novels aspire to a greater totality than does Wolf; she aims not for a full objective picture of the Nazi era or of the present, but a productive confrontation with objective reality from a critical, subjective perspective.

Critics on both sides of the Berlin Wall have faulted Wolf for the ways in which she links the Nazi period to the present. Ranging from Mayer's vituperative attack in the West [32] to Auer's explosion in the East, [33] reviewers have argued that she includes too little of the totalitarian present in the Soviet bloc countries, or that she criticizes the GDR from a politically incorrect, "abstract," and "subjective" outlook. If she has already incensed East German critics, it seems hardly realistic for those in the West to demand a more direct indictment of her own country. Any reader in the GDR would understand clearly enough Wolf's references such as that to Mühsam's widow in a Stalinist camp or that to the suicide of Lenka's teacher, who could not cultivate the "virtues" of suppression and adaptation still required thirty years after Nazism. [34] She does detail more of the horrors of Nazism than of Stalinism, but this focus is, after all, her subject: the formative patterns of her

---

32.   Hans Mayer, "Der Mut zur Unaufrichtigkeit," *Der Spiegel* (March 17, 1977).

33.   Annemarie Auer, "Gegenerinnerung. Über Christa Wolf: 'Kindheitsmuster,'" *Sinn und Form* 4 (1977), pp. 847-878.

34.   Roland Wiegenstein, "Kassandra hat viele Gesichter," *Merkur* vol. 31, no. 10 (October, 1977), p. 933.

childhood. Furthermore, the basic narrative structure, the break-down of Wolf's authorial personality into three parts, demonstrates her conviction that her generation will continue to live with dam-aged psyches in a state of self-alienation until they too confront the Nazi legacy in their totalitarian past. [35]

In contrast, Wolf's contemporary Hermann Kant avoids the present altogether in *The Stay* (1977), an East German novel fre-quently compared with *Patterns of Childhood*. Although the transformation of Kant's hero from a guilty to a morally sensitive human being is frequently moving and more nuanced than earlier versions of such tales, the novel seems hermetically sealed off from the context of the decade in which it was written, all too simply rounded off and enclosed in form. No such transformation com-pletes *Patterns of Childhood*: the first-person narrator has not fully accommodated the alienated third-person Nelly; the work of mourn-ing the past remains incomplete, left for the reader to continue.

Wolf's open work has nonetheless its formal weaknesses: the text can be disjunctive, unfinished, and indecisive; its simple language sometimes falters and rings flat compared to the poeti-cally rich expressions of Johnson or Handke. Yet the very quality of disjunction, incompletion, and indecision may be a strength when one considers the reality with which Wolf is grappling. The "unbelievably entangled matting" of feelings in the one who was partly ignorant yet implicated in the guilt cannot be accommodated by the routine novel; those entangled feelings, rather, are left undistorted, unprotected, accessible, and unfinished. [36] The work's power seems to confirm Adorno's dictum, cited at the outset of this study: the unspeakable resists the structuring of language and aesthetic form itself. As Wolf reaffirms at the close of her work, she will not allow the "boundaries of the speakable" to limit her. The scrupulous, unsparing self-scrutiny that results has no equal in

---

35.   Neil Jackson and Barbara Saunders, "Christa Wolf's *Kindheitsmuster* - An East German Experiment in political autobiography," *German Life and Letters* 33 (1979/80), pp. 320-321.

36.   Trommler, p. 599.

all other German literature on Nazism. Perhaps Wolf's self-awareness as a woman, and thus an "outsider," helps to fuel her critical perspective on the ideologies of her social environment and thus propels her tireless wrestling for the inner authenticity that defies the limits of the established novel form. Certainly some men share her suspicion of socially prescribed attitudes; the male precursors Wolf identifies are, significantly, writers like Büchner: alienated, critical observers on the fringes of mainstream society.

The narrators of these three works of the seventies study the formation of their own and their parents' identities in a historical context. Both Handke's account of his mother's crushed sense of selfhood, and Wolf's of her split psyche, pause to explore alternative developmental directions and leave open possibilities for change at the end. In contrast, Johnson's Gesine may search for concealed truths, but her fate seems sealed: she will repeat the mistakes of her parents. The determinism of the modernized and yet closed world of Johnson's novel appears to echo *Doctor Faustus*: the large-scale historical cultural development fated since Luther to erupt in fascism becomes the personal-scale family history of individual weakness destined to repeat itself in the future. Thus the two relatively closed novels of our study are similar in their answers to the questions "How could that happen?" and "How have we become who we are?"

The further the Third Reich recedes into history, the more possible it becomes to encapsulate it as simply part of the past. The question "How have we become who we are?" can help to prevent such evasion and thus now supplements well the question of the earlier novels of the epoch, "How could that happen?" By tracing the personal imprints of their own or others' past attitudes and behavior, Johnson, Wolf, and Handke confront readers with a legacy in the present they cannot ignore. Only the open works hold out hope that we can become any different from what we were. But all three of them reveal the personal magnitude of the continuing wound in humanity.

Selected Bibliography

The bibliography lists primary sources first, then secondary sources in three categories: (1) Works on the Individual Authors; (2) Relevant General Literary Criticism; (3) Extra-Literary Works Related to Nazism or the Postwar Period.

PRIMARY SOURCES

Böll, Heinrich. *Aufsätze-Kritiken-Reden*, Vols. 1 and 2. Munich: Deutscher Taschenbuch Verlag, 1969.

_____. *Billard um halb zehn*. Munich: Knaur, 1963.

_____. *Erzählungen-Hörspiele-Aufsätze*. Cologne: Kiepenheuer & Witsch, 1964.

_____. *Frankfurter Vorlesungen (1963-64)*. Munich: Deutscher Taschenbuch Verlag, 1968.

_____. *Neue politische und literarische Schriften*. Cologne: Kiepenheuer & Witsch, 1973.

_____. *Werke*, Vol. 10, ed. Bernd Balzer. Cologne: Kiepenheuer & Witsch, 1978.

Grass, Günter. "Ben and Dieter: A Speech to the Israelis," trans. Helen Mustard, Venable Herndon, and Ursula Molinaro. *New York Review of Books* (June 1, 1967): 18-20.

_____. *Die Blechtrommel.* Frankfurt am Main: Fischer, 1962.

_____. *Über das Selbstverständliche.* Berlin: Deutscher Taschen-buch Verlag, 1965.

_____. *Über meinen Lehrer Döblin und andere Vorträge.* Berlin: Literarisches Colloquium, 1968.

Handke, Peter. "Ich bin ein Bewohner des Elfenbeinturms." In *Prosa Gedichte Theaterstücke Hörspiel Aufsätze.* Frankfurt am Main: Suhrkamp, 1969.

_____. *Wunschloses Unglück.* Salzburg: Suhrkamp, 1974.

Johnson, Uwe. *Jahrestage,* Vols. 1-3. Frankfurt am Main: Suhrkamp, 1970-73.

Mann, Thomas. *Doktor Faustus.* Frankfurt am Main: Fischer, 1947.

_____. *Gesammelte Werke,* Vols. 9, 10, 11 and 12. Oldenburg: Fischer, 1960.

_____. *Schriften zur Politik.* Frankfurt am Main: Fischer, 1970.

_____. *Sorge um Deutschland.* Frankfurt am Main: Fischer, 1957.

_____. *Tagebücher,* ed. Peter de Mendelssohn. 4 vols. (1933-1934, 1935-1936, 1937-1939, 1940-1943). Frankfurt am Main: Fischer, 1977-1982.

Wolf, Christa. *Kindheitsmuster* (first published in GDR in 1976). Darmstadt: Luchterhand, 1981.

_____. *Lesen und Schreiben. Aufsätze und Prosastücke.* Darmstadt: Luchterhand, 1972.

"Diskussion mit Christa Wolf," *Sinn und Form* vol. 28, no. 4 (1976): 861-888.

SECONDARY SOURCES

1. Works on the Individual Authors

Abbe, Derek van. "Metamorphoses of 'Unbewältigte Vergangenheit' in *Die Blechtrommel*," *German Life and Letters* 23 (1969/70): 152-160.

Adorno, Theodor. "Zu einem Porträt Thomas Manns." In *Noten zur Literatur III*. Frankfurt am Main: Suhrkamp, 1965.

Apter, T. E. *Thomas Mann: The Devil's Advocate*. London: Macmillan, 1978.

Arnold, Heinz Ludwig. "Gespräch mit Günter Grass," *Text und Kritik* 1/1a (October, 1971): 1-26.

_____. *Im Gespräch: Böll*. Munich: Richard Boorberg, 1971.

_____, ed. *Text und Kritik* 33 (Heinrich Böll issue). Munich: Richard Boorberg, 1972.

Auer, Annemarie. "Gegenerinnerung. Über Christa Wolf: 'Kindheitsmuster,'" *Sinn und Form* 4 (1977): 847-878.

Bahr, Ehrhard. "Metaphysische Zeitdiagnose: Kasack, Langgässer und Thomas Mann." In *Gegenwartsliteratur und Drittes Reich*, ed. Hans Wagener. Stuttgart: Reclam, 1977.

Baker, Donna (a.k.a. Donna Reed). "Nazism and the Petit Bourgeois Protagonist: The Novels of Grass, Böll, and Mann," *New German Critique* 5 (Spring 1975): 77-105.

Bance, A. F. "The enigma of Oskar in Grass's *Blechtrommel*," *Seminar* vol. 3, no. 2 (Fall, 1967): 147-156.

Barbu, Eugen, and Deleanu, Adrei Ion. "Serenus Zeitblom." In *Sinn und Form Sonderheft zu Thomas Mann.* Berlin: Rütten & Loening, 1965, pp. 134-143.

Baumgart, Reinhard. "Der grosse Bänkelsang," *Neue deutsche Hefte* 65 (December, 1959): 861-63.

_____. *Das Ironische und die Ironie in den Werken Thomas Manns.* Munich: Hanser, 1964.

_____. "Statt eines Nachworts: Johnsons Voraussetzungen." In *Über Uwe Johnson*, ed. Reinhard Baumgart. Frankfurt am Main: Suhrkamp, 1970.

Beckel, Albrecht. *Mensch, Gesellschaft, Kirche bei Heinrich Böll.* Osnabrück: A. Fromm, 1966.

Berendsohn, Walter A. *Thomas Mann, Künstler und Kämpfer in bewegter Zeit.* Lübeck: Max Schmidt-Römhild, 1965.

Bergsten, Gunilla. *Thomas Manns "Doktor Faustus." Untersuchungen zu den Quellen und zur Struktur des Romans.* Stockholm: Svenska Bokförlaget, 1963.

Bernhard, Hans Joachim. *Die Romane Heinrich Bölls. Gesellschaftskritik und Gemeinschaftsutopie.* Berlin: Rütten & Loening, 1970.

Blackmur, R. P. "Parody and Critique: Mann's *Doctor Faustus.*" In *Eleven Essays in the European Novel.* New York: Harcourt, Brace & World, 1964, pp. 97-116.

Blomster, W. V. "The Demonic in History: Thomas Mann and Günter Grass," *Contemporary Literature* 10 (Winter 1969), 1: 75-84.

Boa, Elizabeth. "Günter Grass and the German Gremlin," *German Life and Letters* 23, no. 1 (January, 1970): 144-151.

Bock, Klaus. "Geschichtsbegriff und Geschichtsbild bei Thomas Mann," dissertation, University of Kiel, February 21, 1959.

Boehlich, Walter. "Thomas Manns *Doktor Faustus,*" *Merkur* 2, no. 4 (April, 1948): 588-603.

Bohnen, Klaus. "Argumentationsverfahren und politische Kritik bei Thomas Mann." In *Gedenkschrift für Thomas Mann. 1875-1975,* ed. Rolf Wiecker. Copenhagen: Text & Kontext (1975): 171-191.

Boulby, Mark. *Uwe Johnson.* New York: Ungar, 1974.

Brode, Hanspeter. "Musik und Zeitgeschichte im Roman. Thomas Manns 'Doktor Faustus.'" In *Jahrbuch der Deutschen Schiller-Gesellschaft 1973.* Stuttgart: Kröner, 1974.

_____. "Die Zeitgeschichte in der 'Blechtrommel' von Günter Grass. Entwurf eines textinternen Kommunikationsmodells." In *Günter Grass: Ein Materialienbuch*, ed. Rolf Geissler. Neuwied: Luchterhand, 1976.

_____. *Die Zeitgeschichte im erzählenden Werk von Günter Grass: Versuch einer Deutung der "Blechtrommel" und der "Danziger Trilogie."* Frankfurt am Main: Peter Lang, 1977.

Burns, Robert A. *The Theme of Non-Conformism in the Work of Heinrich Böll.* Coventry: U. of Warwick, 1973.

Butler, E. M. *The Fortunes of Faust.* London: Cambridge University Press, 1952.

Caltvedt, Lester. "Oskar's account of himself: narrative 'guilt' and the relation of fiction to history in *Die Blechtrommel*," *Seminar* vol. 14, no. 4 (1978): 285-294.

Carlsson, Anni. "Das Faustmotiv bei Thomas Mann," *Deutsche Beiträge* 3 (1949): 342-362.

_____. "Der Roman als Anschauungsform der Epoche. Bemerkungen zu Thomas Mann und Günter Grass," *Neue Zürcher Zeitung* (November, 1964).

Dawson, J. S. "Interpretation of Dictatorship in the works of certain modern German authors." Ph.D. dissertation, Universtiy of Toronto, 1963.

Diersen, Inge. *Untersuchungen zu Thomas Mann.* Berlin: Rütten & Loening, 1965.

Diller, Edward. *A Mythic Journey: Günter Grass's "Tin Drum."* Lexington: The University Press of Kentucky, 1974.

"Diskussion zu Thomas Mann," *Sprache im technischen Zeitalter* 5, nos. 17/18 (1966): 70-79.

Dittmann, Ulrich. *Sprachbewusstsein und Redeformen im Werk Thomas Manns.* Stuttgart: Kohlhammer, 1969.

Elliot, John R., Jr. "The Cankered Muse of Günter Grass," *Dimension* 1 (1969): 516-523.

Enderstein, Carl O. "Heinrich Böll und seine Künstlergestalten," *The German Quarterly* 43, no. 4 (November, 1970): 733-748.

Feuerlicht, Ignace. *Thomas Mann.* New York: Twayne, 1968.

Fischer, Ernst. "*Doktor Faustus* und die deutsche Katastrophe." In *Kunst und Menschheit*, pp. 37-97. Vienna: Globus, 1949.

Fischer, Heinz. "Sprachliche Tendenzen bei Heinrich Böll und Günter Grass," *German Quarterly* 40, no. 3 (January, 1967): 372-383.

Freedmann, Ralph. "The narrative worlds of Günter Grass," *Dimension* (1970): 50-63.

Futterknecht, Franz. *Das Dritte Reich im deutschen Roman der Nachkriegszeit. Untersuchungen zur Faschismustheorie und Faschismusbewältigung.* Bonn: Bouvier Verlag, 1976.

Gelley, Alexander. "Art and Reality in *Die Blechtrommel,*" *Forum for Modern Language Studies* 3, 2 (April, 1967): 115-125.

Gerlach, Ingeborg. *Auf der Suche nach der verlorenen Identität. Studien zu Uwe Johnsons "Jahrestagen."* Königstein/Ts.: Scriptor Verlag, 1980.

Golik, I. J. "Die Kälte der Dekadenz. Zur Kritik des Modernismus im Schaffen Thomas Manns," *Weimarer Beiträge* 17, no. 3 (1971): 151-170.

Greif, Hans-Jürgen. *Christa Wolf: "Wie sind wir so geworden wie wir heute sind?"* Bern: Peter Lang, 1978.

Gronicka, André von. *Thomas Mann.* New York: Random House, 1970.

_____. "Thomas Manns *Doktor Faustus,*" *Germanic Review* 23, no. 3 (October, 1948): 206-218.

Grothmann, Wilhelm. "Die Rolle der Religion im Menschenbild Heinrich Bölls," *German Quarterly* 44 (1971): 191-207.

Günter, Eberhard, et. al., eds. *Kritik 77: Rezensionen zur DDR-Literatur.* Halle-Leipzig: Mitteldeutscher Verlag, 1978.

Haase, Horst. "Charakter und Funktion der zentralen Symbolik in Heinrich Bölls Roman *Billard um halb zehn,*" *Weimarer Beiträge* 10, no. 2 (1964): 219-226.

Hage, Volker. "Vom Einsatz und Rückzug des fiktiven Erzählers. *Doktor Faustus* -- ein moderner Roman?" *Text und Kritik* (Thomas Mann issue) (1976): 88-98.

Haiduk, Manfred. "Der Gedanke des antifaschistischen Widerstandes bei Thomas Mann," *Wissenschaftliche Zeitschrift der Universität Rostock* 9 (1960): 53-59.

Hamburger, Käte. "Anachronistische Symbolik: Fragen an Thomas Manns Faustus-Roman." In *Gestaltungsgeschichte und Gesellschaftsgeschichte*, ed. Helmut Kreuzer, pp. 529-553. Stuttgart: Metzler, 1969.

Hamm, Peter, "Verrückte Lehr- und Wanderjahre," *Du* 19, no. 12 (1959): 132-136.

Hatfield, Henry. "Can One Sell One's Soul? The Faust Legend." In *Great Moral Dilemmas in Literature*, ed. Robert M. MacIver, pp. 83-97. New York: Harper, 1956.

_____. "Death in the late works in Thomas Mann," *Germanic Review* 4 (1959): 284-288.

_____. *From "The Magic Mountain": Mann's Later Masterpieces*. Ithaca: Cornell University Press, 1979.

_____. "Günter Grass: The Artist as Satirist." In *The Contemporary Novel in German*, ed. Robert Heitner, pp. 115-134. Austin: University of Texas Press, 1967.

_____. "The Magic Square, Thomas Mann's *Doktor Faustus*," *Euphorion* 62, nos. 3/4 (1968): 415-420.

_____. *Thomas Mann.* New York: Knopf, 1961.

_____. "Two Notes on Thomas Mann's *Doktor Faustus,*" *Modern Language Forum* 34 (1949): 11-17.

_____. "Der Zauberer und die Verzweiflung. Das Alterswerk Thomas Manns," *Wirkendes Wort* 12, no. 2 (1961): 91-102.

_____, ed. *Thomas Mann: A Collection of Critical Essays.* Englewood Cliffs, New Jersey: Prentice-Hall, 1964.

Heller, Erich. *The Ironic German.* Boston: Little, Brown & Co., 1958.

Henning, Margrit. *Die Ich-Form und ihre Funktion in Thomas Manns "Doktor Faustus" und in der deutschen Literatur der Gegenwart.* Tübingen: Niemeyer, 1966.

Henze, Eberhard. "Die Rolle des fiktiven Erzählers bei Thomas Mann," *Neue Rundschau* 76 (1965): 189-201.

Hermsdorf, Klaus. "Aufforderung zur Tat," *Neue Deutsche Literatur* 11 (1960): 144-147.

Hill, Linda. "The Avoidance of Dualism in Heinrich Böll's Novels," *Germanic Review* 56 (1981): 151-156.

Hillmann, Heinz. "Günter Grass's *Blechtrommel.* Beispiel und Überlegungen zum Verfahren der Konfrontation von Literatur und Sozialwissenschaften." In *Der deutsche Roman im zwanzigsten Jahrhundert,* vol. 2, ed. Manfred Brauneck. Bamberg: C. C. Buchners, 1976.

Hoffmann, Leopold. *Heinrich Böll: Einführung in Leben und Werk.* Luxemburg: Sankt Paulus, 1965.

Hollington, Michael. *Günter Grass: The Writer in a Pluralist Society.* London: Marion Boyars, 1980.

Hye, Roberta T. *Uwe Johnsons "Jahrestage": Die Gegenwart als variierende Wiederholung der Vergangenheit.* Bern: Peter Lang, 1978.

Jackson, Neil and Saunders, Barbara. "Christa Wolf's *Kindheitsmuster*: An East German Experiment in Political Autobiography," *German Life and Letters* 33 (1979/80): 319-329.

Jaeckel, Günter. "Die alte und die neue Welt: Das Verhältnis von Mensch und Technik in Heinrich Bölls Roman *Billard um halb zehn*," *Weimarer Beiträge* (1968): 1285-1302.

Jendreiek, Helmut. *Thomas Mann: Der demokratische Roman.* Düsseldorf: Bagel, 1977.

Jendrowiak, Silke. *Günter Grass und die "Hybris" des Kleinbürgers: "Die Blechtrommel" -- Bruch mit der Tradition einer irrationalistischen Kunst und Wirklichkeitsinterpretation.* Heidelberg: Winter, 1979.

_____. "Die sogenannte 'Urtrommel': unerwartete Einblicke in die Genese der *Blechtrommel* von Günter Grass," *Monatshefte* 71(1979): 114-115, 172-186.

Jeziorkowski, Klaus. *Rhythmus und Figur: Zur Technik der epischen Konstruktion in Heinrich Bölls "Der Wegwerfer" und "Billard um halb zehn."* Bad Homberg: Gehlen, 1968.

Just, George. *Darstellung und Appell in der "Blechtrommel" von Günter Grass: Darstellungsaesthetik vs. Wirkungsaesthetik.* Frankfurt am Main: Athenäum, 1972.

Kahler, Erich. *The Orbit of Thomas Mann.* Princeton: Princeton University Press, 1969.

Kaufmann, Fritz. *Thomas Mann: The World as Will and Representation.* Boston: Beacon Press. 1957.

Kaufmann, Hans. "Gespräch mit Christa Wolf," *Weimarer Beiträge* 20, no. 6 (1974): 90-112.

Klussmann, Paul Gerhard. "Thomas Manns *Doktor Faustus* als Zeitroman." In *Thomas-Mann-Symposium, Bochum, 1975,* ed. Paul Gerhard Klussmann and Jörg-Ulrich Fechner. Kastellaun: A. Henn, 1978.

Koopmann, Helmut. "Günter Grass: Der Faschismus als Kleinbürgertum und was daraus wurde." In *Gegenwartsliteratur und Drittes Reich,* ed. Hans Wagener. Stuttgart: Reclam, 1977.

_____. *Thomas Mann: Konstanten seines literarischen Werks.* Göttingen: Vandenhoeck & Ruprecht, 1975.

Lange, Victor. "Thomas Mann: Tradition und Experiment." In *Thomas-Mann-Symposium, Bochum, 1975,* ed. Paul Gerhard Klussmann and Jörg-Ulrich Fechner. Kastellaun: A. Henn, 1978.

Lehnert, Herbert. "Satirische Botschaft an den Leser: Das Ende des Jugendstils." In *Gestaltungsgeschichte und Gesellschaftsgeschichte,* ed. Helmut Kreuzer, pp. 487-515. Stuttgart: Metzler, 1969.

———. *Thomas Mann: Fiktion, Mythos, Religion*. Stuttgart: Kohlhammer, 1965.

Lengning, Werner. *Der Schriftsteller Heinrich Böll*. Munich: Deutscher Taschenbuch Verlag, 1969.

Linder, Christian. *Böll*. Reinbek bei Hamburg: Rowohlt, 1978.

Lindsay, J. M. *Thomas Mann*. Oxford: Basil Blackwell, 1954.

Linn, Marie Louise. "Doppelte Kindheit: Zur Interpretation von Christa Wolfs *Kindheitsmuster*," *Der Deutschunterricht* 30, no. 2 (1978): 52-66.

Loschütz, Gert, ed. *Von Buch zu Buch: Günter Grass in der Kritik*. Neuwied: Luchterhand, 1968.

Love, Ursula, "'Als sei ich . . . ihr *geschundenes Herz*': Identifizierung und negative Kreativität in Peter Handkes Erzählung *Wunschloses Unglück*," *Seminar* 17(1981): 130-146.

Lukács, Georg. *Essays on Thomas Mann*. Trans. Stanley Mitchell. New York: Grossett & Dunlap, 1964.

Lyon, James K. "Words and Music: Thomas Mann's Tone-Poem *Doktor Faustus*," *Western Humanities Review* 13 (1959): 99-102.

Mainka, Jürgen. "Thomas Mann und die Musikphilosophie des XX. Jahrhunderts." In *Gedenkschrift für Thomas Mann, 1875-1975*, ed. Rolf Wiecker. Copenhagen: Text & Kontext (1975): 197-214.

Mander, John. "Variations on a Tin Drum," *Encounter* 19, no. 5 (1962): 77-84.

Mann, Katia. *Meine ungeschriebenen Memoiren*, ed. Elisabeth Plessen and Michael Mann. Frankfurt: Fischer, 1974.

Mann, Michael. "Adrian Leverkühn: Repräsentant oder Antipode?" *Neue Rundschau* 76 (1965): 202-206.

Mason, Ann L. "Günter Grass and the Artist in History," *Contemporary Literature* 14, no. 3 (1973): 347-362.

_____. *The Skeptical Muse: A Study of Günter Grass's Conception of the Artist*. Bern: Herbert Lang, 1974.

Mayer, Hans. "Günter Grass and Thomas Mann: Aspects of the Novel." In *Steppenwolf and Everyman*. Trans. Jack Zipes, pp. 181-199. New York: Thomas Y. Crowell Co., 1971.

_____. "Der Mut zur Unaufrichtigkeit," *Der Spiegel*, March 17, 1977.

_____. *Thomas Mann: Werk und Entwicklung*. Berlin: Volk und Welt, 1950.

Mecklenburg, Norbert. "Faschismus und Alltag in deutscher Gegenwartsprosa: Kempowski und andere." In *Gegenwartsliteratur und Drittes Reich*, ed. Hans Wagener. Stuttgart: Reclam, 1977.

Meyerhoff, Hans. "Thomas Mann's Faust," *Partisan Review* 16 (1949): 93-96.

Michelsen, Peter. "Oskar oder das Monstrum," *Neue Rundschau* 83 (1972): 722-740.

Migner, Karl. "Der getrommelte Protest gegen unsere Welt," *Welt und Wort* 15, no. 7 (1960): 205-207.

Miles, Keith. *Günter Grass*. New York: Barnes & Noble, 1975.

Miller, Leslie L. "Uwe Johnson's *Jahrestage*: The Choice of Alternatives," *Seminar* 10, no. 1 (1974): 50-70.

Mommsen, Katharina. *Gesellschaftskritik bei Fontane und Thomas Mann*. Heidelberg: Lothar Stiehm, 1973.

Motylowa, Tamara. "Die Erneuerung des Realismus." In *Sinn und Form Sonderheft zu Thomas Mann*, pp. 123-133. Berlin: Rütten & Loening, 1965.

Müller-Seidel, Walter. "Sprache und Humanität in Thomas Manns *Doktor Faustus*," *Acta Germanica* 3 (1968): 241-256.

Nägele, Rainer. *Heinrich Böll: Einführung in das Werk und in die Forschung*. Frankfurt am Main: Athenäum Fischer, 1976.

_____. "Heinrich Böll. Die grosse Ordnung und die kleine Anarchie." In *Gegenwartsliteratur und Drittes Reich*, ed. Hans Wagener. Stuttgart: Reclam, 1977.

Neuhaus, Volker. *Günter Grass.* Stuttgart: Metzler, 1979.

Neumann, Bernd. *Utopie und Mimesis: Zum Verhältnis von Aesthetik, Gesellschaftsphilosophie und Politik in den Romanen Uwe Johnsons.* Kronberg: Athenäum, 1978.

Nieraad, Jürgen. "Pronominalstrukturen in realistischer Prosa: Beobachtungen zur Erzählebene und Figurenkontor bei Christa Wolf," *Poetica* 10, no. 4 (1978): 485-506.

O'Neill, Patrick. "Musical form and the Pauline message in a key chapter of Günter Grass's *Blechtrommel,*" *Seminar* 10 (1974): 298-307.

Oswald, Victor A. "Full Fathom 5: A Note on some Devices in Thomas Mann's *Doktor Faustus,*" *Germanic Review* 24, no. 4 (1949): 196-204.

Parry, Idris. "Aspects of Günter Grass's Narrative Technique," *Forum for Modern Language Studies* 3, no. 2 (1967): 99-114.

Petriconi, Hellmuth. *Das Reich des Untergangs.* Hamburg: Hoffmann & Campe, 1958.

Plard, Henri. "Über die *Blechtrommel,*" *Text und Kritik* 1/1a (1971): 27-37.

Prodaniuk, Ihor. *The Imagery in Heinrich Böll's Novels.* Bonn: Bouvier, 1979.

Pross, Harry. "On Thomas Mann's political Career." In *Literature &* *Politics in the Twentieth Century*, eds. Walter Laquer and George Mosse. New York: Harper & Row, 1967.

Reddick, John. "Eine epische Trilogie des Leidens?" *Text und Kritik* 1/1a (1971): 38-51.

Reed, T. J. *Thomas Mann: The Uses of Tradition.* London: Oxford University Press, 1974.

Reich-Ranicki, Marcel, ed. *In Sachen Böll.* Munich: Deutscher Taschenbuch Verlag, 1971.

Reid, James Henderson. *Heinrich Böll: Withdrawal and Reemergence.* London: Oswald Wolff, 1973.

Rice, Philip Blair. "The Merging Parallels: Mann's *Doktor Faustus*," *Kenyon Review* 11, no. 2 (1949): 199-219.

Richter, Frank. *Günter Grass: Die Vergangenheitsbewältigung in der Danzig-Trilogie.* Bonn: Bouvier, 1979.

_____. *Die zerschlagene Wirklichkeit: Überlegungen zur Form der Danzig-Trilogie von Günter Grass.* Bonn: Bouvier, 1977.

Richter, Hans. "Moralität als poetische Energie," *Sinn und Form* 29, no. 3 (1977): 667-678.

Rilla, Paul. "Notizen zu Thomas Manns *Doktor Faustus*," *Dramaturgische Blätter* 4 (1948): 145-155.

Rothenberg, Juergen. *Günter Grass: Das Chaos in verbesserter Ausführung: Zeitgeschichte als Thema und Aufgabe des Prosawerks.* Heidelberg: Carl Winter, 1976.

Sautermeister, Gert. "Zwischen Aufklärung und Mystifizierung: Der unbewusste Widerspruch in Thomas Manns *Doktor Faustus*," *Anti-faschistische Literatur* 3 (1978): 77-125.

Schaper, Eva. "A Modern Faust: The Novel in the Ironical Key," *Orbis litterarum* 20, no. 3 (1965): 176-204.

Scharfschwerdt, Jürgen. *Thomas Mann und der deutsche Bildungsroman.* Stuttgart: Kohlhammer, 1967.

Scher, Steven Paul. *Verbal music in German Literature.* New Haven: Yale University Press, 1968.

Schiffer, Eva. "Politisches Engagement oder Resignation? Weiteres zu Uwe Johnsons *Jahrestagen*." In *Der deutsche Roman und seine historischen und politischen Bedingungen*, ed. Wolfgang Paulsen. Bern: Francke, 1977.

Schlee, Agnes. *Wandlungen musikalischer Strukturen im Werke Thomas Manns.* Frankfurt am Main: Peter Lang, 1981.

Schonauer, Franz. "Günter Grass: Ein literarischer Bürgerschreck von gestern?" In *Zeitkritische Romane des zwanzigsten Jahrhunderts*, ed. Hans Wagener. Stuttgart: Reclam, 1975.

Schwab-Felisch, Hans. "Lämmer und Büffel," *Neue deutsche Hefte* 7, no. 67 (1960): 1058-1060.

Schwarz, Wilhelm Johannes. *Der Erzähler Günter Grass.* Bern: Francke, 1969.

_____. *Der Erzähler Heinrich Böll.* Bern: Francke, 1967.

Seiferth, Wolfgang. "Das deutsche Schicksal in Thomas Manns *Doktor Faustus*," *Monatshefte* 41, nos. 3/4 (1949): 187-202.

Sokel, Walter H. "Perspective and Dualism in the Novels of Böll." In *The Contemporary Novel in German*, ed. Robert Heitner, pp. 9-35. Austin: University of Texas Press, 1967.

Sontheimer, Kurt. *Thomas Mann und die Deutschen.* Frankfurt am Main: Fischer, 1965.

Spender, Stephen. "Thomas Mann's *Doktor Faustus*," *The Nation* 167 (1948): 634-635.

Sprengel, Peter. "Teufelskünstler. Faschismus - und Ästhetizismus-Kritik in den Exilromanen Heinrich, Thomas und Klaus Manns," *Sprache im technischen Zeitalter* 79 (1981): 181-195.

Stein, Jack M. "Adrian Leverkühn as a Composer," *Germanic Review* 25, no. 4 (1950): 257-274.

Stephan, Alexander. "Christa Wolf, *Kindheitsmuster*," *New German Critique* 11 (1977): 178-182.

Stern, J. P. "From Family Album to Literary History," *New Literary History* 7, no. 1 (1975): 113-133.

Sternberger, Dolf. "Deutschland im *Doktor Faustus* und *Doktor Faustus* in Deutschland," *Merkur* 29 (1975): 1123-1140.

Stresau, Hermann. *Heinrich Böll*. Berlin: Colloquium Verlag, 1964.

Szemere, Samuel. *Kunst und Humanität*. Berlin: Akademie Verlag, 1967.

Tank, Kurt Lothar. *Günter Grass*. Berlin: Colloquium Verlag, 1968.

Ter-Nedden, Gisbert. "Allegorie und Geschichte: Zeit und Sozialkritik als Formproblem des deutschen Romans der Gegenwart." In *Positionen des Erzählens*, ed. H. L. Arnold and Theo Buck. Munich: Beck, 1976.

Trommler, Frank. "Epische Rhetorik in Thomas Manns *Doktor Faustus*," *Zeitschrift für deutsche Philologie* 89 (1970): 240-258.

Tuska, Jon. "The Vision of *Doktor Faustus*," *Germanic Review* 40, no. 4 (1965): 277-309.

Uhlig, Gudrun, ed. *Autor, Werk und Kritik I: Heinrich Böll, Günter Grass, Uwe Johnson*. Munich: Hueber, 1969.

Vaget, Hans Rudolf. "Kaisersaschern als geistige Lebensform. Zur Konzeption der deutschen Geschichte als geistige Lebensform in Thomas Manns *Doktor Faustus*." In *Der deutsche Roman und seine historischen und politischen Bedingungen*, ed. Wolfgang Paulsen. Bern: Francke, 1977.

Vormweg, Heinrich. "Uwe Johnson. Bestandsaufnahmen vom Lauf der Welt." In *Zeitkritische Romane des zwanzigsten Jahrhunderts: Die Gesellschaft in der Kritik der deutschen Literatur*, ed. Hans Wagener. Stuttgart: Reclam, 1975.

Voss, Lieselotte. *Die Entstehung von Thomas Manns Roman "Doktor Faustus": dargestellt anhand von unveröffentlichten Vorarbeiten.* Tübingen: M. Niemeyer, 1975.

Wallmann, Jürgen P. "'Das Vergangene ist nicht tot.' Zu Christa Wolfs neuem Roman," *Deutschland-Archiv* 3 (1977): 310-312.

Weiss, Walter. "Peter Handkes *Wunschloses Unglück* oder Formalismus und Realismus in der Literatur der Gegenwart," *Austriaca* (1975): 442-459.

Wendt-Hildebrandt, Susan. "*Kindheitsmuster*: Christa Wolfs 'Probestück,'" *Seminar* 17 (1981): 164-176.

Wiegenstein, Roland H. "Kassandra hat viele Gesichter," *Merkur* 31, no. 10(1977): 989-1006.

Wieser, Theodor. *Günter Grass*. Neuwied: Luchterhand, 1968.

Williams, Wm. D. "Thomas Mann's *Doktor Faustus*," *German Life and Letters* 12, no. 4 (1959): 273-281.

Willson, A. Leslie. "The grotesque Everyman in Günter Grass's *Die Blechtrommel*," *Monatshefte* 58 (1966): 131-138.

Wirth, Günter. *Heinrich Böll.* Cologne: Pahl-Rugenstein Verlag, 1969.

Yates, Norris W. *Günter Grass: A Critical Essay.* Grand Rapids, Michigan: Eerdmans, 1967.

Zeller, Rosemarie, "Die Infragestellung der Geschichte und der neue Realismus in Handkes Erzählungen," *Sprachkunst* 9 (1978): 115-140.

Zorach, Cecile Cazort. "Freedom and Remembrance: The Language of Biography in Peter Handke's *Wunschloses Unglück,*" *German Quarterly* 52 (1979): 486-502.

2. *Relevant General Literary Criticism*

Adorno, Theodor. "Engagement." In *Noten zur Literatur III,* pp. 109-135. Frankfurt am Main: Suhrkamp, 1965.

Auerbach, Erich. *Mimesis.* Trans. Willard Trask. Garden City, New York: Doubleday & Co., 1957.

Baumgart, Reinhard. *Aussichten des Romans oder hat Literatur Zukunft?* Frankfurt am Main: Deutscher Taschenbuch Verlag, 1970.

_____. "Kleinbürgertum und Realismus," *Neue Rundschau* 75, no. 4 (1964): 650-664.

_____. *Literatur für Zeitgenossen.* Frankfurt am Main: Suhrkamp, 1970.

Behn, Manfred. "Neuere antifaschistische Prosa in der DDR," *Sammlung* 1 (1978): 61-70.

Beicken, Peter. "'Neue Subjektivität': Zur Prosa der siebziger Jahre." In *Deutsche Literatur in der Bundesrepublik seit 1965,* ed. P. M. Lützeler & Egon Schwarz. Königstein/Ts.: Athenäum, 1980.

Bienek, Horst. *Werkstattgespräche mit Schriftstellern.* Munich: Deutscher Taschenbuch Verlag, 1962.

Blöcker, Günter. *Literatur als Teilhabe.* Berlin: Argon, 1966.

Boa, Elizabeth & Reid, J. H. *Critical Strategies. German Fiction in the Twentieth Century.* Montreal: McGill-Queens University Press, 1972.

Bosmajian, Hamida. *Metaphors of Evil: Contemporary German Literature and the Shadow of Nazism.* Iowa City: University of Iowa Press, 1979.

Brandt, Thos. O. "Gedanken über die zeitgenössische deutsche Dichtung," *German Quarterly* 33 (1960): 103-116.

Brecht, Bertolt. "Bemerkungen zum Formalismus." In *Gesammelte Werke*, vol. 19, pp. 313-319. Frankfurt am Main: Suhrkamp, 1967.

Brettschneider, Werner. *Zorn und Trauer: Aspekte deutscher Gegenwartsliteratur.* Berlin: E. Schmidt, 1979.

Demetz, Peter. *Postwar German Literature.* New York: Pegasus, 1970.

Deschner, Karlheinz. *Talente, Dichter, Dilettanten.* Wiesbaden: Limes Verlag, 1964.

Drewitz, Ingeborg. "Groteske Literatur: Chance und Gefahr," *Merkur* 19, no. 4 (1965): 338-347.

Durzak, Manfred. *Der deutsche Roman der Gegenwart.* Stuttgart: Kohlhammer, 1971.

_____. *Der deutsche Roman der Gegenwart: Entwicklungsvoraussetzungen und Tendenzen.* 3rd ed, (expanded and revised). Stuttgart: Kohlhammer, 1979.

_____. *Gespräche über den Roman.* Frankfurt: Suhrkamp, 1976.

Duwe, Wilhelm. *Ausdrucksformen deutscher Dichtung vom Naturalismus bis zur Gegenwart.* Berlin: Erich Schmidt Verlag, 1965.

Enright, D. J. *The Apothecary's Shop.* London: Camelot Press, 1957.

_____. *Poets and Conspirators*. London: Chatto and Windus, 1966.

Fergusson, Francis. *The Idea of a Theater*. Princeton: Princeton University Press, 1949.

Frank, Joseph. *The Widening Gyre*. New Brunswick, New Jersey: Rutgers University Press, 1963.

Geissler, Rolf, ed. *Möglichkeiten des modernen deutschen Romans*. Frankfurt am Main: Moritz Diesterweg, 1965.

Gray, Ronald. *The German Tradition in Literature 1871-1945*. Cambridge: Cambridge University Press, 1965.

Hamburger, Michael. *From Prophecy to Exorcism*. London: Longmans, 1968.

Hatfield, Henry. *Modern German Literature*. Bloomington: Indiana University Press, 1968.

_____. "The Myth of Nazism." In *Myth and Mythmaking*, ed. Henry A. Murray. New York: G. Braziller, 1960.

Hermand, Jost. "Darstellungen des Zweiten Weltkrieges." In *Literatur nach 1945*, vol. 1, ed. Jost Hermand. Wiesbaden: Akademische Verlagsgesellschaft Athenaion, 1979.

Hörnigk, Therese. "Das Thema Krieg und Faschismus in der Geschichte der DDR-Literatur," *Weimarer Beiträge* 24 (1978): 5, 73-105.

Horst, Karl August. "Polemik und Totalität: Über die Situation der deutschen Nachkriegsliteratur," *Wort und Wahrheit* 17, nos. 6/7(1963): 440-449.

Jens, Walter. *Moderne Literatur. Moderne Wirklichkeit.* Pfullingen: Neske, 1958.

Kahler, Erich. "Untergang und Übergang der epischen Kunstform," *Neue Rundschau* 64, no. 1 (1953): 1-44.

Kayser, Wolfgang. *Entstehung und Krise des modernen Romans.* Stuttgart: Metzler, 1954.

Klotz, Volker. *Geschlossene und offene Form in Drama.* Munich: Hanser, 1960.

Kreuzer, Helmut. "Neue Subjektivität: Zur Literatur der siebziger Jahre in der Bundesrepublik Deutschland." In *Deutsche Gegenwartsliteratur: Ausgangspositionen und aktuelle Entwicklungen,* ed. Manfred Durzak. Stuttgart: Reclam, 1981.

Langer, Lawrence. *The Holocaust and the Literary Imagination.* New Haven: Yale University Press, 1975.

Liddell, Peter. "Janus and the Social Dichotomy: Facets of Socialist Realism in the East German Novel in the 1970s," *Seminar* 17 (May, 1981): 114-129.

Lukács, Georg. "Art and Objective Truth." In *Writer and Critic & other Essays,* ed. & trans. Arthur D. Kahn. New York: Grosset & Dunlap, 1971.

Mayer, Hans. *Deutsche Literatur seit Thomas Mann.* Reinbek: Rowohlt, 1967.

———. *Literatur der Übergangszeit.* Berlin: Volk und Welt, 1949.

———. *Der Repräsentant und der Märtyrer.* Frankfurt am Main: Suhrkamp, 1971.

———. *Von Lessing bis Thomas Mann.* Pfullingen: Neske, 1959.

———. *Zur deutschen Literatur der Zeit.* Reinbek: Rowoht, 1967.

Milch, Werner. *Kleine Schriften zur Literatur- und Geistesgeschichte.* Heidelberg: Verlag Lambert Schneider, 1957.

Nägele, Rainer. "Geschichte und Geschichten. Reflexionen zum westdeutschen Roman seit 1965." In *Deutsche Gegenwartsliteratur: Ausgangspositionen und aktuelle Entwicklungen,* ed. Manfred Durzak. Stuttgart: Reclam, 1981.

Osterle, Heinz D. "The Other Germany: Resistance to the Third Reich in German Literature," *German Quarterly* 41 (1968): 1-22.

Reich-Ranicki, Marcel, ed. *Deutsche Literatur in West und Ost.* Reinbek: Rowoht, 1970.

Richter, Hans Werner, ed. *Almanach der Gruppe 47.* Reinbek: Rowohlt, 1962.

Sokel, Walter H. *The Writer in Extremis.* Stanford: Stanford University Press, 1959.

Steiner, George. *Language and Silence.* Middlesex: Penguin, 1967.

Trommler, Frank. "Realismus in der Prosa." In *Tendenzen der deutschen Literatur seit 1945*, ed. Thomas Koebner. Stuttgart: Kröner, 1971.

_____. "Der zögernde Nachwuchs: Entwicklungsprobleme der Nachkriegsliteratur in Ost und West." In *Tendenzen der deutschen Literatur seit 1945*, ed. Thomas Koebner. Stuttgart: Kröner, 1971.

_____. "Zur aktuellen Situation der DDR-Literatur." In *Deutsche Gegenwartsliteratur: Ausgangspositionen und aktuelle Entwicklungen*, ed. Manfred Durzak. Stuttgart: Kohlhammer, 1981.

Walter, Hans-Albert. "Deutsche Literatur im Exil: Ein Modellfall für die Zusammenhänge von Literatur und Politik," *Merkur* 25 (1971): 77-84.

Wehdeking, Volker Christian. *Der Nullpunkt: Über die Konstituierung der deutschen Nachkriegsliteratur (1945-1948) in den amerikanischen Kriegsgefangenenlagern.* Stuttgart: Metzler, 1971.

Will, Willfried van der, and Thomas, R. Hinton. *The German Novel and the Affluent Society.* Manchester: Manchester University Press, 1968.

Winter, Hans-Gerhard. "Von der Dokumentarliteratur zur 'neuen Subjektivität': Anmerkungen zur westdeutschen Literatur der siebziger Jahre," *Seminar* 17, no. 2 (1981): 95-113.

Zeller, Michael, ed. *Aufbrüche: Abschiede. Studien zur deutschen Literatur seit 1968*. Stuttgart: Klett, 1979.

Ziolkowski, Theodore. *Dimensions of the Modern Novel: German Texts and European Contexts*. Princeton: Princeton University Press, 1969.

3. *Extra-Literary Works Related to Nazism or the Postwar Period*

Adorno, Theodor. "Was bedeutet: Aufarbeitung der Vergangenheit." In *Eingriffe*. pp. 125-146. Frankfurt am Main: Suhrkamp, 1963.

Adorno, Theodor, Frenkel-Brunswik, Else, Levinson, Daniel J., and Sanford, R. Nevitt. *The Authoritarian Personality*. New York: Harper & Row, 1950.

Allen, William Sheridan. *The Nazi Seizure of Power: The Experience of a Single German Town 1930-1935*. Chicago: Quadrangle Books, 1965.

Arendt, Hannah. *Eichmann in Jerusalem*. New York: Viking Press, 1965.

Aron, Raymond. "The End of the Ideological Age?" In *Social Thought in America and Europe*, ed. David M. Kennedy and Paul A. Robinson. Boston: Little, Brown, & Co., 1970.

Barraclough, Geoffrey. "Article II on The Liberals and German History," *New York Review of Books*, November 2, 1972.

Bell, Daniel. "The End of Ideology in the West." In *Social Thought in America and Europe*, ed. David M. Kennedy and Paul A. Robinson. Boston: Little, Brown and Co., 1970.

Benjamin, Walter. "The Work of Art in the Age of Mechanical Reproduction." In *Illuminations*. Trans. Harry Zohn, pp. 219-253. New York: Harcourt, Brace and World, Inc., 1968.

Berning, Cornelia. *Vom "Abstammungsnachweis" zum "Zuchtwart."* Berlin: de Gruyter, 1964.

Bracher, Karl Dietrich. *The German Dictatorship: The Origins, Structure, & Effects of National Socialism*. Trans. Jean Steinberg. New York: Praeger, 1970.

Childs, David. *Germany Since 1918*. New York: Harper & Row, 1970.

Craig, Gordon A. *Germany 1866-1945*. Oxford: Oxford University Press, 1980.

Dahrendorf, Ralf. *Society and Democracy in Germany*. Garden City, New York: Doubleday, 1969.

Deutscher, Isaac. *Marxism in our Time*. Berkeley: Ramparts Press, 1971.

Eisner, Lotte. *The Haunted Screen.* Trans. Roger Greaves. Berkeley: University of California Press, 1965.

Fest, Joachim. *Das Gesicht des dritten Reiches.* Frankfurt am Main: Ullstein, 1969.

Fromm, Erich. "Fascism as Lower-Middle-Class Psychology." In *The Place of Fascism in European History.* ed. Gilbert Allerdyce, pp. 36-48. Englewood Cliffs, New Jersey: Prentice-Hall, 1971.

Hamilton, Richard. *Who voted for Hitler?* Princeton: Princeton University Press, 1982.

Handt, Friedrich, ed. *Deutsch: gefrorene Sprache in einem gefrorenen Land: Polemik, Analysen, Aufsätze.* Berlin: Literarisches Colloquium, 1964.

Haug, Wolfgang Fritz. *Der hilflose Antifaschismus.* Frankfurt am Main: Suhrkamp, 1970.

Holborn, Hajo. *Germany and Europe.* Garden City, New York: Doubleday, 1971.

_____. *A History of Modern Germany 1840-1945.* New York: Knopf, 1969.

Hughes, H. Stuart. *Contemporary Europe.* Englewood Cliffs, New Jersey: Prentice-Hall, 1966.

Jaspers, Karl. *The Question of German Guilt.* Trans. E. B. Ashton. New York: Capricorn Books, 1961.

Kater, Michael. *The Nazi Party: A Social Profile of Members and Leaders, 1919-1945.* Cambridge: Harvard University Press, 1983.

Klemperer, Victor. *"LTI" Die unbewältigte Sprache.* Munich: Deutscher Taschenbuch Verlag, 1969.

Kracauer, Siegfried. *From Caligari to Hitler.* Princeton: Princeton University Press, 1947.

Kühnl, Reinhard. *Deutschland zwischen Demokratie und Faschismus.* Munich: Hanser, 1969.

_____. *Das dritte Reich in der Presse der Bundesrepublik.* Frankfurt am Main: Europäische Verlagsanstalt, 1966.

Lebovics, Hermann. *Social Conservatism and the German Middle Classes 1914-33.* Princeton: Princeton University Press, 1968.

Lichtheim, George. *The Concept of Ideology and Other Essays.* New York: Random House, 1967.

Lubasz, Heinz. "Hitler's Welfare State," *New York Review of Books* (December, 1968): 33-34.

_____, ed. *Fascism: Three Major Regimes.* New York: Wiley, 1973.

Lukács, Georg. *Die Zerstörung der Vernunft.* Berlin: Aufbau, 1954.

Mills, C. Wright. "On the New Left." In *Social Thought in America and Europe,* ed. David M. Kennedy and Paul A. Robinson. Boston: Little, Brown and Co., 1970.

Mitscherlich, Alexander and Mitscherlich, Margarete. *Die Unfähigkeit zu trauern.* Munich: Piper, 1967.

Moore, Barrington. "Fascism as the heritage of Conservative Modernization." In *The Place of Fascism in European History,* ed. Gilbert Allerdyce, pp. 127-143. Englewood Cliffs, New Jersey: Prentice-Hall, 1971.

Mosse, George L. *The Culture of Western Europe.* Chicago: Rand McNally & Co., 1965.

_____. *Nazi Culture.* Trans. Salvator Attanasio et al. New York: Grosset & Dunlap, 1968.

Neumann, Franz. *Behemoth: The Structure and Practice of National Socialism 1933-44.* New York: Harper & Row, 1966.

Rauschning, Hermann. *The Revolution of Nihilism,* Trans. E. W. Dickes. New York: Longmans, Green, & Co., 1939.

Reich, Wilhelm. *The Mass Psychology of Fascism.* trans. from manuscript of the third edition. Albion: Albion Press, 1970.

Ringer, Fritz K. *The Decline of the German Mandarins: The German Academic Community, 1890-1933.* Cambridge: Harvard University Press, 1969.

Schoenbaum, David. *Hitler's Social Revolution: Class and Status in Nazi Germany 1933-1939.* Garden City, New York: Doubleday, 1967.

Stern, Fritz. *The Politics of Cultural Despair.* Garden City, New York: Doubleday, 1965.

Sternberger, Dolf; Storz, Gerhard; and Süskind, Wilhelm E. *Aus dem Wörterbuch des Unmenschen.* Munich: Deutscher Taschenbuch Verlag, 1970.

Stollmann, Rainer. "Fascist Politics as a Total Work of Art: Tendencies of the Aesthetization of Political Life in National Socialism," *New German Critique* 14 (1978): 41-60.

Viereck, Peter. *Metapolitics: From the Romantics to Hitler.* New York: Capricorn, 1965.

Weber, Eugen. *Varieties of Fascism.* Princeton: Van Nostrand, 1964.

Index